Luminous

The Psychology of
Enlightenment

Luminous

The Psychology of Enlightenment

Aubrey Degnan, Ph.D.

Cover Photograph
Aubrey Degnan, Ph.D.
Layout and Cover Design
Vicki Anne Crane

First Paperback Edition
Copyright © 2005 by Aubrey Degnan, Ph.D.
ISBN 0-9774496-2-9
First Edition Cover Design
Tom McConnell

Second Paperback Edition
Copyright © 2023 by Aubrey Degnan, Ph.D.
ISBN 979-8-9875778-2-0
eBook ISBN 979-8-9875778-1-3

Published by Miracle Publishing Group
www.miraclepublishinggroup.com

I dedicate this book to the wisdom teachings that have touched my life. I dedicate this book to all sentient beings and to each of you, your children, and your ancestors. I dedicate this book to my children, their families, and our future generations. I ask that the merits received through these actions be quickly and completely passed to all souls. I am grateful for this opportunity to be of service.

I humbly bow to the great Enlightened Minds who have far surpassed my level of understanding and cultivation. The guidance of my teachers stretches me beyond the limitations of my conceptual mind, opens my heart into compassion, and moves my soul into spaces beyond my wildest imagination. This is a living transmission of esoteric teachings, beyond anything publicly taught.

This ancient journey is within the power of each of us to complete. This book is about the transformation of my life and the Enlightenment of my soul. My soul drinks deeply as the heavens open to me.

I am but in kindergarten.

May you be inspired, may you be uplifted and encouraged because this transformation can happen to you.

May whatever merits are accumulated through the writings in this book be dedicated to all sentient beings.

Contents

Foreword

As my student, Dr. Aubrey Degnan has received serious spiritual training for four years. I have taught her sacred and secret Divine wisdom and knowledge. She is a totally devoted student. She has reached Soul Enlightenment.

Her book can lead you on your spiritual journey and offer Divine Guidance. I hope that everyone reading this book will receive blessings, guidance, and spiritual nourishment from it.

I am sending her to the world to offer spiritual teaching and guidance. I send my spiritual blessings with her and her book.

Master Zhi Gang Sha
San Francisco, California
September, 2005

Preface

The first published edition of *Luminous* reflected my journey at that time. The book sold out. Now, new readers are asking for this guidance to help them live through these chaotic times. There is a hunger to transform chaos, polarization, and depression into peace, connection, and joy. To do this, we need to deeply heal our wounds, initially psychologically and physically. In turn, this healing evolves into a deeper spiritual connection with our Soul.

This second edition of *Luminous* is updated into both an eBook and print. This new edition contains 65 tools, carefully highlighted for the reader to practice in daily life. These are meditations in action. To realize the full impact of any meditation, practice it for 24 hours! This will bring you, the reader, a progression from a more ego-based or limited consciousness to an expanded state of Being.

These essential steps, quite simply put, are to first *relax*. Take a few minutes to become present in the here and now, to feel your senses and exhale deeply. Quiet your mind. This leads to a portal of stillness that some find in walking in nature. We see the exquisite beauty of trees, sky, and hear the birds. Second, *accept* our own humanity to have self-compassion. These two simple practices are gateways to expanded states of consciousness.

Today, I live more quietly on a ranch. Tom and I integrate this meditative approach into our workshops and retreats, using our animals to help students drop into their senses and be in nature. Our rescue mustangs, initially quite wild, now bring joy to those who visit our land. We help people feel better. These precious moments of breaking free from our pain are the building blocks of creating a happier life. These are the blessings that come with the process of Awakening spiritually.

The Path becomes the Teacher. We learn to not push the river and in turn, the river carries us.

In deep gratitude, I thank those who have helped me publish this new edition: Annie for her impeccable feedback, careful design layout, and the depth of her understanding the purpose of this book. I thank Tom for his enduring and continual support, ideas, and love. I also express deep gratitude for being with others who choose to dive deeply into their innermost core being. When we go there together, I simultaneously see the magnificence of our uniqueness and the Oneness of all.

And to you, the reader, I wish you the realization of your deepest aspirations in this life. May you each be blessed with light and love.

Aubrey
October 2023

Introduction

In this book, I will share with you important spiritual wisdoms that help us awaken to Enlightenment. These wisdoms come to me through my teachers over the past 30 years. Now, many wisdom teachings come to me directly. Some may think these wisdoms are to be kept secret. Others may think the experiences generated by the practice of the wisdom teachings are to be kept private. I deeply honor their position and humbly disagree.

Now is the time in our universe to share, to try to put into words that which is beyond word and concept. The challenge is to remain humble and pure in intent. It is time to get out of the small teacup containing our mind and prior experiences and enter instead the vast space that surrounds any object. It is within entering the emptiness of the unknown that the true wisdoms will come to you.

I ask of you, dear reader, to temporarily place to one side your logical thinking and allow other aspects of your mind to receive the teachings and experiences that are in this book. This is a process that I, too, have done for years, calling it "putting my mind on the shelf." This will allow you to receive what I describe in this book on the deepest level within your soul. This book can then bring to you direct transformation that is alchemical and spiritual. I believe there is something contagious in sharing mystical knowledge and Enlightenment. It literally can help you to awaken spiritually. This is one of several purposes of this book.

Having been a student of the journey of the soul from ego to Enlightenment since childhood, I always first experience the meditations, tools, and teachings that come to me. I seek the truth of what works best and quickest. These truths I then pass on to others. It is these truths that are in this book.

The beauty of your individual experience is that each of you will have a slightly different truth and a slightly different way of opening to the Divine. Another purpose of this book is to rekindle the spark within your soul and lovingly help you to open to your own experience, truth, and Enlightenment.

I begin by sharing my personal life, including insights gleaned from my years as a professional psychologist. I am a mother of two beautiful, successful, well-adjusted, and spiritual children with their own children. I also share this personal background because some of you may recall the teachers who gave me a precious piece of the puzzle.

It is my hope that this book will also be received as a contribution to the field of psychology. I propose a paradigm shift from the usual approach to psychotherapy into viewing the human mind from the perspective of the Divine Mind, or God Consciousness, or Buddha Nature, also known as Enlightened Mind. Having attained this expanded state of consciousness, we now view the reality of our human condition from this perspective. May this be known as the Psychology of Enlightenment.

The remainder of this book gives examples of the different states of consciousness accompanying this new paradigm. I offer tools to assist you in realizing these states. Some of these tools are practices transmitted to me that I have permission to pass on. Others are my own. Please note the footnotes at the end of this book that will help you identify the origins of these precious teachings. The spiritual abilities that accompany expanded consciousness are discussed, stories are presented, and my direct experience is shared. By following this format within each chapter, I hope to clearly present the experience, its significance, and application in your daily life.

As a teacher, I incorporate these tools into my own work, adding my creativity and inspiration. When I am offering a healing or a blessing and something happens that has never happened before, I trust in the Divine to show me and guide me. This quality of trusting that the wisdom will come as I am offering service is what I have come to call the Unknown. I now understand that within the Unknown and its spontaneity, we open to directly receive wisdom teachings.

What is written in this book is my truth as it actually happened. There are times of bliss and pain, joy and sorrow, struggle and freedom.

Thank you all for being with me in this lifetime and giving it the richness of our times together.

Part I

In Kindergarten

Chapter 1

I Am But in Kindergarten

As I enter the darkened temple, I tighten my shawl around my shoulders. While the room is still cold from the night, I am comforted to sit so close to my loved ones. I drape a second blanket across my knees and tuck in the edges, preparing for our meditation.

Deep inside, I feel so at peace, so grateful to be sitting with my spiritual teacher, next to my beloved Tom, in a semicircle of nine close disciples. I look up to see my teacher seated on the elevated platform. He too is draped with blankets. This special meditation is only for the assistant teachers. The others are still sleeping.

I need do nothing but sit and deeply open myself to his teaching. I have no outside concerns. I feel complete and present.

I have no inkling that the most precious gift possible, the very wish of my entire life, the pursuit of 30 years, is about to come to me.

Collectively, our voices follow his words. "Dear God and Heaven's Team, we ask to be of Universal Service…" His gentle words guide my focus as my attention moves from my ears down to the center of my chest. All of me is concentrated in my heart chakra. I feel a pulsing and a heat that builds into pressure, as though all the energy in my body has left my extremities and moved into my heart chakra.

I am following his words in rapt concentration. My soul—more essential than my inner child, my purest light—sits now in the very center of my chest. My soul is shining brightly with the nourishment of this focused concentration.

Following his guidance, my soul begins to send light out into the universe. I see with my inner vision a multitude of light rays going out from my chest.

I feel I could explode with its pressure and intensity. I send my light in 360 degrees, in all possible directions into the universe. I see my light rays going like laser beams directly into thousands upon thousands of individuated souls. I see their hearts receiving my light rays. Their hearts light up with a golden bursting like the explosion of a thousand suns.

Now the power of this light from the hearts of all these souls focuses back upon me and enters my heart chakra from all directions. They are returning the light, a multifold returning of the light from so many beings simultaneously.

This intensity is beyond anything I have ever experienced. It is coming from all around me! There is so much light! The light pours into my heart and then explodes into the thousands of cells within my own body. The intensity continues to build! Each cell is now illuminated in a white and golden light!

I am on fire in this light! I am like a Christmas tree with luminous and powerful lights in every particle! Surely there can be no more than this for I might explode!

Yes! There is more and it comes mercilessly in its power overtaking me in its light! Within each luminous cell there is now a soul, a being of light that is pure white. These luminous shining souls, all thousands upon thousands of them gather together in a power and a concentration that sweeps all the energy into a ball of light.

This, in turn shoots, back out into the universe as infinite balls that transform into shafts of light. It is like lightning that is sent back out into the universe in a rapid projectile. Millions of white shafts of light go in 360 degrees into each soul that has now subdivided into infinite luminous cells.

The light is expanding and exploding into waves and layers. This is the light of infinite souls.

Suddenly I am lost…gone, gone, gone beyond. I am catapulted into a dimension of pure light and pure Oneness. There is golden liquid swirling around me. There is no longer a me. I am becoming the golden swirling moving light.

Then there is white light without any movement. A stillness of infinite whiteness opens into vast space, smooth, peaceful, endless, silent. Soaring in infinite golden white light there is no sense of time. Moving like rings of golden light around planets in a disc-like motion. Interchanging movement and stillness, all in light. The explosions and power quiet into a slow sense of suspended stillness. I am pure white light, constant, brilliant, and gentle.

I do not know how long this is going on. O cherished and blessed state!

Time goes by without me. Gradually, figures are moving around me. I am quite removed from them. They could be anything. I have no continuity with their forms, no recognition of what I now see. I stay in the light. The state of light is more present than external forms and yet not altered by anything. I am quivering in my body. I feel disorientated. My tears are coming.

I am still in the light... of the light. Curiously, the state continues as my body tentatively rises off the pillow. My friends are moving slowly to go downstairs for breakfast. I am the last to rise. The light rises with me. Together, we move down to the bottom of the stairs. I am seeing light everywhere I look. Nothing alters the experience that is still unfolding.

I stand dazed and barely moving, allowing others to walk past me. Gazing inquisitively, from only inches away is Peter. The question in his eyes changes to a beautiful smile. His eyes are equally brilliant as he recognizes that I, too, am in the cherished state of Enlightenment. "Congratulations!" he says. He is my dear friend. He is often present with me as these blessings arise. He sees this moment, and for this I am grateful!

I am in the food line, disoriented and not connecting with any desire to eat. I flow past the breakfast buffet holding a bowl. The brilliant light is with me. I look into the cereal bowl that convention says I must now fill with food. I want to just peacefully rest in the light. There is no friction between eating or not eating, walking or not walking, holding a bowl and staying in the light. I begin to perceive the bowl in a new way. It is a quite empty and well-worn white bowl. From this constant light the bowl now has a precious and quite beautiful quality. I see the cuts and scrapes of many utensils that have hit its edges and worn this bowl through years of use.

Yet there is a light emanating from this bowl. It actually shines at me. I cup it gently in two hands. It is now the precious begging bowl that ancient sages have used seeking alms. It is the begging bowl of the Enlightened Ones. It is my empty bowl radiating light.

I walk to the table with my empty bowl and sit down. Everyone at the table is eating. I just sit and smile quietly.

I am receiving spiritual teachings from my bowl. My bowl is empty and yet full at the same time. Form is emptiness and emptiness is form. I am seeing the fullness within the space in the bowl. This bowl is actually full—light is sitting in it like a puffball. The light has substance.
People now leave the table, and a deep quiet surrounds me. Interesting to be both in this gentle constant light and also in my physical body. I am coexisting quite comfortably.

As I walk outside, I feel the sun's warmth inviting my cells to stretch beyond my skin like fine filaments into the morning air. Birds are calling and the redwood needles glisten. My senses reach like tentacles to taste the delights of so much life and brightness. My heart feels peace and gratitude. My mind is still. There is nowhere to go, no urge to speak. I rest in this light for the day. Outside activity does not seem to touch the light inside.

I feel forever altered as my deepest wish is being granted. For 30 years, I have prayed to realize Enlightenment, wishing each night upon seeing the evening star, "Star light, star bright, first star I see tonight, I wish for Enlightenment for all sentient beings tonight."

All my work, all my studies, all my adventures have brought me to this precious day. On June 23rd, 2002, my wish is being granted. Indeed, this is a gift from God.

Chapter 2

Unfolding of the Path

Gratitude

Within each and every culture abides this ancient journey of the soul passed down through oral teachings, art, and ritual from generation to generation. The most powerful teachings are often kept secret, reserved for only the ears of a top-level disciple as the spiritual master prepares for their transition. It is rare to receive these teachings and transmissions that are the keys opening us to true transformation within a single lifetime.

As I study and learn these carefully guarded secrets, a deep peace descends upon me. I breathe in the perfection of the light of the universe and see the sparkle of the raindrop upon each leaf. Let us begin the journey by thanking each of you for giving me the opportunity to write, to be of service, and to uplift your soul through my words.

Together, we will join our thoughts and our hearts to enter spaces that many say cannot be conceptualized. Yet, I believe we need to share, to attempt to connect our individual experiences with the ancient poetic and mystical songs of the Enlightened masters throughout time. We must try to understand. We may also open in the process.

This book is about the unfolding of the path and how to make it smoother each day.

How does this precious and ancient journey unfold? Why is it sometimes called "the path of crazy wisdom?" Here are some guiding spiritual principles to help us:

- ❖ First. Realize our soul undertakes this journey.
- ❖ Second. Create a sacred space through beginning all practices in the state of prayer. Our soul speaks through prayer to all souls in the entire universe, those in physical form and those in the soul world.
- ❖ Third. Create an internal sacred space, a golden urn to hold and carefully protect our unfolding.
- ❖ Fourth. Recognize the nature of our humanity contains suffering and struggle. When we experience these struggles, obstacles, or difficulties we can see them as potential lessons. Learn what is to be learned and then let go.
- ❖ Fifth. Practice nonattachment to our ego, the very roots of our personality, justifications, blame, judgment, and expectation. Practice nonattachment to the very pattern of our habitual thinking. Practice nonattachment even to the outcome of our journey, peak experiences, and hope for Enlightenment. Nonattachment allows us to enter and remain in the Emptiness—one aspect of the Enlightened Mind.
- ❖ Sixth. Enter the profound state of consciousness where you directly receive wisdom teachings and guidance from the highest saints, buddhas, God, or the Universe.

Seeing My Soul

Two years before I experience entering the state of Luminous that I have just described, I meet my special teacher. He calls this relationship bringing me "through the door." What brought me to his door was the use of a single word: Soul.

One day in April 2000, I am seated in an alcove of windows overlooking San Francisco. I am in Effie Chow's apartment with her sister. We are planning the upcoming International Qigong Conference. As the Grande Dame of Qigong in this country, Effie Chow is gifted at presenting Qigong Masters in the West. She brings medical Qigong into the mainstream of public awareness through her annual conferences. She plays a national role, brilliantly organizing the White House Commission on Complementary and Alternative Medical Policy.

I have a vision of a press event for her upcoming Qigong Conference. Effie is kind, allowing me to bring the press event to fruition. I gather six powerful Qigong Masters, asking them to demonstrate their healing abilities with volunteers suffering from a serious physical illness. We invite Western scientists who are actively researching the effects of Qigong and healing. Members of the press will be able to question all three groups. To select these Qigong Masters, I review their biographies. Only one in the entire program uses the word, "Soul." His photo jumps out at me. "Yes, I am going to see what he has to say about the soul!" This is a moment of recognition— my first contact with Dr. Zhi Gang Sha.

At the time, I am writing about soul, struggling to express its essential nature. I read various Chinese texts. Why is soul so important? My pump is primed and hungry!

The presentation goes quite well. The atmosphere is supercharged. Researchers are tracking the Qi levels before and after each Master's healings. The press is both skeptical and involved. One of the photographers comes forward. She has such a toothache that it is most difficult for her to film this event. This is exactly what I had hoped: someone from the press would spontaneously experience a direct healing! Her toothache is dramatically reduced. She can smile again.

The next morning Dr. Sha speaks about the "Role of the Soul in Healing." We are in the San Francisco Marriott, and he chants, invoking spiritual beings. He is dressed quite formally in a dark blue suit. His hair is cut very short. He wears glasses. His outer demeanor is formal, while his inner-directed lecture goes beyond the boundaries of conventional Medical Qigong. He simply leaps over traditional limitations to get to the heart of the spiritual discussion. Within minutes, the direction of my life changes.

I drink in every word. I feel the nourishment going to my core. The impact of the truth transfixes me.

He speaks about the Soul within each of us, within every physical entity, and within the invisible spiritual world. He speaks about the on-going essence within us that moves from one lifetime to another. He speaks about the wondrous matrix of interconnectedness between us. He speaks about the soul of each organ and each cell within our physical bodies. He speaks about where to find our soul within our body. He speaks about how to bring our soul into its rightful position of guiding our lives.

I close my eyes. He guides me to actually see my own soul. Sure enough, sitting in my belly, my Lower Dan Tian, is a beautiful small golden Buddha in front of a peaceful still sea. I weep tears of gratitude.

I find my soul!

My Buddha speaks to me, healing a pain in my shoulder from a car accident. "Send light to your shoulder." In these precious moments, so much is happening: I am seeing internally, I am hearing internally, I am actively healing myself.

My cells are vibrating in a massive rearrangement. There is a chaotic inner activity. I feel a shifting, a new order emerging. Images from my past sweep before my eyes as disparate pieces of a puzzle. Then the images begin to resettle and a new integration begins. There is a new matrix emerging that makes me feel different.

I begin to see. I begin to hear. My soul is becoming the captain of my ship. After 30 years of meditation and study, a new solidity and confidence settles down just in front of my spine. My years of chanting mantra while driving my car, ALL were food for this moment. This new understanding feels more accurate than what I have previously known.

Within this very first hour with Dr. Sha, I reconnect with myself. I am peaceful and solid. Joy and wisdom combine to give me *myself*. I understand the significance of this event and feel immense gratitude. Within my life, there have been many experiences, visions, and cognitions. Yet to be able to put it all together and to truly understand what it means within my psyche is an exquisite gift. I am moved to tears. A quality of relief brings energy and life force into my face.

My God! My life begins to make sense. I am elated! I am on the road again! I have been in the desert for many years. I was the little red caboose of the engine that said, "I think I can. I think I can, I think I can." I had fallen off the tracks and was lying on my side in the limitless orange sand of the Sahara, so alone that I didn't even recognize the desert.

This single class is far more than just another mystical, feel-good experience. Wisdom teachings are clearly presented—with a road map to Enlightenment. The many nights of wishing, "Star light, star bright, first star I see tonight, I wish for Enlightenment for all sentient beings. That is my wish tonight." For years I held this secret so as not to spoil the wish. On this day, events and habits spanning many years make sense. As though somebody adjusted the microscope, I can see! This gentle soul is telling me what I am looking at, and its significance.

With renewed energy, I feel washed and cleansed. It must be visible. As we come to our lunch break, my dear friend Patricia Smith takes one look at me and exclaims, "Wow! What happened to you? Whatever that is, I want some of it!" Patricia is a nurse who has played a significant role in bringing medical Qigong to the Santa Cruz area and to the Land of Medicine Buddha retreat center. Years earlier, she suffered paralysis and depression and could not continue in her role as a hospital administrator. As part of her own healing, she turned to medical Qigong. Her inspiring story is part of a series produced by NBC Dateline on "Qigong for Healing." Her story is also included in a PBS documentary, "Power Healing with Master Sha." Her sophisticated understanding of Qigong significantly contributes both to her clients and the field.

When I see my soul in my lower belly, it is not a small girl or boy as Dr. Sha intimates. My image is different, and it takes three years for me to know why. For souls who are just beginning on the path, this soul is in our lower belly. However, as the soul progresses, through study and hard work, through blessings and karma clearings, this soul grows and is next placed in the heart.

I see my soul as a small golden Buddha. I didn't dare to share this out loud because it was not the little girl or little boy. A year is to pass before my dear friend Peter calls me, "Little Buddha." I am not comfortable with being a Little Buddha, as it seems self-inflated. Another few months are to pass by before I hear of the teachings that state you must be willing to acknowledge your own Buddha Nature. It is an internal jump that is not easy and filled with potential false pride. Yet there is a deeper truth that has nothing to do with me. It is this: we are all of The Source. We are all of the Buddha Nature, the God Nature. This potential is within each and every one of us.

It is my deepest hope as I write today that your soul will resonate, connecting with mine, and find this spiritual roadmap helpful.

Prayer

Only within these past few years have I come to understand the impact and purposes of prayer. Prayer is sacred communication with all souls, souls in physical form and souls without form.

Prayer connects us with the Heavenly Host, God, and Enlightened Masters. Prayer is knocking on the door, inviting a conversation with God. Prayer is both the asking and the dialogue.

Loving prayer is the essence of healing the souls of every cell that is sick or weak. Remote prayer is intentionality calling upon the living consciousness within DNA and RNA to heal at a distance.

Prayer is a communication for any purpose including finding a job, selling your home, and resolving issues in a relationship.

Prayer is giving a gift of love, healing, or blessing to another soul.

Prayer is the context, like two bookends in which to do all sacred work, including healing and psychotherapy.

Prayer can address your own personal life, the lives of family and friends, and the very existence of all souls in the entire universe. The scope of prayer reaches from the personal to the universal.

Prayer is saying hello to the soul world that surrounds us and guides us in our daily physical existence.

In an audacious moment, with the hope of an innocent child reaching for a desired fruit, I ask Dr. Sha, "What do I need to do to realize Soul Enlightenment in this coming year?" He answers, "Mantra. Do your mantra, give unconditional service, do not think of yourself. Unconditional service is doing whatever is asked of us or in front of us. There is no higher or lower. Not thinking of yourself. It will happen automatically in the state of prayer. Our minds are not on ourselves."

The World Within the Golden Urn

We are about to enter the world within this golden urn. In time, this golden urn will also dissolve into emptiness and light.

Visualize a bowl or urn made of 24 karat, pure, glistening, and radiating gold. Its edges are scalloped into delicate curves like the shape of flower petals reaching into infinite space. It is within this golden bowl that the spiritual journey unfolds. This golden urn is a metaphor which holds the context or the description of the inner journey. Within this golden urn, there are specific spiritual principles that must be followed for successful transformation to occur. It may be likened to alchemy for the soul.

Allow your mind to stretch, to try on ideas, concepts, and experiences that will help us open into places beyond your imagination. Simultaneously, reconnect with prior spiritual or peak experiences, possibly when you were a child and so very open. We have forgotten our own intuitive wisdoms as the pressures of our daily lives constrict our souls. Now we open and stretch again.

The path unfolds in front of us. The path is unique to each person. Sometimes we fall off the path. That, too, is part of the path. The path has obstacles. The path can be fast and somewhat precarious. The path can be tediously slow. The path has great heights of bliss and bottomless abysses of darkness. The path is both in form and formless. The path has no linear time dimension. The path is filled with synchronicity and coincidence. The path may take a lifetime to understand the meaning of specific events. The path ultimately takes us further into the now that opens like a multidimensional funnel into light, emptiness, and power. This is therefore, with this last understanding, the journey that never needs be made because you are already there.

Struggle and Obstacles

Do not mistakenly think that this journey is easy. It is not. In fact, it is quite difficult, requiring tenacity, courage, willingness to let go, patience, humility, and even detachment from thinking you are "special" because of your aspirations. Sometimes it is necessary to burn, baby, burn. Then one must ask, "Just who is burning?" Yes, as we all know, the one burning is our ego, our sense of false self, the very goals of materialism and money that our culture values and instills in us as impressionable children.

We must be willing to let these cultural values have less import in our lives while simultaneously living in our modern society. This path need not be taken by running to the hills and the nearest cave. This path literally unfolds as your path, the one in front of you at this time. Realizing this is itself a spiritual guideline of accepting and looking for the lesson in the situation being presented. Understanding this we need to cultivate an attitude that looks for the lessons rather than looking to blame.

One key element on this path is encountering obstacles. These obstacles are a form of spiritual challenging or testing. We need to quickly recognize what is spiritual testing and learn how to move through these phases. These obstacles provide the essential opportunities necessary for spiritual transformation such as clearing of karma, letting go of preconceptions and expectations, practicing obedience to the Divine, letting go of self-centeredness, giving of service to others, purifying our thinking, strengthening our physical body, and preparing our soul to carry intense light. Throughout this life and prior lives, we have acquired habitual patterns that are karmic and these patterns must be broken and the concurrent lessons learned.

It has taken me three years to understand the process of spiritual testing, to recognize it as it begins, and to know how to get through these painful experiences. On the path to Enlightenment, the process of spiritual testing will show you the face of your own ego. Ego is our personality, our habitual thinking, and our emotional tendencies. Together, they create our belief system, values, goals, perspective on life, any event, relationship, or person. The process of spiritual testing creates a tension, and like a rubber band can be stretched until it breaks, thereby freeing us of ego. Enlightenment happens when we are free of ego, even momentarily.

Centuries ago, the Greeks included stories about spiritual testing in their mythology. The Gods would challenge mere mortals. If the mortals pass the test, they thereby become demigods. Hercules is a good example because he wanted to become a demigod, much like we strive for Enlightenment.

Hercules is given a single day to clean the Augean stables—filled with horse manure (old karma) so thick the average human being could barely walk in it. He thinks and thinks. It seems impossible. Then he looks over his shoulder and sees a river running a hundred feet from the stables. He is suddenly inspired. Why not use the flow of the river to wash the stables? So, he diverts the river and sends the water into each stall in the stable. By the end of the day, he is finished.

This wonderful myth shows how Hercules uses inspirational thinking to solve his dilemma. His solution is thinking beyond the conceptual mind. It is an archetypal connecting with the universe to receive an answer to his struggle. The river is life's energy. Hercules becomes friends with a source of energy greater than himself and thus fulfills his task given by the Gods.

When I am only six, I read this story. It stays with me all my life. How interesting that these Greek gods and demigods have both emotions and weaknesses. Now I understand more deeply the meaning of struggle, perseverance, inspiration, and rising to a new level. The stables are my karma of lifetimes. I have much to clean out to realize full Enlightenment.

Spiritual testing will stretch your preconceptions, such as thinking that healing means the physical body will recover. When a client does not recover and in fact dies, how can I make peace with this dilemma? Did I let them down? Who has the power to heal? What does healing mean? These are only a few of the many questions that come when being tested as a spiritual healer. Sometimes these conflicts crescendo within me. I struggle to understand.

In this book are stories of life and death, deep sorrow, and truly exquisite moments of sweet bliss. I share my own conflicts and hardships such as how to survive financially while offering free service to the poor. Can I charge for giving a blessing when blessings are from God? No. All right then, how do I survive in this physical world while offering service?

The reason this chapter is titled "Unfolding of the Path" is that moral dilemmas such as these cannot be answered overnight. It takes time to find our way, to cultivate purity, sincerity, and fortitude. There is also the issue of balance. We are human beings in a physical world. We are also spiritual beings living out only one incarnation at the moment.

Non-Attachment

A second key element on this path is practicing non-attachment. This includes not only one's ego or sense of self, it includes all positions or states of consciousness along the entire path to Enlightenment. It includes Enlightenment itself and all the levels of Enlightenment that unfold subsequently.

Non-attachment becomes a way of life. It does not mean not caring or being emotionless. Rather, non-attachment has a quality of smooth, letting go, mature understanding of ever-changing realities. It is a state of non-grasping. Therefore, in the non-attachment there is a strength of knowing that all is in transition between form and formless. So why get involved or upset? Ah, but the ego does get upset and invested in outcomes. This is a dilemma.

Here is my spiritual test as it relates to non-attachment. My teacher says not a word about my Enlightenment experience, not even privately. I am silent. It seems to me an opportunity to turn inward and be with the truth I directly experience. I reassure myself by saying, "If it is my truth, then surely I do not need any acknowledgement." Yet my insecurities wish for his smile.

Four months after my Enlightenment experience, I am alone with him in his small apartment. He tells me, "Bow down," indicating I am to prostrate with my head to the floor in front of a photograph of his teacher in China. As my head touches the carpet I hear his words, "You will realize the highest level of Enlightenment. You will be seriously tested 3 or 4 times more and will pass."

Where many people come to Master Sha for healing, I come to him for Enlightenment. Nothing more is said on this point. In fact, I begin to think he has forgotten this evening. I recall he made such a big event about Peter Hudoba's Enlightenment only a year prior. With Peter, a neurosurgeon from Canada, Master Sha asked him to write about his experiences and these pages are often shared with the public. In fact, upon many occasions, I am the person to read Peter's story.

For two years, my teacher and I stay in this silence on this point of my Enlightenment. Until one day, we are alone in a small chiropractic clinic. The room is no more than eight feet long and four feet wide. I remind him gently about my experience of Luminous. It is as if the conversation had never occurred before. "I will ask God," he says. "Yes, you are Enlightened." "Awesome!" my soul shouts inside me, "I am affirmed." Now you may find it strange that he would "forget" or choose not to discuss such an event. Yet this is most like him. You just never know what is coming at you. He certainly keeps me on my toes.

Perhaps another two months go by before my teacher makes a big announcement to his students of my realization of Luminous. Even then he speaks only of soul Enlightenment, something he hopes others will realize. Among his group of more than a hundred close students, I am the second person to receive this recognition. By this time, nothing moves my inner emotions. I feel neither joy nor pride nor reprimand because it took so long. I feel just quiet inside, detached and solid in my own truth. I know that *now the real work begins.*

We are a diamond in the rough. It takes a good teacher—kind, skillful, intelligent, perceptive, and tough—to wield spiritual sandpaper and polish our facets of life experience into beings of pure light. There is an ancient Chinese saying, "Yan shi chu gao tu. Serious master produce high level disciple."

Witnessing Enlightenment

I cannot begin to tell you the power, the impact, the meaning to me of witnessing the actual Enlightenment experience happen in front of my very eyes. My lifetime has been consumed with the spiritual quest. For decades, I pray each night for Enlightenment for all sentient beings. I read and study the path to Enlightenment…yet all this is from a distance, a separation. Then, one day…

In August 2001, Tom and I are at Sam's house in Moraga. The door opens and people are coming into the seminar. As I stand near the hallway, two men enter. One is Dr. Sha and the other I do not know and see only his back. I approach to greet Dr. Sha and the second man turns his head to look at me. We are perhaps three feet apart. I am taken aback for his eyes are turbulent and swirling with light and power. I have never seen eyes in this condition. Inside I am saying, "WHAT has happened to this man!" Then, his deep voice with its European accent says, "Hello, I am Peter." As is often the case, all his "hellos" have a big smile and radiant eyes beaming out to the beholder.

The previous day, Dr. Sha is with Peter by the ocean in San Francisco. He tells Peter to "just open, fully open," and Peter, a meditation practitioner for 25 years, does just that. He realizes a partial entry into a powerful Enlightenment experience.

During the next few hours at Sam's house, Peter's opening continues, especially when Dr. Sha is chanting for a long time the Eighty-Seven Buddhas mantra of compassion. I am only a few feet away from Peter as he realizes the Buddha level of Enlightenment.

His cheeks are flushed and his pores are sweating. There is heat coming off of him. He is shaking, trembling, and bows down with his head to the floor. I see his back convulsing as his muscles ripple with the energy. I am transfixed, sensing the explosion within the room.

Many of us in the room see purple light inside our own bodies and golden light around the people in the room. We all feel such an exquisite energy that moves us to tears. Peter is on his knees, tears passing over his cheeks, his body shaking.

Dr. Sha continues chanting, calling on one Enlightened being after another. I, too, am opening and, for the very first time, I can feel myself merging into their magnificent presence. Their qualities are so different. I feel them inside my body: graceful, soft, fluid Quan Yin; solid, strong, penetrating, deep blue Medicine Buddha; youthful, regenerative, kind Jesus; tall, bearded, wise, gentle, scholarly Lao Tzu. Then a white lotus opens in my heart. Peter is moving with the rhythm of the microcosmic orbit. I am beyond words and thoughts…inarticulate, disorientated, and quiet.

I know this day and this event is most special. I ask Peter if I may meet with him later to learn more about what is transpiring. He graciously accepts. Two days later we meet. I bring my video camera to try to document his transformation. I ask him to carefully describe his inner experience of Buddha Enlightenment. He describes the power of energy and light shooting up through his chakras and blowing out through the top of his head and entering the state of Divine Bliss and union with God. However, it is not until we complete the filming that he lets the shield over his eyes fall. I look deep inside to witness a newly born volcanic explosion of primordial depths, an energetic swirling mass of power. It is almost too much to enter, and I lower my eyes like a shy little girl in the presence of universal creation.

I learn that Peter is a neurosurgeon who escaped from Communist Czechoslovakia with his wife. In the middle of one dark night, they were on foot trying to avoid the police and the border guards. Peter tossed the coins of the I Ching to tell him which way to go for safety and ultimate political freedom. Peter is a good example of cultivating the Golden Urn and trusting his spiritual teachings in a pinch.

Conversing With God

The third key element on this path is the aligning of one's soul with the Divine. This aligning has several facets. First is the practice of obedience to the will of God, however you come to understand this. Second is entering into conversations with God, or what I will call flow. Third is living a daily life with compassion, kindness, and purity of mind.

As the path progresses, our life transformation becomes more real and tangible. It may often be difficult to have the same dialogues with family and friends that before was usual. This leads to a paradox wherein you are simultaneously more open to a direct connection with the Divine, and yet estranged from your prior network. Further, what in many psychological groups is viewed as sharing, you can now see is really complaining or self-aggrandizing. Neither of these last two qualities will help you become more pure or humble within your own mind. Habitual negative thinking and repetitious idle chatter feed the ego in a manner that does not nurture the cultivation of higher states of consciousness. There is a direct and immediate negative emotion that follows a negative thought. This is "funny thinking." Thus, words of gossip, self-importance, complaints, and judgments are all negative thinking. This is not the direction I wish to pursue. So, with whom can there be a dialogue?

The door closes to an old way of thinking and speaking with others. And another door opens. For me, the opening of the door leads to conversations with God.

These conversations take two forms: prayer and flow. Prayer is the invoking of the Divine. Flow is receiving the message from the Divine. This is the conversation.

In the bigger picture, this guidance from the Divine may come in many forms: visual, sound, and synchronistic events or thoughts. Flow is an aspect of this guidance. I begin to pray and learn the profound impact of prayer upon healing soul, mind, body, and relationships. Then I learn how to speak with God directly.

At first, there is a single word that comes forth: Love. I am but a little baby learning a new way to communicate with the Divine. Later an entire book comes forth in perfect order with its table of contents leading the way. This is a blessed and golden state wherein my soul connects directly with God. I even learn how to speak publicly and spontaneously from within this state.

I ask God for guidance in the writing of this book. What am I to say? What am I not to say? More importantly, what will have the greatest impact upon the soul of the reader?

I sit quietly, praying to the countless Enlightened Ones, to God. I focus on my heart. No expectations, concepts or thoughts. I enter the Emptiness, open my mouth, and the words flow out into this book. There is a golden hue about my study. We begin and these are the words I receive:

"Oh, my Child
You are learning well.
Listen
Listen
Listen
For my words are
Everywhere.
I crescendo in the rainfall
Pouring my blessings down upon your head
Cleansing you.
Guiding you.
Ask
Just ask."

Flow comes as wisdom teachings out of the Emptiness.

The Task

Within the spiritual journey, there exist lineages of teachers and teachings. Some teachers are in the soul world and some are in the physical world. It is essential for one's progress to be respectful to all of them and to their wisdom. Your physical teacher is one of the vehicles through which the teachings come. As you progress on the path, these teachings also come directly from God.

When your teacher gives you something to do, DO IT!! I am given a task.

"Aubrey, you must write your book about your own Enlightenment and your transformation over the past year and a half. Write about what is testing, opening your spiritual channels, your Message Center, and your Enlightenment." My teacher, Master Sha, continues, "People need to understand these."

In this modern day and age, I receive a call on my cell phone while I am grocery shopping at Safeway. I sit down on the worn green wooden bench outside the glass doors, quietly listening to his voice. His tone is deep, as if softened by his trip to his ailing father in China. "Yes. Yes, I will do this," I tell him.

As I gaze at the golden hills and the swaying trees across the highway, he gives me a teaching. "Teaching is ten times faster than meditation! Write your book!" (September 2002)

Chapter 3

Beginning

The desire to fully awaken is a powerful magnet drawing us to the spiritual path. As children, we may not be able to articulate these feelings, yet we know the peace that comes when we walk in nature, watch the eternal rolling of the ocean's waves, feel the soft dirt of plowed fields. This peacefulness goes deep into our bones, a lullaby of nature. As adults, we yearn for this peace. Yet it is deeper than peace that we seek. This magnetic pull is behind the never-ending questions of a two-year-old, behind the "Why?" that follows every answer you give them. These whys are like the eternal waves of the ocean: answer them and you tell the child about the principles of the universe and creation.

I begin my conscious journey when I am but two years old. Because I am often sick, I spend a lot of time in bed. My mother turns my bed upside down, raising the mattress so I can look out at San Francisco Bay. One day, as I am gazing at the Golden Gate Bridge, I am suddenly in the sky and flying quite fast between its spans, heading downward into somebody. My mother and father love to sail on the bay. They do so just before my mother gives birth to me. I experience my soul coming into my mother's womb while she is out sailing on the bay. I instantly know, in a child's quite matter-of-fact manner, that this is my soul. I feel and see the flight. Often in my adult life, I share this realization. I keep thinking someday someone will say, "Yes, I had a similar experience," but so far no one has shared this.

Between two and four, I have another matter-of-fact realization. My paternal grandparents are farmers who live in the gentle countryside of Sebastopol, a little town 50 miles north of San Francisco. My mother often sends me to their farm to recover from an earache or cold. I associate the countryside with getting well. Every morning, Grandma turns on the radio to listen to Walter Cronkite reporting the news from overseas. We are sitting in the kitchen eating hot cereal and watching the cold frost on the grasses outside. She is burning wood in the firebox of the old stove to take the chill out of the air. Grandma listens so intently to the news, hoping my father will return soon, hoping he will live through this long war. I see her pain. My "knowing" tells me my father may not return. I may never know my father. Poor Grandma.

My life has now two distinct paths. With my upper class German Jewish mother, I live in The City. We eat dinner at a formal table. People come to discuss intellectual matters. They discuss the war from the safety and comfort of a distant shore. With Grandma and Grandpa, I pick fruit from the apple trees and kick dirt in the orchards. They are Christian farmers. Grandma has some Native American blood. From her, I inherit the name Aubrey, her family name. Her mother was a midwife and healer. Perhaps this familial line helps me become a spiritual healer.

Between two and eighteen, I frequently travel from one side of my family to the other. Many impressionable moments occur with both. When I am six, my father returns from the war. He, too, becomes a key influence. Each time I return to be with either parent, that path continues seamlessly from where I left off. I do not share the experiences I have with one parent with the other. My lips are sealed. This child's survival technique, years later, becomes a psychologist's ability to keep the confidences of others.

Life with My Mother

When I am about three, my mother teaches me that I have the power to direct my own dreams. I am having bad dreams, and she wishes to help me. Being herself in Jungian analysis, she finds the dream state significant. When I am four, I have a nightmare about scary witches. While I am inside the dream, I remember what my mother says. I climb to the very top of this gnarly cypress tree. The witch is chasing me. It is terrifying. "Mommy told me I have the power to direct my dreams!" Armed with this power, I decide to fly. The witch is too heavy, and I fly away.

So, I cultivate the ability to fly in the dream state. Sometimes I fly over entire cities and high mountains. Sometimes I am clumsy and bump into things. Sometimes I fall and sometimes I soar. It takes many years to get good at this.

It is not until I meet my first Tibetan lama that I hear the term for this practice. They call it Dream Yoga. Apparently, I am practicing sky walking—one of the siddhis or powers that comes as you progress on the path to Enlightenment.

Thank goodness I come from a family who is open to psychic phenomena. My uncle, Michael Hughes, is a psychic who is tested by Stanford University. He is placed in a Faraday cage to isolate any random electric currents while they research his psychic abilities.

I remember sitting in the small white kitchen in Uncle Michael's home in Laurel Canyon in Los Angeles. I am six years old. I look up at the old-fashioned glass door. Suddenly, I see little people sitting on two of the wooden frames that hold the lower panes. They are just resting there quite jovially. "Mom! Mom! I see the little people in the window!" I am so excited. At the time I do not know I am seeing with my third eye. Both Mom and Uncle Michael assure me that Leprechauns are indeed watching us. It all seems so natural. My uncle has many spirits in his house.

My mother is quite psychic herself. As an adolescent, she sees her elder brother could be hurt in a car accident. She implores him, "Please, Buddy, don't go! Don't go out now!" He ignores her pleas and is indeed hurt in an accident. Many times, she tells me this story. It frightens her to see into the future and she avoids her intuitive side as an adult.

However, by the time of her death she is seeing again. She reports there are little cats in the closet. Men from the play *The Three Penny Opera* are seated in the living room. We speak many times about the difference between hallucination and seeing spirits. I know now that there are moments in life when "the veil is thin" between the physical and the spiritual realm—when we are close to dying, when we are quite ill, or when we are in shock.

In spite of the struggles within our relationship, my God, how grateful I am now as I reflect back on the many doors, both external and internal, that she opens for me. I so miss her. Tears come to my eyes. On that very last day, she says, "I wish we could have had one more good conversation." She is on her way out. It is the last time I see her. Two days later, I am placing long-stemmed blue iris around her body as she lies in her four-poster bed on the top of Nob Hill. She is only two blocks from Master Sha. She was scheduled to meet him that afternoon. Instead, in his workshop that morning he prays for her passage into the soul world.

Now I understand these spiritual openings from the vantage point of Enlightenment. For a long time, these openings are isolated phenomena.

Like a slow-motion movie of a flower opening—the bud opens in short, jerky motions until suddenly it is in full bloom.

I am raised outside organized religion. My father calls the giant redwood trees his cathedral. I can well understand—these majestic trees with light streaming through from heavens to the soft, quiet earth! My mother is an atheist; yet her grandparents attend synagogue. My uncle explores matters of the soul in poetry while my cousin becomes a physicist.

I am given a rather broad hand of cards in this diverse background. Nobody teaches me religion. I am a seeker on my own, searching for Enlightenment.

I recall one warm spring Sunday when we are living in Carmel. I am eight. I walk into the back of a church trying to somehow become a part of whatever is going on here. I see people kneeling and then sitting. "Why do you kneel down?" It seems you kneel because everyone else does. This is not a good enough answer for me. The next week I go to another church. I want to know why people are doing what they are doing. I am seeking and yet not knowing even how to ask the questions.

My great-grandparents attend Temple Emanuel, and my mother thinks this may help me. I go with them into a beautiful, curved roof temple with golden walls. In front of me is a ruby red cabinet with gold tiles. It contains the Torah. I am impressed by the sense of reverence and richness of spirit. So, I enroll in classes with other teenagers. This lasts perhaps three times. The classroom feels bare, the atmosphere thin. The teaching is by a book. There is nothing alive for me. This does not touch my burning hunger to know and understand the sacred journey.

So where is the sacred journey? Where is the living transmission, the living energy that I can feel? When I am sixteen, I am given the chance to visit Egypt. It is here I have my first living energy experience…I knew I have lived there before! It makes me weep.

Life with My Father

My father in his early twenties spends hours at the formal dining table of my mother's parents. He, too, listens to lengthy discussions of the intelligentsia from the protected ambiance of distant shores. These discussions turn his stomach. They create an ethical dilemma. As a young doctor he cannot bear sitting on the sidelines. So, he leaves my mother and their luxurious life to join the British in World War II.

My father volunteers to go to war when I am not even a year old. He lives in London during the bombings by the Germans, working as a member of the British Royal College of Surgeons. I do not see him for the next six years. I cry when Perry Como sings, "Oh my papa, to me you are so wonderful. Gone are the days when you would take me on your knee. Gone are the days when you would change my tears to a smile." I so miss the man I do not know.

Out of this yearning for my father comes a dedication to his values—one of the guiding forces of my life. He calls it, "Always take care of the poor and the suffering." The power of this resolution is not a conscious decision. There simply is no other way. This becomes one of the profound connections between my soul and the goals of my teacher, Master Sha. Both my father and Master Sha have a profound dedication to service.

One precious morning in Uncle Michael's home, I quietly tiptoe into the living room where I see a figure under the soft white blanket on the sofa next to the stone fireplace. My mother promises me that when I wake up, HE will be there. I cry at the fulfillment of her promise. HE is there! After all the hours of suspense, feeling the despair and hope of dear Grandma as she listens to the radio, after all my hidden tears listening to Perry Como, here he is. His toes stick out one end of the blanket and his head sticks out the other. He is alive. He comes home to get me!

That very day, at age six and a half, we travel by train to the county hospital in Martinez, where he has just secured a job. He lets me count his few remaining coins during that train ride. He is quite broke. We arrive at the county hospital and he takes me directly to his "home." He sleeps in a building adjacent to the hospital. It is the abandoned juvenile hall.

I clearly remember that first night when he tells me to go to bed. He will be right back. The walls are khaki colored, worn cement. There are no chairs, no furniture. It is bare. There are bars in the doors and on the windows. I hear the walls screaming. I try to push away the energies coming at me. I never imagined that children could be locked up! I am terrified. I huddle in a thin blanket on the naked steel coils. I dare not sleep. This is my first weekend visit with him.

My earliest memories of the county hospital are the crowded main lobby with its rickety cold metal chairs. These chairs are filled with struggling humanity. People are in pain. People are poor. People are bleeding. People are drunk. The county jail bus arrives with prisoners who need immediate attention. I walk through this lobby, intimidated by the nakedness of humanity. I hang onto my father's white jacket. People lean on their chairs, sit in their chairs, and sleep in the same chairs. Babies are crying. So many eyes show gratitude mixed with pain. Voices greet him saying, "Hello, Doc…thank you for helping me."

They are strangers to me, yet they seem to know him so well. I feel safe as long as I am with him. This is so very different than the life of luxury I live with my mother, with its properness, maids, and private schools.

For the next eleven years, I receive an education in humanity and service. It is an opportunity that today's laws forbid. For me, it is an extraordinary blessing. These experiences open my heart to Master Sha some 40 years later. With Master Sha there is a similar flood of humanity, suffering, and loss of hope as people come for healing and blessing. There are many similarities between my father and my teacher—as doctors, as healers, as powerful innovative minds, and as charismatic speakers. In time, I see that their spiritual goals are very different. My father is motivated to help the poor, as he too was poor. Master Sha is motivated to bring Enlightenment to all souls. My father's church is in the Redwood Groves. Master Sha's church is in the light of God. Both are powerful men who can fill an audience's hearts with their poetic and inspirational words. Later, I understand this quality of charisma and poetry comes from speaking in the state of flow where one's soul is connected with the Divine.

During these formative times with my father, I spend weekends, holidays, and later, long summer visits. I love going to be with him. I am able to volunteer in the hospital. At first, he just lets me tag along. I practice becoming invisible and am known as "George's daughter." Sometimes I wonder if I have an identity other than "George's daughter." It seems not. Later, he sends me to different wards for full days and weeks at a time.

A Ten-Year-Old Sees Death

One day when I am ten, there is great excitement. I am following my father on his daily rounds. About a dozen people are hovering around the doorway to one room. I continue to follow my father as people make a path for him to quickly enter. I am shocked by what I see. There is a man burnt to a crisp. He is a fireman. There has been a terrible fire in one of the canyons, and he was trapped. His skin is gnarly, blackened, charred. "Doc, Doc, take me out!" he cries. "Let me die!"

His mind is so clear. He knows he has no life to live, and he begs to die. My father orders the meds. The man quiets down as the sedatives take effect. He asks my father to give a message to his wife. "Doc, Doc, tell her I love her. Tell her I forgot to wish her happy birthday. Oh God, Doc how could I forget to wish her happy birthday as I rushed out the door? I am so sorry. Doc, tell her I am so sorry."

At this point, someone in the room realizes I am watching all this and shuttles me out the door. I stand still in the hall, absorbing what I am seeing. I see that a body in deep pain may still have a clear mind. I see these are separate. I also see the nakedness of truth and how he faces his truth in crisis. I see crisis for the first time. I see the impact of shock. I see how a life happens in moments. I see impermanence. I see that love needs forgiveness. I see that his hurry to rush out the door led him to forget to tell his wife his love for her and to wish her happy birthday. I learn so much about our priorities and that often we have them backwards.

All these teachings stay with me throughout my life. They become the backbone of my perspective about life. As an adult, I am at ease with trauma and crisis because of many such experiences in the hospital. Bearing witness to the nakedness of the fireman's humanity facing his death gives me the foundation to work with trauma in law enforcement and the military. I am more comfortable with this nakedness than with the social airs of those with power or prestige. This is a profound, shocking, and eye-opening teaching for a ten-year-old.

My father speaks to me many times about trauma. He alludes to the blankets placed over the British hospital's windows, protecting them from being sighted and bombed by German airplanes. He mentions the constant shrieking of air-raid sirens day and night. He tells me about multiple wounds. All these images are painted into my mind through his words. He never speaks about himself or the impact of these days and years upon him. He speaks of trauma as something he learned to face so he could help suffering soldiers seeking refuge and fighting for their very life and limb.

For years, he endures the bombings of World War II. He joins the British before the US entered the war, possibly more keenly aware than other Americans of the danger facing European Jews. His motivation is spurred through the dinner conversations in the home of my mother's family as they lavishly entertain cultured Jews, comfortably safe in San Francisco. It is perhaps difficult for these individuals to face the dangers to their families in Germany because of our human ability to deny reality. I think my father is also seeing the disparity of social class, privilege, and war. These forces collectively lead him to join the British. He comes to know war in the chaos and terror in London. In his words, his job was to "sew people back up."

As an adolescent, I follow my father as he moves through a typical day at the county hospital. He is now head of surgery and will soon be given the title of County Medical Director. He works very long hours. To be able to spend time with him, I volunteer for the same long workday—16-18 hours a day.

By the time I am fifteen, the staff at the county hospital is used to seeing me either next to my father or working on the wards for days at a time. The following year, Dad decides I need to spend a month at a time on key wards so that I can really be "put to work."

My rotation begins in surgery. I am taught how to scrub before entering the operating room, how to set up the surgical trays, and how to prep someone's abdomen before the doctor uses the scalpel. I see inside abdomens, legs, hearts, and even testicles. I hear the sound of a saw cutting through bone.

Then I am moved to X-ray, assisting in positioning patients and developing film. In time, I even do the entire chest sequence unassisted. I see bones and skeletons. The radiologist and technicians help me spot fractures or tissues masses. I assist with barium procedures that show the stomach and intestinal tract. I am fascinated.

Then I am rotated to the ward for the elderly. I see the helplessness and isolation of old age. I somehow think the elderly are always old and do not realize they were once young. This may sound strange, but I did not have the sequence of youth, adult, old age, and then death as a reality we all face. During my time with geriatric patients, I learn how to make beds while the person is still in it and unable to get up. I empty their urinals and try to suppress my gag reflex at its smell. I wash their wrinkly bodies. I feel stifled on this ward. The air is suffocating in its stillness.

I rotate from geriatrics to OB/GYN, assist in the birthing of babies. The mothers are often so young, barely sixteen or eighteen. Their friends come to the hallways and hang out while the young mother gives birth. It is a party! The full moon seems to bring babies being born and more inmates fighting who rush to emergency seeking sutures.

I am rotated into the emergency room. People seem real when they are in trouble. There are no social airs. I am learning how to connect with peoples' hearts. Yet I still have more questions than answers. Why do the doctors automatically tell a paraplegic that he will never walk? Why do they take away his hope? Is there not something that can be done? My heart goes out to the young motorcycle rider asking me for help. He can no longer walk holding his young daughter's hand. Why is there this suffering?

By seventeen, I am learning a great deal about the human mind as it is confronted with illness. It is summer and Dad sends me to the psychiatric ward for three months. It is called J Ward. There is a lockdown section where patients are isolated and constrained to their bed in leather wristbands. I see patients crazily "acting out," either to attract attention or to scare people away. I also watch them in an instant become lucid, knowing who and where they are. In these lucid moments, I find them often more honest and accessible than the staff and doctors. They speak with me and connect in a heart-to-heart dialogue. Then suddenly, they re-enter whatever reality they had just left. They hold postures with arms raised to the ceiling for hours at a time. How can this be? My arms get tired after a few minutes! I am witnessing altered states of consciousness that have very heavy psychiatric labels placed upon them. The unfairness of this labeling process is shocking.

I come to know many of the patients on this ward. There is a sixteen-year-old boy from a middle-class family. They call him a delinquent because he doesn't come home on time to the curfew set by his parents. He is referred to as "acting out," "angry," and "defiant." To me, this seems like many of my friends and really no big deal. It is hard to understand what comes to pass. The head nurse, Maxine, a large woman with a powerful deep voice, a no bullshit attitude, and a good nose for realism, invites me to a hearing for this young man.

It is a hot summer day, and I am sitting in the small staff room with a very large wooden table in the center. This is the "hearing" that Maxine wants me to observe. Until this moment, all that I really know about psychiatrists is that they spent time with each patient behind closed doors. These little cubicles feel confining, and I did not want to enter. So, I had not met any of the psychiatrists until this hearing.

In this staff room is the chief psychiatrist, the county representative, Maxine as the head of the psychiatric ward, and the boy's parents. I see piles of records on the table. I contract my body so as to not be engaged, hoping no one will ask me a question. Somehow, I do not feel safe. I sense many conflicting agendas. Maxine thinks this young adult does not need further treatment. The parents are vehement that their son is truly disturbed and beyond their care. The psychiatrist advocates increasing the treatment by referring him to another institution. The county representative falls in line with the psychiatrist, not wanting the county to finance further care. The parents continue to push their point. I can see they are truly at odds with their son and quite angry with him. They are lashing out at this unmanageable adolescent—using "treatment" as a punishment.

I wonder when their son will be asked to join us. But he never comes. There is no intent to include him in the hearing. He is a minor, chattel, a disenfranchised person. The decision is to transfer him to an institution, equipped to give electroshock treatments. This means locking him up for many more months.

As one adolescent to another, I emotionally ally with him. I believe his story. I promise to visit him, as I can see he truly has no one on his side. Several weeks later, I go to the San Francisco mental institution where he is getting his new treatment. The elevator is old and squeaky with tarnished green steel walls—more like a freight elevator than one for people. The ward is locked. I have to wait until they let me enter. As he approaches, I am shocked. This is not the same boy I saw only weeks ago. This person is gaunt, his eyes filled with terror. He looks like a 40-year-old, worn-out man. He bursts into tears, begging me to help him get out of this torture chamber. He tells me they strap him to the table, frying his brain as his body jolts in convulsions. It is a terrible punishment that his parents demand he endure. He is a prisoner.

I leave our visit devastated, never to see him again. I am reeling in my own shock. So many questions are circling around inside my head. How can parents commit their own child to this horror? How can one side see "getting home late" and another side see "insanity"? I am witnessing the suffering caused by concepts, caused by our thinking.

When I am with the patients, many relate to me so straight and direct, speaking from a deep core place. The puzzle is, I cannot find that core place in the psychiatrist. Why? Why are people in crisis more accessible? Certainly, they are more accessible than my mother's social friends and the psychiatrist. I am fascinated. It seems to have to do with the comfort and illusion of safety in roles.

Dad does not like psychologists or mental health workers. I have the impression he thinks they are as wacky as their clients. Unfortunately for Dad, I become a Humanistic Psychologist rather than an MD. He is gracious about my choice and never shows any disappointment or regret.

He continues to teach me about the role of service and the importance of helping others. He says, "Always watch out for the little people." He means the poor, the isolated, and the lonely.

The summer draws to a close. I am absorbing the education that life itself brings. This is much more interesting than the lengthy intellectual debates at my mother's formal dining table. I find the dinner hour boring. Besides, I have to wear my shoes to the table!

Life with My Mother Continues

In my sophomore year, we travel to Rome. Arriving at the Sistine Chapel, I see the whiteness of the large marble statue of David at its entrance. My mother tells me people kiss the toe of David in reverence. This is why his toe is so worn down. As we walk into the Chapel, perhaps 40 by 100 feet, I feel such grandeur of a presence—more palpable than paintings and marble alone can express. Voices echo. Sounds of shoes reverberate off the stone walls. People walk and talk in hushed tones. Everyone feels this indescribable presence.

The ceiling of the Chapel opens my mind into my first cognitive realization of spirit and song of the Heavens. How could someone paint up that high? How could this painter, Michelangelo, conceive of all these images? What are these colorful and majestic pictures? As my eyes and neck turn and turn to gaze at the ceiling, one spot holds my attention. It is the hand of God touching the out-stretched fingers of Adam. God is surrounded by angels, billowing clouds, and golden light. It is the hand of God touching humanity.

This is the first extensive and complete vision of God I have ever seen. I ask my mother to give me a replica of this fresco of God's hand and man's hand touching. Today, 30 years later, this painting is part of my shrine.

These external visions of God coupled with European masters' Renaissance paintings have a lasting impact. However, at the time the endless depictions of angels and golden billowing clouds seem somewhat ho-hum to my adolescent veneer of boredom. I walk slowly down long corridors in museums without feeling anything stir in my heart.

Later, I have many direct experiences of God, God's heart, and heaven. My soul travels to God and these images appear as the God painted in the Sistine Chapel, only with total light and no form. I know God as a Presence of Light. Michelangelo, a great mystic, was pointing in this direction.

My mother next takes us to tour the underbelly of humanity. Going from depicted bliss to pain becomes my first clear taste of the up and down, seesaw nature of the journey of the soul. How perfect! How symbolic!

It is a natural progression to go from the vision of God to the bowels of the catacombs, to the very tombs of those who died during the Roman Empire proclaiming there is a God. The Romans chased the Christians into these underground tunnels where they had fled for their lives. The Christians created labyrinths of pathways under the earth to hide from the Roman soldiers. As we walk through the catacombs, there are open tombs that rest like bunk beds stacked one upon another. We wander in candlelight through these caverns of packed dirt until we come upon large open meeting areas, and then more labyrinths of tombs. We walk for miles in this seemingly endless curving cemetery until we are liberated into the light of day many miles from Rome. I taste the freedom of fresh air. The Christians must have felt the same relief as they came out into this open meadow.

Together, my mother and I walk through the progression that occurs many times within the history of humanity. It is the fundamental religious disagreement that leads to the persecution and annihilation of millions of souls. It is the progression of man's intolerance of others' beliefs. In God's name, we slaughter disbelievers. It is an appalling vein of humanity.

Mother exposes me to this horror that is so deeply embedded in our collective karma. This is her teaching. She shows me. I feel it and smell it and walk in it. I never forget this lesson.

The next day, we fortify ourselves with strong Italian coffee in the comfort of our hotel. She tells me we are going to the site of the Roman Games. I flirt with the bus boy. Life is easy at the moment. We travel to the Roman Colosseum and enter ground level into the large, circular tiered brick structure. It appears much like a football stadium, only so much older. She shows me where the horses and chariots raced around the outside.

We walk below the ground into tiny cells with windows just high enough to see the dust of the Colosseum's arena. Here, the prisoners waited to compete with one another, freedom promised upon killing their adversary. No matter what game is played, almost everyone dies. Gradually, I learn that the winner also loses his life. It is not a game. Just as this realization of the true picture comes to me, it must also have come to those who were imprisoned. They were forced to fight, then they, too, were killed while the bloodthirsty crowds cheered. What horrible atrocities. I can feel screams coming from the ancient walls. I can feel the anguish of the trapped victims.

My mother gives me a good education in the history of man and the suffering we have inflicted on one another. This is culture? Surely it is not cultured behavior. She takes me to sites of history, sites of death, and sites of cultural greatness. Her tutelage is a gift.

If these are examples of how people fight over questions of the existence of God, how then do people deal with a physical embodiment of the spirit of God? What about Jesus?

As if to answer that question, my mother takes Patti, my college roommate, and myself to Israel. We are nineteen. We begin in Nazareth, the town of Jesus's early adolescent years. We are taken to the actual site of his family home. We enter through a low doorway, immediately descending into a rounded underground cave. The stairway is curved and cut into the tightly packed orange desert earth. The walls, the floor, and the stairs are made of the same orange clay. Everything is startlingly barren.

I have no relationship with Jesus as a child or adolescent. Being in his home does not move me at this time.

Later, we go to Jerusalem to visit the chapel of the Last Supper. There are many engravings on the walls, a table in the center. Years later this room comes to me in a dream where the golden spirit of Jesus is in the air hovering above his disciples. I am seeing Jesus with my third eye while in the dream state.

In 2002, I see Jesus again when Master Sha comes to dinner in our home. Today, I have a profound and direct relationship with Jesus. My mind wants to figure out how does this work? I go from no relationship with Jesus to directly experiencing the light of Jesus flowing through my heart and hands in blessing and healing?

My early years lay the foundation for spiritual Awakening into Enlightenment.

Chapter 4

Good Teachers Hurt

I learn early on that good teachers are tough. Good teachers can hurt you. It is up to you, and only you, how to receive this tough love.

One hot sticky day in New York City, I am in leotards with the door open to a small courtyard. There are about 25 dancers in the room with me. The walls are all mirrored. We are somewhat nervous, as the Grande Dame of Modern Dance is about to make a personal appearance to correct us. This is seen by each of us as a great, if not somewhat intimidating, moment. It is a great honor to be part of her school at the age of sixteen.

Martha Graham glides rapidly into my body space, leans over, and pinches the inside of my thigh in an effort to get more turnout of my leg. I am jolted by this physical and definitely painful intrusion into my body. She won't let go! I am forced to bend beyond what I thought was possible! Then she glides on to the next sweating young student.

Sexual Hanky-Panky

I manage to avoid sexual intercourse with my teachers. It is hard to admire them when they take advantage of my vulnerability as a woman. I survive their passions and egomania while still being a respectful student. As the years pass, my women friends become more at ease, telling their stories of seduction by a respected teacher. But it takes a toll on a deeper philosophic level: trust. It seems the closer I get to the "inner circle," the greater the chance of sexual hanky-panky. It is a two-way street. While the teacher (say it is a man) may abuse the power of his position, the female student uses her seductive nature to also conquer his power. This abusing of power and role is only one face of the ego flaws that are still present even in a high position. Luckily, very early on I see that even a great teacher has ego flaws. It is up to me to separate these flaws from the body of knowledge he is transmitting, to throw out the bath water but keep the baby.

I am standing on the edge of a meadow where the land suddenly drops off into the tumultuous Pacific Ocean. This juxtaposition between gentle meadow and dashing cliffs reflects the confusion and shock I feel inside. A dear friend of mine, a beautiful young woman, has committed suicide. She fell in love with Fritz. He took advantage of his power and his persona and crossed the boundaries of psychiatrist and lover. He is a sexy and brilliant man who loves younger women. Some might say he is indiscriminately lecherous. Personally, I stay away from him in the hot tubs of Esalen.

Fritz Perls, M.D.

As synchronicity would dictate, I hear that a brilliant Gestalt therapist, Fritz Perls, has recently arrived from the East Coast and is looking for a "large living room" in which to hold his workshops. I am 27, single, sexy, a bit naïve, and very drawn to understanding more about the human psyche. So, I grab the opportunity and open my home to Fritz. Fritz looks like an old oak tree with powerful gnarly energy spreading out into its branches. He has a gruff manner, a deep, vibrant voice that cuts through bullshit.

One weekend a month, he stays at my house in Berkeley. This lasts for one year. These two-day training sessions are very intense. The room holds 20 to 25 people, all eager to learn about the "Here and Now" approach of Gestalt psychotherapy.

Each of us experiences the infamous Hot Seat, that special place of honor, the empty chair at Fritz's side. Sitting in the hot seat, we start to tell our stories, our dramas to which we are dearly attached. Fritz falls asleep…and snores! We keep talking, bumbling along, unable to interrupt ourselves. All eyes rivet upon the student flailing to express himself. Why is Fritz sleeping? We certainly don't understand why he suddenly wakes up, barking some directive at the hot seat. It is fascinating trying to see, to hear, and to follow. What IS this man doing? How can he track what is being said when he is snoring? Does he have some sixth sense for authenticity?

I do not yet have the ability to enter his mind and follow his thinking. It looks very puzzling. Yet this is the beginning of my training under powerful teachers. It is the beginning of learning how to enter into someone else's mind. By the time I am studying with my latest teacher, I consciously request in my mind his permission to travel where his consciousness is going. With this permission, I can travel into spaces in the universe I never dreamt even existed!

One day, I am in the hot seat in Fritz's house in Big Sur, emerging from a deep piece of work. I open my eyes and hear the loud sound of the surf crashing on the cliffs below. It is as though I am hearing it for the first time. It is so loud! I don't recall hearing any sound before I began. I am so startled! The light outside the open windows is golden, and the room is filled with little squiggly movements of electricity. I realize the sound and the light were there all along. *I* was not present.

This is my first conscious awareness that my inner thoughts and constant dialogue prevent me from hearing and seeing. This stark contrast between being open and being consumed by my inner voices becomes the foundation for serious meditation practice. I get it! I graphically understand the difference. I was not present. My senses were overpowered by my thinking and anxiety. The doorway into the NOW opens! I break through into an expanded state of consciousness! I will always remember this moment.

Gestalt is the study of the Here and Now. Just as the hot seat process brings one into the present, Fritz's work with the dream state does as well. The doorway of the dream state makes a lasting impression on me.

Fritz maintains that all dreams are unfinished situations. He shows us how to complete any dream in the NOW. We sit next to him and follow a specific sequence: "First," he requests, "tell your dream in the first person, present tense." Good. We run through the entire dream from beginning to end.

"Now," he adds, "become each key person in the dream. Say 'I am so and so.' Describe yourself as that person. Now, slowly recreate the dialogue with another person in the dream. Before you answer as the second person, repeat 'I am so and so.' And describe yourself."

This second recreation of the dream sequence deepens our understanding of each character and its emotions and demands. On a more subtle level it is an opportunity to see my own projections onto the characters in my dream. This is a foundation experience for seeing the power of projection and its illusory nature. The positions of each character become more crystallized. Simultaneously, the person telling the dream goes deeper into the dream world and brings a more ripened version of the dream state into the workshop room. Characters in the dream state are encouraged to fully voice their thoughts. Just when there is nothing left to say, Fritz demands you speak the unspoken. Without fear of reprimand, we push the boundaries of the dream further.

We replay the dream a third time, the way we would have liked it to be. To feel free to change the ending, or to create an ending where there was no prior resolution, to truly bring the dream into the NOW. This powerful merging of waking reality and dream reality has two results: it brings healing into the psyche through the dream state, and it opens the inner doors between conscious and unconscious material.

Fritz believes the dream is a reflection of the personal psyche. I believe him for years until I meet my first Tibetan lama. This belief is quickly broken. There is a powerful dynamic with my teachers starting: first trying on their teachings, then allowing these beliefs to be shattered! Part of the Enlightenment Journey is the breaking of all beliefs! We must be willing to break attachments, including what we are convinced is truth!

A third teaching from Fritz is seeing the power of remote work and how the soul world knows everything!

This day changes my life. My four-year-old daughter is off for the day with her father, whom she hasn't seen for six months. It is his first visit since our divorce. I am still in love with him, a handsome, bright psychologist and poet. I hope he will return to me, and I cling to this hope for the four years of our separation. Fritz knows my daughter from Big Sur, where she frolics in the tubs or rushes into his seminar room in the middle of a video recording session. He knows I have a beautiful little daughter.

Fritz calls me to the hot seat to have a dialogue with her father. As her father's voice emerges, the strength of his resolution to separate from me is so clear. It is equally clear how I yearn to reconnect our family. The stuckness of a broken marriage and the anguish of my broken dreams are vividly elucidated.

"Now," says Fritz, "pick up a big pair of scissors." I do this and hold the scissors in my mind. I trust Fritz. I do not know where he is going with this image. "Are you willing to let go of this marriage completely?" *Ouch.* He is cutting to the core, asking me to let go of my promises, my hopes, my loyalties, my pain. I see where he is taking me, and I cannot escape. The people in my living room are watching intently. There is no way out. Everything is going in slow motion and hanging on the empty spaces in the dialogue. I feel pushed not only beyond my comfort level, but beyond my readiness. I am stuck. I am standing in the way of my own river of life! I am attached.

Fritz tells me to strongly grip these large scissors in my hand. "Now see the cord between you and your ex-husband. Cut that cord!" he barks. I do.

I am not 100% behind this! But I cut the cord anyway. I make a leap into new territory.

It is the experience of standing on the precipice and leaping into the abyss…or is it leaping into the space of freedom? It is a loss of control. It is the unknown. Years later, this process of leaping into the unknown, of going beyond my mental constructs becomes a daily venue with Master Sha. He is a master at moving me beyond my own self-imposed boundaries. Good teachers hurt.

Years later, my ex-husband tells me that very afternoon when I am cutting the cord, he meets his future wife. They "dance the night away."

Claudio Naranjo, M.D.

Claudio Naranjo, dark-haired, bearded, thin, with penetrating yet laughing brown eyes, is a Chilean psychiatrist. Claudio has a keen intellect with a conscious veneer of humor and sarcasm. He highly regards the role of the fool in the Tarot as the keeper of divine inspiration. His gift is his mind, and his handicap is the same. I have seen him with his heart open and filled with light. I have seen him depleted of that very light. To learn from Claudio, one must meander with him in his non-linear storytelling and have a high tolerance for leaving the original point. His stream of consciousness presentation style has left many a good student behind. While this may be frustrating to the ego and the cognitive mind, it is really quite an excellent practice in loss of control.

Initially, I know of Claudio as a parent in that my daughter and his son attend the same school in Berkeley. However, a most unfortunate accident occurs and his son is killed in Big Sur. My heart goes out to him as a parent.

At about the same time, Claudio is returning from South America where he went to study under Oscar Ichazo. While there are many tales about this period in his life that can be better presented through those personally at his side, I must share a key vignette. Claudio spends 40 days in the Chilean desert, a rough, isolated, and barren setting. During this intense retreat, Claudio realizes Enlightenment. The word of this event travels to Berkeley with hushed hints that he will teach esoteric wisdoms from an ancient Sufi lineage.

Upon hearing of this possibility, I am immediately touched with that quality of knowingness…knowing I must contact him. Two very significant teachings are to come to me while studying under Claudio: the passing of Baraka and learning the Enneagram. In a dream, I am told to go to Claudio's house, and upon awakening I call him to make an appointment.

Claudio receives me warmly and invites me to return on a special day when he will officially begin his teaching. As part of the first day's initiation in the Sufi tradition, we sit in his back yard. There are 40 people all dressed in Berkeley's finest hippie tradition. It is springtime. This precious day is to be known as Baraka Sunday.

Claudio puts on Bach's *Concerto in D Minor* and sits down in the center of the circle. He begins to look deeply into the eyes of someone only a few feet away from where I am in this circle. He slowly turns to the next person, now only three feet from me. I am unsure of what is happening and yet feel the magnetic pull increasing. He fixes on my eyes and the energy begins to build. I am transfixed by his gaze. He turns to the next person and the next until he has met each of us in this transpasso or passing of divine blessing. He is inseminating each of us with baraka, the seeds of Awakening. Golden dewdrops of heavenly blessing fall upon each of us present.

This is a seminal moment in my spiritual journey. It is the seed of my own Awakening that culminates while studying with Master Sha. It takes 30 years to mature the seed into an embryo that is now born as an infant into the Enlightened state.

Claudio so generously gave and gave of his light. I feel he gave to us and then was worn down. This may be a key observation. While we are learning how to realize Enlightenment, we also need to learn how to sustain and nurture this blessed state.

The second significant teaching that Claudio passes to us is the Enneagram. The lineage of this Enneagram is passed from Oscar Ichazo to Claudio. The origins of the Enneagram come from an ancient Sufi order, the Sarmouni in Afghanistan. This is the same tradition that brought the personality work embedded in the Gurdjieffian Institute and that was tailored to the needs of Gurdjieff's ego.

However, in Oscar's case, this body of knowledge was imparted to him as a complete teaching. Apparently, Oscar was selected by the Sarmouni as an experiment upon the Western mind. The Sarmouni were most familiar with the Eastern mind, and this was their chance to see if their teaching could work and transform a mind from the Western Hemisphere.

Claudio, along with perhaps 20 other seekers went to train with Oscar in Chile. It was a difficult time and yet the rewards were great for Claudio returned to Berkeley with eyes that shine, revealing his Enlightened Mind. Oscar went on to found Arica that spread throughout the US as an esoteric school. Claudio is one of Oscar's first students. I, in turn, am one of Claudio's first students.

The Enneagram of Personality Types is a fascinating body of knowledge that enables anyone to clearly see the patterns of their ego. It includes ways to meditate and remove the tenacious roots of our personality.

This intense study of my ego is one side of the coin to liberation. Master Sha is to bring the second side of the coin. And as Tarthang Tulku, my Tibetan root guru loves to point out: two sides of one hand is still one hand. One side will have more darkness and the other side will have more light. Hold up your hand and you will see this teaching!

With Claudio, I begin serious meditation practices. One day during a retreat, I go downstairs into a basement room to chant. I feel energy moving inside like a volcano trembling. I had dropped acid with my mother the day before, and needless to say I am still quite open! I sit facing a blank wall about six feet away from me. "Om, Ah, Hung, Om, Ah, Hung." I chant and chant and tremble and tremble. The fire at the base of my spine is intense. Suddenly, a powerful thrust of energy picks me up from my cross-legged position by my bottom and tosses me upside down in a somersault into the wall. I land upside down on my head. Heat is pouring out of my body. I am sweating. I feel and see a spiraling energy going up my spine and out my head. I am blasted open in my kundalini. The sound "hum" vibrates into an explosion rising from my coccyx to my head.

Claudio's toughness always comes with a wry humor. In many ways he epitomizes the jokester. As one of Claudio's assistants, I am assigned to teach the Jesuits in Chicago. This is what happened.

I am in Claudio's study waiting for him to give me final assignments of the material I am to cover this weekend with the Jesuits. His eyes get that mischievous sparkle. Something is up! I can smell it.

"Aubrey, I have a task for you." This means he has a personal test for me, a serious challenge delivered through his laughter. "You are to teach the Jesuits tantra!"

"What?" My silent voice shrieks! How can I teach a celibate priesthood sexual tantra? There are priests and nuns in this group! They have never even met me in person! We have had contact through phone calls over the past twelve months. Besides, I know some of them are homosexual! Celibate, gay, elderly, and strangers to me. How can I gain their trust! This is an absurd Claudio trick!

He continues, "The final closing of your weekend is to end with tantric practice, naked in meditation! You figure it out and do it! This is your task!" And with that, the front door is opened and I am ushered out, stumbling, yet nodding my head. Claudio means naked tantric practice, not just mental tantric images. "Oh dear…" And off I go to Chicago.

Mind you, as a student, I have been well taught to rise to the occasion when given a task or homework. It is just that the stakes keep rising!

I have a good rapport with this group through their representative, Bob Eagan, a Jesuit. I know that my connection with him is strong enough that if I ask him to do something, he will. I also know that the group highly respects Claudio. They have done substantial work on themselves. They are this weekend finishing the Fisher Hoffman process of healing relationships between themselves and their parents. In the group's mind, I am coming for the ritual completion of this emotional and spiritual healing. So, their expectations are for closing ritual, blessings and love. Mine are the same— with the boundaries just slightly expanded!

"Bob, I need to ask you something." This is how I begin that Friday night upon my arrival. "I want you to select maybe two or three people in this group and ask them to follow your lead on Sunday. I want them to do exactly what you do. Can you think of whom this might be?"

"Oh yes, definitely there are three people whom I can trust in this way," Bob answers.

"Good. Sometime Sunday afternoon I will stand up. When I stand, I want you to also stand. And then for those three people to follow your lead. Are you clear? This is most important. That is all I will say for now, so be prepared."

Whew, step one is now in place.

Sunday comes. We are meeting in the faculty lounge of the Jesuit college. The group is very open emotionally. Tears are flowing as people forgive their mothers and fathers. Love is now the topic. Love and forgiveness of all past pains. People are letting go of their emotional stuck points. A sense of freedom and relief fills the room. I look over to Bob, whom I carefully placed directly opposite me in this circle. Pachelbel is playing. I ask the group to remain in silence for the next practice we are going to do.

I stand up. Bob stands. Three more people stand. The rest of the group stands. We are all facing each other in the circle. I undo the button on my long skirt. It falls to the carpet. Bob undoes the button on his pants and lets them slide to the carpet. The other three are following and two more pairs of pants and a skirt now drop to the carpet.

There is the counter motion of hesitation, but the weight of five people already disrobing moves the rest of the group. The other fifteen people ever so slowly let their pants or skirts fall. One nun, who is in her late fifties, stands stoic. Nobody is noticing her refusal because they each are so involved in their own internal friction. She backs away from the group and heads to the door. I know this is a most tentative and vulnerable moment. It would be so easy for others to simply bolt. No one else even sees her going.

I reach for my blouse and pull it off my shoulders and head. Bob, bless him is doing the same. So are the next three. So then follow the other fifteen, priests and nuns and lay members. We are in our underwear. The Jesuits and I are in our underwear in the faculty lounge!

I remove my bra and panties and immediately sit back down in my place in the circle. Quickly Bob does the same for there is some comfort in sitting on the carpet. Everyone follows suit until all of us are totally naked seated on the floor.

I begin chanting, "Ommmmm…" The group chants, eyes close and there is momentary safety. Most of the people in the room have never seen a naked body of the opposite sex. It is quite comforting now to hide behind closed eyes, neither seeing nor being seen.

"Now turn to the person next to you and face them…good, close your eyes again and continue chanting…your body is your temple…your soul came into a body…your body is the temple that God designed…your body is beautiful and pure…" I continue in this manner, introducing the notion of temple to help reduce fear and prior prejudice or beliefs about the body as separate from the soul. I am trying to help them break through conceptual barriers and prior beliefs about the negation of the body.

Suddenly, a voice chimes in, "Yes, my body IS my temple!" It is the very dean of the college! He is the first to break through the silence. It is an enormous jump. When the priests and nuns hear his words, it gives them permission to move beyond their prior belief system into the HERE AND NOW.

Eyes begin to open. They look around at one another in the circle. They are relaxing. The atmosphere in the room significantly shifts and softens. People are facing their partner. There are eight dyads. Everyone is sitting cross-legged on the floor. Pachelbel is playing its heart song and can now be heard on a deeper level inside each person's mind. Openings are happening in the room. I ask, "Please now listen to this music. Feel the love. Gaze into the eyes of the person across from you. Deeply gaze and hold your eyes open. Look into their soul. Breathe. Relax. Gaze."

The atmosphere is shifting into golden light that is palpable in the space. Each dyad is gazing into one another's soul. Now we chant, "Ommmmm…" together. The energy and the light continue to build. I continue to guide them with my voice saying, "Let your eyes now very slowly look upon the temple, the body, of the person in front of you. See the beauty that God has given to each of us. Relax. Just look. Up and down. [Pause.] Up and down." The subtlety of the gaze is loaded with mixed emotions. Wanting to look, curious, judgmental, embarrassed, relieved, intrigued, forbidden. The emotions are a veritable flood of energy.

"Relax, know that you are seeing a beautiful temple of the soul." We come back on track into the golden space. "Rest now within the eyes and the pupils of your partner." Safety again. The golden light is calm in the room. "Bring your hands together in the prayer position. Bow your head to your partner. Sit quietly with eyes closed." We meditate together for a few minutes allowing each person to regroup inside.

I ask the group to slowly put their clothes back on. We begin to share the experience. Priests and nuns are stunned by this tantric practice. They report golden light. They directly went into the light. In the light there is no judgment. This they now learn for themselves. Their bodies are as spiritual as their souls. It is a seamless moment of Oneness.

Thus, I complete my task for Claudio. Good teachers are tough.

Tarthang Tulku, Rinpoche

In terms of his cultivation of the Enlightened state of being, Tarthang Tulku, Rinpoche is the most realized and powerful spiritual teacher I have yet met by the time I am 30. He is one of the first Tibetan teachers to come to the Bay Area. His Holiness the Dalai Lama has not yet arrived for his first visit. The world of Enlightenment is still quite new and uncharted terrain in the West.

Claudio introduces his students to Rinpoche one warm summer day in Berkeley. We are sitting in an old university hall on the north side of campus. We sit cross-legged in silence with our eyes closed. Rinpoche sits on a slightly elevated platform. Time passes. Silence continues. "Perhaps nothing is going on here," I say to myself. "It is all so quiet." I peek out of my half-closed lids to behold an absolutely amazing sight. There is a Golden Buddha in front of me. His skin is golden. His demeanor is majestic and magnetizing. Somehow, Rinpoche has completely transformed himself into a Buddha! I sit and stare absolutely dumbstruck. I had never heard of such a phenomenon.

My curiosity and sense of smell for authenticity leads me to study with this Rinpoche. He offers a two-month summer intensive for practicing health professionals. Twenty-five of us join him in an experience that is forever life changing. In the years to come, several of his students realize Enlightenment. Rinpoche is a bit of a renegade from traditional Tibetan Buddhism, and he makes us his Western experiment. He wants to know if the Western mind can be trained as the Eastern mind. To that end, he gives us practices that in Tibet are given only after you are accepted for the three-year retreat. We bypass the preparatory stage and are catapulted into the powerful hidden teachings. We spend the next two months, dawn to dusk, five days a week with him. On the weekends, we have to do 24 hours of meditation practice on our own and report our experiences the next Monday.

Although I lack continuity in my practice, Rinpoche continues to open me further into peak experiences. I do not know what these experiences mean or what to do with them. When I report back to him, he just smiles and nods.

We learn a breathing technique focusing upon fire in the belly. As part of this sequence, he introduces a very sweet chant called Maha Sukha or Great Bliss. This opens my lower belly center, connecting me with the intimacy of the universe. This is my first taste of Divine Bliss. *[See the Chapter on "Opening Spiritual Channels" for a complete description of this practice.]*

That autumn, he asks me to teach Kum-Nye, which is a body/mind relaxation class with a form of self-massage designed to open our chakras. I become one of the early teachers at his Nyingma Institute, a tall and beautifully painted, in the traditional Tibetan style, building on the northern end of U.C. Berkeley campus. Later, he even asks me to write an article about Kum-Nye in *Gesar News,* his quarterly journal.

In the fall, I take my children to school by 7:30 in the morning and continue into the hills of Berkeley's Tilden Park, where I spend the next three hours meditating outside. Rinpoche gives us the secret Sky Meditation. It upsets high-level students even today when I refer to this Sky Meditation because we are not supposed to know about it. Even Rinpoche got in trouble with his peers for giving out such secrets.

I lie down on the hillside facing the morning sun. I relax my body as deeply and fully as possible without falling asleep. In this alert yet quiet state, I turn my gaze to my eyelashes. Each lash captures rainbow light and quivers with the microscopic movement of my eyelid. I take this movement to be an indication that my nervous system is not yet sufficiently quiet. So, with great intent I quiet down until there is no reflective light movement on my eyelashes. Only at this point do I feel ready to begin.

I gaze onto the infinite sky. My eyes are open halfway. Each instant when there is an attaching to a particular space in the sky, I cut through that attachment with a sharp knife-like intent. In Vajrayana Buddhism this is the vajra sword—sharp, powerful, and swift. It is the symbol for cutting through any attachment. I am as a samurai in the sky. Cutting through any stopping point. Slice through the sky. Continue further into the vast space. Cut through any place my eye lingers. Go further and further and further into the vastness.

Suddenly the total sky, almost in a discernable pop before my eyes, stands totally still, uniform, pale blue and so very empty—an endless smooth glide of emptiness. The utmost silence is upon me. This is the Shunyata, the great Void state of consciousness.

I do not know how long I rest in this place. It is long enough to drink deeply of this unique experience of total emptiness.

Suddenly, the whole experience changes. Where there has been infinite emptiness, there is now the image of Guru Padmasambhava filling the entire sky! This being literally fills the sky! He comes swiftly almost as if the force of his presence popped out with a push into my awareness. He has a quality of being thrown at me from within the emptiness. He comes from the vastness of the emptiness. I am so startled to see this great teacher who brought Buddhism from India to Tibet in 700 AD. There are texts, sutras (poems), and termas (hidden teachings embedded in rocks, rivers, and Enlightened Minds) that expound his great wisdom. It is said that he was born in a lotus flower that grew out of the mud. Symbolically, this captures the inspiration and hope that abounds in all souls: that out of the mud, suffering, and struggle of our humanity, we can be reborn into the beauty and fragrance of the lotus flower.

I have never heard of Padmasambhava or anyone else being thrown into my awareness out of the sky! I return to Rinpoche and tell him that the great Vajra Guru came to me in the sky. Rinpoche merely looks at me and says, "I wish I had that relationship with Vajra Guru." Rinpoche is totally understated. I intuitively knew that this experience was directly related to Rinpoche's relationship with Padmasambhava. What I did not know was how this all works. How does an Enlightened Being make contact with a high-level teacher on the physical plane? And even more astounding, "How does this connection get passed to me?" What IS Rinpoche doing?

From this day forward, I continue to chant the Vajra Guru mantra. "OM AH HUNG VAJRA GURU PADMA SIDDHI HUNG." This is one interpretation of its meaning:

OM: the sound of creation
AH: the sound of the void
HUNG: the wisdom compassion in my heart and the universe
VAJRA: sword-like cutting through
GURU: fully realized master teacher
PADMA: born of the lotus flower
SIDDHI: highly realized of all abilities and powers
HUNG: the wisdom compassion in my heart and the universe

I chant this mantra when I drive my car. I bow down to Vajra Guru every morning when I first awaken. I may understand this deep connection only upon my death and passage into the spirit world. Whatever it is, it lives within me.

Six years ago, I made a pilgrimage with my son, Adam, to Tibet where we visit the caves and monasteries of Vajra Guru Rinpoche. The night we arrive, the moon is full, shining down upon one of the caves across the valley from our hotel. It is said that Padmasambhava sat there in meditation. That just happens without a plan. The next day, we take a boat across the rushing river to visit a special monastery dedicated to Padmasambhava. In the back of a darkened hall, surrounded by butter lamps and sticks of incense, is a statue of gilded gold of Padmasambhava that is over 40 feet tall. It is awesome to sit before this statue.

It is Tarthang Tulku, Rinpoche who in 1972 changes my consciousness forever. I am deeply grateful. He helps me to open my Central Channel, the Oma Tube that sits in front of the spinal column. I can see my chakras hanging like beautiful flowers off the deep green vine of this tube. The tube itself is thin and golden. This is my energy body, my spiritual body.

My spiritual channels begin to open with energy and spiritual abilities. Because Rinpoche is a master of Dream Yoga, I encounter him many times in my sleep. Just as Fritz Perls taught me that all the contents in the dream state is an aspect of me, Rinpoche teaches me just the opposite. This is one of my early lessons about attachment to the belief systems that first help us grow and then hinder our growth. We learn to let go of outgrown perceptions to progress beyond them.

And then the unthinkable happens.

I am kneeling in front of Rinpoche in Padme Ling, his monastery. He agrees to see me in person even though there is no class or event. "Rinpoche, I want to tell you that I am moving to the wilderness of Mt. Shasta." "What?" he asks, raising his voice. He is livid with me! I have no idea what I am doing that invokes this anger. I assume I will continue to teach and study with him. Then I quickly add, "I also want to thank you for all the teachings you give to me in the dream state." This is another matter that was kept silent previously. I feel like I am stammering for ways to acknowledge and appease him. Interrupting me, he thunders, "And there will be no more!"

That was it. With his vajra sword, he cuts me off. I am dumbstruck. No warning. No hint that, as a student, I do not have the right to make this decision. After all that he has given me, after the many connections that are cultivated, he just cuts me off. There is nothing I can say. The pain of loss of connection with my teacher is devastating. The damage is done.

So that very month, when I am 35, I take my two young children and move onto the holy mountain of Mt. Shasta. We are four miles down a dirt road in the wilderness with a dream to open a dharma center in an energy vortex. There are three adults, greenhorns at best to surviving in the wilderness. We build three domes before the heavy winter storms bring over 14 feet of snow.

In this setting, I complete my doctoral dissertation on "The Evolution of Awakening: Transpersonal Psychology as a Tool for the Transcendence of Ego." I place my old-fashioned manual typewriter on an old yellow picnic table in the middle of a meadow in the middle of the woods. I see this as my three-year retreat. Students begin to come to study with us. We are invited to make a presentation in town.

The first public talk we give is at the local metaphysical bookstore. It is on "Dreams." I ask the audience to volunteer a dream. One young man, a total stranger, stands up and says, "Last night I had the strangest dream. A man in orange and purple robes came to me. He said his name was…something like 'Tartag Tulke Rinpo' or something close to that." I ask him, "Was it Tarthang Tulku, Rinpoche?" "Yes! Yes! That was it! Who is that?"

I am as mystified as I have ever been with the experiences and teaching of Rinpoche. I am excommunicated, yet here is a total stranger that Rinpoche visits in the dream state. Rinpoche knew how to contact me, one last time.

30 years pass. Rinpoche opens a famous retreat monastery in Northern California. I submit my name for a public tour. It is denied.

Good teachers hurt.

I become a ship without a rudder, a student without a teacher. Life becomes my teacher, and the lessons are many.

(left to right) myself, June Degnan (my mother), His Holiness the Dalai Lama, Senator Dianne Feinstein, San Francisco Mayor Frank Jordan, Richard Blum (Chairman of American Himalayan Foundation; sponsors His Holiness' trips to the U.S.)

His Holiness the Dalai Lama comes for his first visit to the West and performs a compassion ceremony at a dharma center near our home. We place a thangka (traditional Tibetan painting) of the Mandala of Compassion on the wall for that ceremony. I have many occasions of personally being blessed by His Holiness. Tibetan lamas visiting the United States stay in our home in Berkeley. Sister Palmo, the British assistant to the sixteenth Karmapa, makes her final retreat on our land in the wilderness of Mount Shasta.

I continue my inner psychological training, doing Reichian body work with Joe Busey. Here my chakras open more fully and evenly. I tolerate great amounts of energy or qi moving through my body without the jerking or trembling or shaking of new students first exposed to this electrical current.

Sometimes my clients teach me. One day, I am concluding the Fisher-Hoffman Process with my client, a clinical psychologist. He is a most logical man. On the last day of our work, he suddenly bursts into tears and starts to shake. He is experiencing himself as an infant being run over by a plow in a dirt field. He just cannot figure this out. I suggest he speak in the following weeks with his mother or brother. Was there a child run over by a plow? The answer comes back "yes." It's a family secret. A generation before my client was born, a baby was born and killed. Was he that baby in a prior life?

This haunting question stays with me. How can we access this soul wisdom? What is the impact of a prior lifetime's moments of death upon the soul who re-enters the physical world? These questions stay with me for many years.

It is not until my work with Master Sha that I understand we are having dialogues with peoples' souls. In the Fisher-Hoffman Process, we are having soul communication in the client's inner sanctuary. We are clearing family karma without having the correct words to describe what we are doing, its significance, and ramifications. We are on the right track, but at the kindergarten level.

However, according to Enlightened teachers such as Tarthang Tulku, the gifts of psychic, healer, telepath, medical intuitive, and clairvoyant are only signposts on the path to Enlightenment. Many, many teachers and students overlook this point. They become seriously lost by their attachment to their gifts. Consider you are on the highway headed towards San Francisco. You see a sign that says 48 miles to San Francisco. If you think you are now in San Francisco, you have seriously lost your perspective. It is like that.

So, although I am learning valuable wisdoms about the human psyche, I am straying from the lightning path to Enlightenment that I followed with Tarthang Tulku, Rinpoche. There are Sufi tales about being lost in the desert on the spiritual quest. I read at least a dozen of them during my time with Claudio. It is getting on your donkey facing backwards.

I taste peak experiences and collect pieces of the holy map. My kundalini opens my spiritual channels. I taste Emptiness. My lower belly opens, and I make love with the universe. Guru Padmasambhava comes to me filling the sky. I see his presence with my third eye wide open. I receive teachings, travel, and fly in the dream state. I am awake in the dream state. However, I am also lost.

My inner life comes to a grinding halt. The pendulum swings from the fertile spiritual setting of California to a more physical world focus. Life takes one of those abrupt turns and I find myself in Senegal, working for the State Department as the Regional Psychologist of West Africa.

While living these three fascinating years in Africa, inside I am spiritually blocked. An internal symbol appears and reappears: train tracks run far out into the Sahara, going up and down over the sand hills. There is a little red caboose on the train tracks. It is the caboose that belongs with the little train that said, "I think I can. I think I can." But now the tracks end in the sand, and the little red caboose falls on its side. All alone and lost in the desert.

I am the fallen little red caboose. I am lost just like the Sufi tales describe. They call this stage in the spiritual journey "being lost in the desert." I am so lost I do not even remember reading these tales aloud to others. This is how deeply I am lost.

I just do not understand that this internal vision is my soul both telling me and visually showing me my lost condition. I am psychologically sophisticated enough to understand that this is symbolic. However, Western Psychology is so very limited in matters of the soul. I do not understand that I have third eye vision and that this gift is a direct channel to the voice of the Universe.

Ten years pass before I manage to find my way. Being lost in the desert is a spiritual test. Even upon returning to California, it takes another three years to reconnect with the river of teachings flowing into us through the great Eastern teachers. They are the predominant gatekeepers of direct transmissions and the living energy of Enlightenment.

My beloved daughter, Brett, brings me into the world of Qigong Masters. One day, she brings me to the Land of the Medicine Buddha, the very site of my Enlightenment three years later. This time it is to meet the Qigong Master, Bingkun Hu. He is a sprightly man with warm brown eyes and a body as fluid as rivers. I learn much from him about qi, the meridians, and channels of this precious life force. He tells me I move my qi quite well. Yet

I still don't understand exactly what he means. I just know I love to move, to dance!

All these paths, all these blessings, all these peak experiences, and each and every one of my teachers, including my parents and children, each and every precious soul has brought me to this moment. I am blessed with the solid foundation of a serious student. I have far to go and yet I trust my own nose. I am guided. I hear the guidance that rings o so sweetly in my ears. I am coming out of the desert. I am coming to the forefront of my own soul's journey. Dear God, I am ready!

Master Zhi Gang Sha, M.D.

Who is this charismatic, high energy, powerful, intelligent Chinese physician? Who is this Spiritual Master integrating soul wisdoms with medical models? Beyond his professional role, beyond his spiritual teachings, beyond his physical body, who is this Soul of Light? What is his relationship to God? How is it that Jesus, Quan Yin, and Amitabha manifest around him? Who is this soul so profoundly committed to serving the Universe and helping all souls realize Enlightenment? Is this hokey or is this an amazing journey? Who is the real Master Sha?

One day, Dr. Sha comes to our houseboat in Sausalito for dinner. I scurry to prepare a roast lamb, one of his favorite meals. Everything is just so, the table is set and pretty, the food is hot and perfect. I am the hostess wanting everything to go according to plan, MY plan or sense of perfection.

As is often the case when one is a student, my plan comes up against the plan of the Universe. Perfection is not what my ego is convinced it is! Perfection is in the Isness of what is!

This is one of those challenging moments: the meal is hot. Tom and I sit down with Dr. Sha at the table. Dr. Sha leads the prayer, bringing in God, Heaven's Team, countless Enlightened Master Healers and countless Enlightened Master Teachers and countless souls to eat first…And they do! His prayer goes on and on! He is asking for peace in the Universe and compassion and Enlightenment for all souls…and much, much more, going on and on.

I go through stages: nervousness about eating while the meal is hot gradually changes to becoming more present to what is actually occurring right here at the dinner table. I begin to HEAR his words. They echo so deeply inside me. All my life I have wished for Enlightenment for all souls. Here is a man voicing this in prayer, out loud, in our home. I am so moved my tears begin to flow. I cannot stop the flood of tears as my emotions open to the depth of his compassion and requests of God on behalf of the entire universe. I reach for my napkin to wipe my nose. I try to contain my tears, but I am like a running stream.

I hear Dr. Sha ask God directly to please be present.

I am momentarily startled by the directness. Certainly, I have heard many members of the clergy speak of executing a holy event in the Presence of God, but I had no idea of the possibility of asking God directly to come and be present! But I only have a moment to break this concept and walk into a new reality. I am completely unprepared for what is about to transpire!

There is a force. An invisible, yet palpable fullness, as in a wind with great power, fills the kitchen and enters the dining area from behind and above Dr. Sha's head and shoulders. There is also a quality of blue haze. The enormous presence of God enters.

I am humbled and in a state of awe. Quickly, I grab my napkin, turning my face to the side to wipe my nose and attempt to be more presentable!

Dr. Sha asks me, "Do you have anything to say to God?" This is so powerful. I feel so vulnerable and undeserving. The very question and the opportunity are so immense I must get to the point quickly. I go deep down inside myself to my very core, to the very point of my lifetime.

"I want to realize full Enlightenment so I can better serve others."

Twice Dr. Sha asks. Twice I give the same answer. There can be no mistake here for this is the request of a lifetime directly stated to God.

I am asking for a level of Enlightenment that will bring me wisdom and clarity, and I commit this blessing of consciousness as service to others. What else can one say to God except to ask for His blessing to fulfill the purpose of your life?

There is a several second pause. No words are exchanged. Suddenly—with a suddenness of impact like a bolt of lightning right in front of you, with a suddenness of nothing becoming something—there is a magnificent being standing five feet away at the foot of the dining table.

Jesus stands seven feet tall before me! He is young and strong with light and health emanating from him. I am flabbergasted by this magnificent presence of health. His hair is dark golden, and his robes are deep rust red. His tan skin radiates golden energy that vibrates in the space between us. I directly experience his Healing Presence. Then I receive the realization that He is here to give me Healing Power and capabilities. Dr. Sha is still praying to Jesus, Mary, Allah, and all the great spiritual healers and masters. I continue to stare at Jesus. Please, understand I am a Buddhist. Jesus has never come to me before!

Thus, my Awakening with Dr. Sha begins. Days later while taking a shower, feeling relaxed, this process of opening continues spontaneously. I feel a smack on the side of my head as I am hit with the impact of the Biblical words, "And God spoke." God does speak! And I hear! I can have a conversation with God! And God speaks and I can hear!

This is a literal experience! So much can happen when I just relax and surrender to being without any particular focus or effort.

The realization is like a time warp, collapsing NOW with THEN. THEN simultaneously becomes two different linear time events: the Biblical time when Jesus lived as an adolescent in Nazareth and an event in my childhood when I visited this home. Jesus lived with his family in an underground room that was accessed by walking down curving orange dirt stairs into a round cave-like room. These two times of the THEN collapse into establishing my connection with Jesus in the NOW.

So here I am, a Buddhist since 1970 having insights about Jesus! It is so important to break away from whatever traditions or paths have brought us to where we are and be willing to expand beyond those concepts into the full understanding of the Oneness of the Divine. This is a moment breaking free!

Conversely, 20 years earlier I am sitting in the third row of the Canterbury Cathedral in London on Easter Sunday. The history of this cathedral dates back to 597 AD, when Saint Augustine was sent by Pope Gregory from Rome to establish Christianity to England. The Queen of England, herself a Christian, warmly welcomed Saint Augustine and gave him this cathedral site.

As my son, Adam, and I walk through its chambers filled with stained glass and stone tombs under foot, we are deeply moved by its rich history. Many religious leaders are buried here, and many have been murdered in the cathedral itself, including Saint Thomas Beckett as the church and state issues struggle for power. All this is humbling. We move to the front aisles of the church as the crowd pushes us forward. The current bishop, 104th in line of succession, extends his hand to my son to come forward for the Holy Sacrament. I hold my son back and tell him, "No, we are Buddhists. Don't go." There is a momentary tussle with the bishop. It is I who am prejudiced and limited to following only my Buddhist path. Now with direct understanding of my connection with Jesus, I open into a new freedom.

This is only the beginning. Over the subsequent three years, this connection grows and brings me direct access to the presence and healing powers of Jesus.

Some people come to Master Sha for physical healing. They may experience a protracted spiritual honeymoon. But those close to him, those for whom he has a "big" job—we receive a different journey. It is difficult and yet rewarding. He has given me the task to write about being his disciple and student. He challenges me to describe to others the particular aspects of the journey that many cannot survive.

In the spring of 2002, Master Sha asks me to write his biography for *Common Ground* in a state he calls flow. As I enter into a meditative quiet, the words begin to come. I feel I am doing a fairly good job; however, he has me redo it several times. He does not make it easy! Here is some of what I write that is published under the title, *Why I Came to the West* by Dr. Zhi Gang Sha:

> *My spiritual and healing journey started at age six. When I was only six, I saw a powerful Tai Chi master practicing in the city park near my home in China. ...I trained under the Master 3-5 hours at a time until the sweat poured out of my body. I learned my first basic spiritual laws: to gain power, I had to be disciplined, making no complaints or having negative thoughts.*

Master Sha found the light and calm at an early age. He writes:

> *At ten I met a great Qigong Master. It was here that I first felt the power of the universe. I meditated and meditated until I felt hot and saw the light, then felt the blessing and the calm.*

Master Sha recognized his healing abilities, saying:

> *At 23, during my first year of medical school I was diagnosed with TB. I had to stop my studies for six months to regain my health. I was determined to heal myself quickly. In 1984 that I had my first public recognition of how I had integrated all of these studies to be a more powerful healer. The Ministry of Health of China had sent me to Beijing where I met a senior doctor from Lionghua Shanghai University, Dr. Cao Xin. Dr. Cao fell while playing volleyball, broke his back and couldn't move at all. Although other doctors treated him with acupuncture, cupping, and massage, nothing worked. He asked me to help. I placed my hands upon the tendons of his legs. Immediately, he felt a sudden surge of great pain from the stimulated tendon. I told him to sit up. To his doctor's amazement, he did. This miracle story spread quickly throughout the Ministry of Health and I was asked to teach Qigong and Tai Chi for the foreign physicians of the World Health Organization during 1984-86. I was discovering secrets that were not available to the great university, the deeper secrets of healing on the level of the soul.*

Then he entered into the true passion of his soul, soul wisdom:

> *I gradually developed the ability to communicate with and learn from spiritual teachers in the spiritual world.*

During this first year, Dr. Sha himself is also growing and coming into his true role. While his introduction to me is as a medical doctor and a healer, somewhere within the first year of my studies with him, he begins to introduce himself as Master Sha.

His true love and his own sense of life mission is to be a spiritual leader. He always prefers to teach about the Soul World in its many aspects. He introduces himself through *Power Healing,* as this set of concepts may be easier for the Western mind to understand and practice. Yet his consistent goal is to deepen the Soul wisdom teachings.

Within two years, Master Sha is publicly identifying his mission as bringing Soul Enlightenment to the entire Universe. His words touch strangers. They cry, feeling the deep truth of his teaching. A flow of humanity attends his workshops, seeking physical and emotional healing. They begin to understand that healing must touch the deepest level inside: our soul. He empowers people to reconnect with their own inner ability for self-healing.

However, going more deeply into dis-ease, the role of the soul becomes crucial. According to Zhi Gang Sha, M.D., and Zhi Chen Guo, M.D., there is a soul in everything: in individual cells, in DNA and RNA, in every organ, every human body, every rock, tree, project, and program. There is a soul in everything that is physical and tangible, and there is a soul in that which is invisible, intangible, and spiritual.

Master Sha is now teaching the power of the soul over matter.

(left to right) George Rask interviewing Master Sha.

Finding a Teacher

While each of the teachers I have previously described contribute significantly to my psychological, physical, mental, and spiritual growth, only one takes me "through the door of Enlightenment." He is the same teacher who brings Enlightenment to another right in front of my very eyes! Finding this very special teacher enjoins a particular history, filled with karmic ties and incomplete relationships that both sides need to finish. Our karmic connections run deep. According to Master Sha, we have experienced a number of lifetimes together.

Within Buddhist teachings, karma exists between people who meet during this lifetime. Relationships such as husband and wife, child and parent, as well as teacher and student are particularly connected in a significant way. It is important to honor these connections, to purify, cleanse, and complete all the threads from our past.

There is a mutual selection between teacher and student, influenced by God, by the highest essence of the Universe—whatever name you wish. It is complex—both human and Divine—and what you make of it. As you saw in my story of Tarthang Tulku, Rinpoche, you can be fired at any moment. The relationship with your teacher is enhanced through blessings, transmissions, teachings, and guidance. You must do the practices to "go through the door."

Traditionally, it is recognized that how we perceive our teacher has a direct impact on our own development. This perception is not merely psychological or projected. It is deeply allowing the Divine to manifest in our teacher and thereby in our self.

Good teachers guide you, carefully pointing out the blessings you receive and the traps of your ego. This guidance is essential. It can cut through lifetimes of struggle and help you realize Enlightenment in a single lifetime.

Through my years with Master Sha, I gain a perspective and clarity on my spiritual life that puts together pieces of a puzzle of diverse peak experiences. Things fall into place that previously made little sense to my conscious mind.

This understanding doesn't come from my usual cognitive or linear thinking. My real understanding comes in aha! moments. I feel my mind bursting open, giving me a vantage point of expansion. I'm amazed how differently I see things with this new perspective—like night and day. These are bursts of realizations of the truths on the spiritual journey. I hold precious these spiritual openings—so rare in a lifetime. My Soul has guided me to this point and now is drinking deeply at the well of Enlightenment. Perhaps this most ancient human journey runs through all cultures and times. The soul cries to go home, to be in peace and light, to find the calming Oneness of God.

Chapter 5

The Psychology of Enlightenment

I would like to offer a new paradigm to psychology that naturally extends the thinking within Transpersonal, Soul, and Spiritual Psychology. I hope this becomes a contribution to the field and brings about a meaningful shift as to how therapy, counseling, and healing are viewed and applied. I will be primarily focusing upon the clinical aspect of psychology. As healers, how we view the psyche is directly applicable to social, community, organizational, and research psychology as well.

I suggest this new paradigm be known as The Psychology of Enlightenment. It begins within a view of the Universe and the human soul from the perspective of an Enlightened Mind. This implies that all expanded states of consciousness addressed within transpersonal psychology are included. However, the latter is viewed from the perspective of occasional breakthroughs into altered states of consciousness. The Psychology of Enlightenment has a more encompassing perspective because it goes further into the condition of our Buddha Mind or Original Mind, also known as Enlightened Mind. How we view our humanity from this position is significantly different. Therefore, how we help others radically shifts and shortens in how much time is needed to help others heal, create, and find their way to a meaningful existence.

Thus, The Psychology of Enlightenment brings new understanding of the journey of the soul from ego to Enlightenment.

This is not developmental or ego-based psychology. It is a clear map, applicable to the Western mind while living a life within our culture, raising a family, and participating in our social structure. It is about viewing the human psyche as an expression of God consciousness. Thus, the process of healing is not focusing upon the regurgitation of traumatic events, or the justification of one's story, rather upon realigning with a profound sense of purpose of one's soul in this lifetime. It is about realizing kindness and acceptance of oneself and others. It is about forgiveness, peace, and harmony. Within the compassion of these emotions, the ability to address grievances that are the more usual topics within therapy is quickly handled.

Everything in the Universe is seamlessly connected, the physical and the spiritual, whether in form or formless, visible or invisible. Paradoxically, we historically make efforts to examine and understand our universe as a whole while collectively and incorrectly separating our totality into segments. This unfortunate systematic division of Oneness leads people to study one segment e.g., physical reality, thinking it accurately reflects the total picture. While physical reality is a part of the whole, its individuality is also magnificent. In one sense, the segmented view of physical reality is a reflection of the whole since all the basic principles and units of physical reality form a unit in itself. Our minds need to openly contain paradoxes without settling for premature conclusions that reduce our true search for truth.

Our universities separate knowledge into departments—history, physics, biology, astronomy, religion—without ever offering an overview of reality in its entirety. The assumption upon which reductionist academia presents its wisdom is a perspective of unenlightened mind. In esteeming the precision of academic knowledge as its "end point" or doctoral levels, we need to ensure we do not become blind to the greater picture. In our culture, we design our social and political structures around this perspective of highly cultivated, yet separate academic pursuits. We constrict our view of reality by accepting academic knowledge of the physical universe as a reflection of the universe in its entirety and forget this is only partial truth.

For a minute, imagine a new paradigm: the most cultivated minds, those who develop a perspective of totality and, thus, realized some level of Enlightenment, guide university academics in restructuring their field. Also, these minds teach students how to open themselves to realize expanded states of consciousness. This approach could be implemented within each department, with professors who chose to participate and the intense desire to expand academia beyond the study of the physical universe and the stepchild of that—human emotion, thought, and consciousness. The result would be a different perspective for these students. Still using the knowledge previously gained, the view would be from the top of the mountain rather than halfway up.

Perception and expectation are tricky in that they both reflect our ego, our prior experience, our belief system, our cultural heritage. At the moment of perception or expectation there is a separation from the truth within the Oneness. For example, if you have five blind men who are each asked to report their reality as they carefully examine and touch a large elephant, you will get five quite different versions of "reality" depending upon what they perceive. While one examines the trunk, another examines the tail, a third examines thick skin, a fourth examines big feet, and a fifth examines tree trunk like legs. Where in all of these perceptions is the view of the whole? How can we then find the truth that this is one whole elephant?

Truth is to be found in the Oneness—the oneness of all phenomena. The universe follows both the laws of physics and the principles of spirituality. From the smallest increment to the largest—subatomic, cellular, organism, and planetary—we share body structures. There exist fields of analysis that help us to discover a total understanding of our Universe. These analytical fields such as science, math, medicine, and philosophy are in a sense substrata to the total knowledge that we collectively are striving to understand and integrate. What I am proposing is a quantum jump, akin to a thousand aha's and from that new position within our own minds, we reengage each academic field and its findings. I am suggesting that to understand our true nature, we must move to the most expanded place in our consciousness and be in touch with the wisdoms that are apparent from this viewpoint. We must awaken to our true nature and our place in the Universe.

I am suggesting a revamping of psychology so that it considers understanding the human psyche or soul within this greater picture of the Universe. I am proposing that the Psychology of Enlightenment begin by standing in the perspective of the Enlightened Mind. The Psychology of Enlightenment includes these elements, which I will attempt in later chapters to answer from personal experience:

❖ **The Role of the Soul.** What and where is the soul? What is the purpose of this lifetime? What are the lessons to be learned? What are the blockages from prior lifetimes? What is karma? What is family karma? How do we communicate with others' souls and for what purposes?

❖ **The Distinctions between Ego and Soul.** Which can best direct this relationship? Why? How can emotional healing from trauma be brought about in only minutes? How can alignment with the Divine heal our physical bodies? How can one heal neuro-associative conditioning and its surface behavior patterns? How can one learn to surrender and open when the ego clearly wants to control? And why is this important?

❖ **The Journey of the Soul.** What are the obstacles along the way? What is the map to understand different mystical states? What are the necessary attitudes to cultivate our progress? How do we awaken our energy centers? How do we sustain a higher and more intense movement of light through our minds and bodies? What is the view of the Enlightened Mind as the soul enters the different levels of Enlightenment? Why does this matter to the individual or to the Universe?

❖ **First stand in the View.** What does this mean? Why does it matter? How can it be applied? Imagine that the tools of our trade, our private and collective practices, all teaching, therapy, counseling, granting of degrees and credentials be entered into by practitioners who themselves are Enlightened Beings.

❖ **Is not each manifestation of soul tainted by ego, belief, and experiences?**

The Psychology of Enlightenment will go beyond the constructs of Humanistic Psychology that gave birth to the Human Potential Movement. The Psychology of Enlightenment will go beyond the concepts of Transpersonal Psychology that address isolated and sporadic altered states of consciousness.

There is now the growing field of Soul Psychology that deals with the profound notion of soul. Its most recent addition is Spiritual Awakening incorporating the potential of spiritual opening. This progression is most exciting.

Many of us in this field have been blessed in our search for wisdom. We have not found it in traditional psychology. We have not found it in institutionalized religion. We have found pieces in esoteric traditions. We have found pieces through various Enlightened teachers in our meditation practices. As I review the many authors in soul psychology, I feel a simpatico as I can see where our lives have crossed. Three years ago, I would not have been able to write from the view that I now can. Having tasted Enlightenment gives me courage to write the rest of this book.

We need to integrate the work of realized spiritual teachers into the practice of psychology. There is a deep hunger among many psychologists to cultivate their own inner practice to the point of realization of Enlightened Mind.

It is time for people to stop reading about the Enlightenment of spiritual masters and yogis in mountain caves, and to place their hope in themselves, to place their commitment in their own souls. You CAN realize Enlightenment in this lifetime.

This is a big jump, because most people tend to give this possibility away to others. People do not understand that by realizing Enlightenment they also forever alter the path of their children and their children's children and an entire lineage of the future. I believe there is much virtue that comes through realizing Enlightenment. It forever changes the karma of the future for the individual as well as their family. This leap can literally recast the very social fabric of our time and culture. This is Universal Service. This is why I believe it is appropriate and even necessary to dare to speak about these matters and to bluntly say what I profoundly believe: "If I can do it, so can you!" This is our human heritage. This is our divine heritage.

Trust your own path. Trust your own unique experience. Just keep going. You will know, beyond any shadow of a doubt when you experience the emptiness, or the luminous, or the powerful undulating Oneness. You will know for yourself.

I applaud each and every one who writes about the journey to Enlightenment, be they Zen monks, philosophers, physicists, psychologists, spiritual leaders, or welders. Why? Because when you come to this place on the path, two different principles guide you:

❖ You know you have not yet arrived, and even if you have, there is so much more to go.
❖ You realize that even if you are still unfolding, it is most counterproductive, and highly ill advised, to state you have arrived, especially given there is nowhere to arrive to and no one to arrive there.

So now we have a dilemma that, in turn, means no dilemma because it is a paradox. One of the secrets of the journey is that you need to open fully and embrace all paradox. In so doing, you actually integrate two seemingly disparate notions into one. If you are a serious student of the journey of the soul from ego to Enlightenment, then you know how difficult it is to speak of Enlightenment. Yet if your motivation is to be of service, to inspire those who seek your guidance, then you must say to all people, "You too have the potential and even the actual opportunity to realize Enlightenment within this single lifetime." And further, "It is essential that you know that!"

Please do remember that realizing even the beginning stage of Enlightenment can happen spontaneously as well as under the tutelage of your teacher. These are gifts from God, the Divine. They can come in many ways. Recall the story of Sydney Banks, a welder and dabbler in humanistic studies. I asked Sydney directly to tell me the story of his Enlightenment and I pass it on to you because it is significant. This is what he told me.

One day, he is sitting in a chair in his living room in Hawaii. He is reading the newspaper when his wife calls him. He doesn't respond immediately so his mother-in-law chimes in and also calls him. They proceed to get irritated with him. Suddenly, the energy spirals up inside him, shooting out the top of his head. All around him and inside him is a swirling mass of light and energy. He looks out the window and sees the ocean, also a swirling mass of light and energy. He is lost totally in the experience that lasts for three days and nights. He emerges from the experience a changed man. He even looks different to his friends.

Based upon this profound and life transforming experience, Sydney has created a successful community-based program called Health Realization. I worked with this program and have seen it transform the thinking and behavior of children and adults in poverty areas riddled with crime and drug addiction. A community in Oakland went from the highest homicide rate to zero homicide, maintaining these statistics for five years. I deeply believe this success is due to the impact of Sydney's Enlightened Mind upon what he then designed. *[For more details, please refer to section on "Malcolm 'Jerry' Williams" in the acknowledgement of teachers at the end of the book.]*

There are many others, realizing these precious states and attempting to bring them back as concepts and guiding principles to serve society and humanity. There are many others that are on the path quite diligently pursuing the higher states of consciousness yet have not yet realized the beginning stage of Enlightened Mind. It is an awkward place to be. They have a perspective of the path, stand on the path, yet have not arrived at the View of the Enlightened Mind.

I propose that once the practitioner, the psychologist, counselor, therapist, psychiatrist stands themselves in the direct experience of Enlightenment, *how* they practice their art will substantially transform. Through this transformation, the new psychology becomes the Psychology of Enlightenment.

The View

The path leads up the mountain. Upon reaching the peak of the mountain, the view changes. It is from this perspective that I am now writing.

The first thing I must say about reaching the peak of the mountain is that there is no mountain. There is no peak. There is no me. There is no reaching.

It is with deep humility that I offer my experiences and realizations. May they be of service to you, the reader.

Come with me. Cast aside all prior concepts. Affirm your intuition, your experiences, your soul. We will together "get out of the teacup," the container of all prior perspectives and enter into the space surrounding the teacup to explore that which we do not yet know.

Knowing

He who knows and does not know that he knows:
    He is asleep. Let him become one, whole.
    Let him be Awakened.
He who has known but does not know:
    Let him see once more the beginning of all.
He who does not wish to know, and yet says that he
    Needs to know; let him be guided to safety and to light.
He who does not know and knows that he does not
    Know: let him through this knowledge, know.
He who does not know, but thinks he knows:
    Set him free from the confusion of that ignorance.
He who knows and knows that he is: he is wise,
    Let him be followed.
By his presence alone, man may be transformed.

                                - Sarmouni Recital, Sufi

When the Buddha said of his Enlightenment, "I am AWAKE," he gave us a clear direction. We need to spiritually awaken. So let us begin from the viewpoint of Enlightened Mind and attempt to clearly describe the indescribable while maintaining humility!

The highest states of Enlightenment are vast beyond any dimension of time or space. While I understand vastness, I am only in kindergarten. I recognize there are many more levels of Enlightenment I have yet to experience. For example, some masters have achieved the level of Enlightenment where you have, "the ability to recall one hundred previous existences and the ability to foresee the circumstances surrounding the next one hundred births." H.E. Kalu Rinpoche described this as the tenth level of Bodhisattvahood [*Foundations of Tibetan Buddhism*, Snow Lion Publications, Boulder, Colorado, 2004, pg. 140.]

What I can address is, within the initial Enlightenment stage, the first level. I have experienced qualitatively different states: intense pure light or luminosity, emptiness, and movement with power. Being in the heart of God—with its boundless love, peace, and exquisite, sweet bliss—follows quite naturally out of the realization of emptiness.

Let me first speak of the Emptiness, or the Void. Here the sound of the silence vibrates in deafening emptiness. The emptiness comes upon you suddenly. It is like being hit on the side of the head. It is shockingly still. It is vast. There is absolutely nothing contained within it. Everything is as if suspended in emptiness.

During my early training, Tarthang Tulku, Rinpoche said, "Pure meditation, on the Nirvanic side, has no field of perception, no center of field, no self. Once color comes, you are in kun-gzhi (lower state). Higher meditation is beyond awareness."

The Emptiness is distinctly different from Luminous. In Luminous all is light, infinite, vast, totally consuming and connected Oneness. There follows powerful movement, undulating light energy. This undulating light power is initially quite like a storm in full glory. It bursts you apart into tiny fragments, spitting you asunder in a thousand directions. Letting go is the only way through. Then the quality instantly changes, and you soar in speeds equal to the power of the light movement. Then you glide, oh so peacefully, uniting with the infinite undulating power. Stay as long as you can. Drink deeply, for this will change your life.

Pause here, dear reader. Close your eyes and be with this last passage. Rest here.

We Fall into The Constrictions of Duality

Within this Oneness that we have just visited is the Empty, the Luminous, and the undulating power. At some very subtle moment you perceive, as distinct from just pure awareness yet within this perception, the origins of "you" begin to take hold. In this manner, you move from a consciousness where are absolutely no distinctions to a consciousness that contains a subtle ego or "I." At this moment, the fall into the constrictions of duality begins.

There are a multitude of very expanded spaces and experiences of consciousness that scatter themselves at the feet of Enlightened Mind. Because they are so close, it can be misleading and we erroneously think we are in the Enlightened Mind. The most simple and yet profound way to be discerning at this point is to ask oneself, "Are there any distinctions at all?" If yes, then you are not in the Enlightened Mind that is pure and naked with no distinctions.

For example, I have been to a space in the universe where light and sound are still one. They have not separated into two dimensions. This was a magnificent realization. This was new wisdom for me. Yet, even this very high experience is not Enlightenment for it has distinctions, e.g., there was a "me" that was quite impressed with what I witnessed and secondly, there was a mass of energy clearly distinguishable as both light and sound. So, there was an "I" and this "I" gave words to this event and stood to the side to witness this.

Let me give another example that I have experienced. There is a split in the farthest reaches of the universe through which one can enter into the pre-time dimension. When one learns how to access this space, one can see into past and future dimensions because they have not yet happened. This is the dimension of simultaneity where all time is occurring in the NOW. This, too, is not Enlightenment, for it has distinctions.

More distinctions arise. Distinctions carry wisdom. Wisdoms are realizations of the principles of the universe and creation. Yet wisdoms and distinctions are both born of separation from the Oneness.

Thus, we fall into duality. The actual experience of this fall is a constriction. You can feel yourself being more squeezed or contained. Realizations flood into the vessel of the soul in a non-verbal and pre-cognitive manner. Paradoxically, the instant each realization is received, the meditator has left the state of Oneness.

As we move from Oneness to Emptiness and to dimensionality, we are progressively limiting our experiences of consciousness. Within dimensionality, be it time, space, light, dark, or galaxies, there abide many realms. This can be viewed like a funnel that is vast at the top and quite narrow in the neck. The top of the funnel goes out into the empty space of Oneness, the funnel itself is quite expanded at first, and then narrows into the state of ego and the physical world.

Heaven and Hell Realms Are Not Enlightened Mind

In terms of the fall from the state of Oneness into duality, even the spiritual realms of great cultures are expressions of separation. The ancient Greek Gods and demigods mix humanity with God Realization. Their liberation into the Oneness is always curtailed by a significant and lethal human failing.

Christians have both Heaven and Hell realms. This view embraces their highest expression of liberation into the Oneness and the agony of lost souls.

The Buddhists have their Hell Realm, Heaven Realm, and Hungry Ghost Realm. Buddhism teaches that these realms are still on the Wheel of Samsara or illusion. Not even heaven is the true liberated state of highest Enlightenment.

Why are these cultural and spiritual expressions of various realms not part of the Enlightened Mind? Because there is a perception that arises within each of the deities, saints, or Buddhas described. Within the moment that perception begins, we fall into duality and a term frequently used in Buddhist psychology, "ignorance." In this case, ignorance refers to forgetting the Oneness, forgetting our roots and our innate potential of a pure and Enlightened Mind. Ignorance implies the subtle layers of personality and ego are forming over our pure mind and we are forgetting our self and our rightful place in the Universe. Ignorance begins with a most subtle pre-thought position that supports separation from the Oneness. So, I am saying here that the mere perception that gives rise to an image or a thought is a fall into duality from Enlightenment.

Siddhis Are Not Enlightened Mind

A further fall out the state of Enlightenment are the Siddhis, the powers or abilities that come as part of the journey toward Enlightenment. I can actually experience the Oneness and from that state experience the smaller, more confined state of the Siddhis. Let me describe this experience. Sometimes when I am in the Oneness, my teacher asks me to "see" with my third eye into a spiritual realm or into the human body. My inner experience is that I must now curtail, rein in, and make smaller my momentary expansion into the Oneness and return to honor his request. I am able to maintain enough awareness to feel and observe the quality of making smaller, of constricting consciousness.

Thus far, I am describing a progressive narrowing of consciousness from that of Enlightenment, be it Emptiness or Luminosity into differentiation, heaven realms, duality, and Siddhis. The construct of saints and Heaven's Realm come from an archetypal projection of the human mind. They also exist in the soul world and allow a connecting into the memory of the human soul. It is a two-way link. Yet, these very saints are also subject to a kind of recycling. They can remain in the various realms, and then must reincarnate into the physical world to do a job, according to the teachings of Master Sha. In any case, they are part of dualistic thinking and have moved out of the state of both Emptiness and Luminosity into a quality of quasi form. Their minds may be Enlightened, but the very perspective we attribute to them of their existence, means they are no longer in the most-vast state of Oneness.

Déjà Vu Is Not Enlightened Mind

The fall continues out of the Oneness into further distinctions. Within the soul memory, we are able to travel in a time dimension that is not linear. Here we have realizations that we have lived before. Not as the personality or ego of today, but rather some aspect of us has been here before, known this before, done this before, met before. The experience of déjà vu or already seen is just a hint of the openings and recognitions that can come to us. The purpose of recollecting past lives is far more serious than the parlor games that our society plays.

Past lives carry unfinished business, old relationships, lessons not yet learned, wisdoms left behind, and the karma or causality that goes with this. Past lives of the individual are only one aspect to be considered. There is karma of a family lineage. There is karma of a nation. There is karma of a religion. There is karma of a generation and an eon.

What then is our relationship to this intricate fiber? How are we to live being simultaneously part of these connections of many generations within the physical realm and yet beings of light in the spiritual realm? These questions must be answered if our lifetime is to be filled with meaning, love, joy, and Enlightenment.

Six Senses Are Not Enlightened Mind

As our consciousness continues to become more and more limited, we approach our entry into the physical plane. The nanosecond any one of our six senses opens the gates of perception into a taste, color, smell, feeling, knowing, or sound, we have fallen into duality. We have, as human beings, separated from the Oneness. The irony is that, as human beings, we have an opportunity to be discerning, to cultivate our intellect and our awareness. Yet this very humanness is ripe for ignorance, attachment, and suffering.

In this fall into duality, we leave the Oneness from which we all arise. We enter the journey that need never be made, for we are already home. Just as the drop of water within the ocean of vastness, we are momentarily distinct, only to be returned to the Oneness.

Going in one direction—toward expansion of consciousness—the senses are a portal to Enlightenment. Here through deep relaxation of both body and mind, we can enter an enhanced awareness of senses and move beyond into the Emptiness. Going in the opposite direction—toward constriction—the senses become a portal to separation from the Oneness. Here the senses lead into a perception that rapidly becomes a thought, such as, "The taste is sweet. The light is golden." For many, this is the area that Transpersonal Psychology has entered.

Both sweet and golden are attributed to higher states of consciousness, yet both sweet and golden have within them the separation from the very state they are trying to simultaneously realize, remain in, and describe. Herein rest the painful paradoxes of our humanity.

Ego Is Not Enlightened Mind

The fall into our humanity continues. One thought is rapidly followed by a second and a third. Within seconds, we have created a pattern of thoughts that lead in turn to a physiological response, often referred to as a gut reaction or emotion. Out of this emotion, we have now a stronger sense of "I" or "me." An attitude is created. Sense, thought, emotion, and now attitude. Fairly soon we will have a complete story line with its justifications and positions that in turn leads to a total belief system. Of course, we take our belief system as an expression of truth, justice, and self-righteousness. We do not question our belief system because it is so carefully buried. This is an area that Humanistic Psychology has entered.

The states of Enlightenment are vast and open. Conversely, the states of ego are confining and limited. The study of personality or ego is mainstream psychology.

This then is the fall of the natural state of mind which is Enlightened into the state of mind that defends and maintains ego. Tarthang Tulku has clearly described moving in the reverse direction to cultivate higher states of consciousness:

> There are stages in the practice of meditation: **1)** Honeymoon where you see colors, feel feelings, hear sounds. **2)** Fascination goes, colors, feelings, sounds go… like an old man who is not too interested in child's play. Any situation is okay, good, bad, whatever. **3)** Nothing really to meditate, as you are a whole beingness all the time. No time, no place, no instruction is needed. *[Teachings from his Human Development Training Program, Berkeley, 1971]*

Having thus described the fall from Oneness, into heaven realms, into our senses, and ultimately into ego, we need to look at the position of the practice of psychology in the West relative to this fall. Unfortunately, our psychology, as compared to Buddhist Psychology, enters at a fairly low level of consciousness, including the study of altered states of consciousness. It is a bare beginning still filled with a separation between my "mystical experiences" and my "normal life."

What Is Enlightened Mind in Daily Life?

Thus far, I have discussed Enlightened Mind as an experience, a state of consciousness. It is transitory in nature, yet its impact remains. Your life is forever changed because of the view you now know to be true.

Enlightenment can be revisited and even more preferable is the ability to rest here as long as possible and as frequently as possible. This is known as "stabilizing" the Enlightened state. Further, there are many levels of Enlightenment. In a sense, in this book, I am only discussing the kindergarten level. There follows grammar school, high school, college, and advanced degrees. Each of these levels contains greater realizations up to and including one thousand simultaneous samadhis. This is certainly geometrically further than a single experience even repeated over time. This, then, is the relative nature of levels of Enlightenment.

To be a fully realized being means to have entered the highest levels of Enlightenment. I am not there. I am merely on the path and attending kindergarten.

Yet, I can tell you from the bottom of my heart, my life is changed. One small example is that the ambition, the drive, the hunger to push the river for success is now instead a state of peace. I laugh with my family as to having no motivation for ambitious activities. I am content to watch the light changing upon the grasses outside my window, and to hear the chickens clucking. It is going full circle from childhood where the soft summer dirt was warm on my feet and returning to this contentment. There is a deep and conscious awareness of the relationship between form and formless and my connection with all that is. There is an ability to detach or let go. I see such beauty before me in the reflection of light upon a blade of grass. I see deeply into people and perceive their struggles. And my personal freedom comes in that I no longer need to rescue them! I can accept their pain and offer compassion. I am more kind. I see the Buddha-nature in all souls and simultaneously see their human struggle.

The Birth of the Lotus Flower Rising Out from the Mud

Given our state of humanity, its struggles, ego, karma, past lives and various obstacles, how can we begin the rise into higher states of being? The mud represents these obstacles for it is dark and hard to see clearly. Yet within this very mud, this very humanity is a multitude of options that when applied correctly can transform our lives into a beautiful flower that receives the infinite sunlight. We begin again the return to our original state. How can we achieve this?

Ultimately, if multi-disciplinary leaders could themselves taste higher states of consciousness, *how* they approach their field, family, and friends would radically shift our world and our future. Just looking at the field of Western Psychology, a significant shift in its collective consciousness could impact many people. So, I am suggesting here that the practice of psychology is key to serving humanity at a time when we truly need healing of our politics, environment, and our hearts. With this vision of service, let me now introduce a select few of the Tools of the Psychology of Enlightenment:

- ❖ **Enlighten the Healers.** First, professionals in the healing arts need to complete their personal work and move into the expansion of their own consciousness. Currently, even the transformational and cognitive disciplines such as Landmark Education, Neuro Linguistic Programming, and Tony Robbins' work are great yet still within the domain of cognition. So here is a start and we need to go further. Once the psychologist, psychiatrist, counselor, chiropractor, acupuncturist, and therapist taste the view of reality and the universe, how we relate to problem solving, relationship issues, career goals, negative emotions, physical illness, alienation, anxieties, and our basic sense of purpose will dramatically shift.
- ❖ **New Tools.** The tools we will use will shift. Light, love, space, the parasympathetic nervous system, and breath will be included.
- ❖ **New Seed Ideas.** Seed ideas and concepts will allow people to switch to a new channel with a more understanding vision including lessons, journey of the soul, karma, habitual karmic thought patterns, illusory existence, impermanence, and the recycling of life.
- ❖ **Speed of Healing.** The speed with which we can heal will shift and quicken. Within a single session or two, issues that previously took months of therapy, reliving childhood crisis and pain, will be healed and let go of with a quality of both understanding and forgiveness.
- ❖ **Accessing Positive Emotions.** We will be able to give people access to positive emotions and to help them sustain these while healing on whatever level they chose to heal.
- ❖ **Opening Spiritually.** We will be able to assist people on their soul journey and help them to open spiritually so that the very perspective they have about their lives will change.

In the following section, I am going to present examples of the process one goes through as you apply these general principles.

❖ **Trauma.** Applying the Psychology of Enlightenment, let me describe how to deal with trauma. I can see the origins of trauma in this lifetime when I work with an individual. I can go further into seeing the family karma and the family theme of struggle that also needs to be healed. Having entered into a state of prayer, I call in the soul of the individual with whom I am working. I call in the souls of each family member going back into 3 generations. Then through identifying the specifics within each of these individuals, parents, grandparents, I enter into a process of cleansing that includes soul-to-soul dialogue that moves to total forgiveness and compassion. Lastly, I ask for healing light and divine love to flow on the actions, behaviors, and karma between people. I do this process while in the state of flow with chanting or singing. *[Some of this will be discussed under "flow" in a later chapter.]*

❖ **Soul Prayer For Healing Relationships.** Call in the soul of your loved one—be it spouse, child, or lover. Begin to speak with them gently, acknowledging their presence. Choose words that balance the condition you wish to change, such that these words are only positive emotions or attributes. For example, if your spouse is afraid of intimacy, then ask the soul in front of you to open to the boundless love and security that comes every day from the Universe. Feel this safety and this love. What you are doing here is balancing a negative state, fear of intimacy, with its antidote of safety and connection. In doing this prayer, you are actually communicating directly with the soul of your loved one. Be patient and do this many times over a couple of weeks. Speak not out loud about your work. You will see results. At the end of your prayer, always say thank you for coming. Be respectful and gentle.

❖ **Barometer of Change of Perspective.** Following the kind of sequence I describe above, I always ask this question of my client or student, "How does this room look to you now, compared to when you first came?" Invariably they will say words such as "brighter," "clearer," "more spacious," or "more peaceful." Then I ask them to claim their experience by saying "I" followed by whatever phase they use to describe the room. "I am brighter," "I am clearer," I am more spacious," or "I am more peaceful." This helps them to claim their new state. It is also a small lesson about perspective. Their new state is clearer, healed or healing, and they are present in the Now. This is my own little barometer reading as to how successfully we both did our healing and blessing session.

❖ **Shifting Out of "Me! Me!" Thinking.** The previous sequence is a good example of what occurs in our consciousness when we shift of ego problems into the present. It truly seems like a new reality. Logically, we know it is the same physical space, yet inside our relationship to this reality has significantly shifted. If you do this a number of times with your clients, they do get the message: I have the power to change how I perceive my universe and the actions that follow.

❖ **Dissolving Negativity.** Once the presence of negativity comes into the client's awareness, be it from an external or internal source, there are a number of ways to transmute this energy within two minutes. This transformation can prevent arguments and ill will between couples as well as totally change the emotions and physiological state of the person initiating this change. This means that long therapeutic sessions that attempt to solve conflicts—internal or external—can be prevented completely. It does not imply that the issue dissolves. It means that the negative emotion, blocked energy, inability to let go, and payoff for staying stuck cannot come into power.

In this proposed new paradigm of Psychology of Enlightenment, I will continue throughout this book to present concepts and tools that can assist the soul in an accelerating manner into the realization of Oneness. In a sense, this is similar to the tenets of development psychology, given that this can occur within a single lifetime. The progression or growth may be continuous and then will inevitably include sudden jumps, or quantum leaps that open the mind to a new perspective. This quantum leap becomes the next rung on the ladder of our understanding.

Relevancy to Western Psychology

Why is this relevant to Western Psychology? Western Psychology, Humanistic Psychology, Transpersonal Psychology, and even Soul Psychology are based upon the premise that an "I" exits. This is an inconclusive assumption based on an unenlightened view wherein only the tails and the ears of the elephant are visible. In the larger picture, this assumption is incorrect.

As part of this premise that "I" exists, the therapist supports the construct that occurs within every session: "I" have a legitimate belief, feeling, and voice. The moment there is this "I" in the mind of the client and the psychologist as well, we have inadvertently helped the ego of the person who comes to us for help, to be justifiably alienated from a) the universal Oneness, b) the person about whom they are complaining, and c) their own soul.

Such a predicament! We wish to help and instead we strengthen the obstacles. We can only teach what we ourselves know to be truth. We can take our clients only as far as we ourselves have gone on this journey.

It is really quite shocking to realize that many of us, myself included, well-intended yet ignorant, have caused longer hours of therapy, created more pain rather than less, and have not come to the deepest issues that move the soul.

Now, I would like to briefly expand the paradigm of Western Psychology by contrasting it with Psychology of Enlightenment.

Western Psychology	Psychology of Enlightenment
Therapist believes "I" exists.	Therapist knows "I" does not exist.
Therapist believes in ego.	Therapist knows ego is illusion.
Therapist focuses for entire session on negative emotions.	Therapist uses tools to heal negative emotions in minutes.
Therapist allows couples to dwell upon negative emotions.	Therapist uses soul-to-soul dialogue to bring couple into loving space quickly.
Therapist supports career goals based on ego drive or money.	Therapist supports career goals based on alignment with the soul.
Therapist seeks to fix situation.	Therapist seeks shift of perspective.
Therapist is better at encouraging expression of negative emotions than bringing forth positive ones.	Therapist is quick to bring positive emotions, including light, love, and forgiveness to the fore.
Therapist focuses upon this lifetime.	Therapist works with past, present, and future lives.
Therapist views struggles as interactive or personality based.	Therapist views struggles as lessons to be learned & purification gained.
Therapist believes in confrontation and dialogue.	Therapist believes in soul-to-soul communication.
Therapist engages ego.	Therapist goes beyond ego.
Therapist rehases stories.	Therapist gets out of the "teacup."
Therapist is logical with some intuitive, creative abilities.	Therapist has realized high level of expanded states of consciousness and teaches client from this view.
Therapist is not Enlightened.	Therapist is on path to Enlightenment.

Given that Western Psychology is primarily the study of the personality or ego and given that Transpersonal Psychology is the transcendence of that ego, both of these bodies of knowledge are focused upon ego. What is this journey the soul undertakes? This is the domain for Psychology of the Soul, a logical continuation of Transpersonal Psychology. Again, I am suggesting a paradigm shift: focus on the soul and its journey. And what is that journey, ultimately? It is the journey to Enlightenment.

The soul is the vehicle that transcends form as it moves through many lifetimes. Ultimately the soul has no identity, just as a drop of water is both a drop and yet part of the whole ocean. For purposes of understanding this vast journey, we must move through a stage where we attribute qualities to the soul. The soul, the ineffable light traveler throughout time and space, squeezes itself into the human form.

At one time, I taught the Enneagram of personality types or ego. I taught the antidotes and virtues to be cultivated. Yet, I truly lacked any understanding of the role of the soul. I personally did not have the wisdom or experience or blessings that I have shared in the first half of this chapter. I could only take others as far as I had gone.

The Buddhist texts are most precise when it comes to understanding and studying the mind and its place in the Universe. Within these texts, there is continual reference to the illusory nature of our existence. Even in the beginning stages of the Enlightened state, it becomes more clear what is meant by illusory.

We are able to see through the denser form of energy that appears to be a solid object and see it is only energy. We can also see and understand that energy has many forms: solid, gas, and nothing. We understand the continual exchange between these states by just thinking about our breathing and how each breath arises from space outside the body, travels into and through the body and cells, and then returns to the space outside. In this simple cycle, there is no distinguishing at what point this breath is me or not me. This breath moves seamlessly between inside and outside. This is a simple example of the seamless Oneness.

Viewed from a more Enlightened state, or even a more expansive state, our physical life, with its trials and tribulations, is simply like a theatrical play, far away and quite transitory. In the Enlightened state, there is so much space and peace and light. Deep inside me this feels like coming home.

How to find our way back home...
How to make the journey that need never be made...
How to return to where we already are...
How to enter into the here and now as a portal to Enlightenment.

Pioneers of Thought, Expression, and Transformation

In the 20 plus years I have practiced as a Humanistic or Transpersonal psychologist helping people with their pain, dilemmas, and hopes, I have seen how psychologists create narrow paradigms inside the teacup. We look for answers and think we are problem solving. This is the best our field can provide without a paradigm shift.

So, within this discourse of this chapter, we are moving from discussions about the inner experience of Enlightenment, the fall into duality as we leave the Enlightened state, and now the beautiful rise out of the fall, returning with awareness and assistance back to the state of Enlightenment. This is full cycle. Some say this is the journey that need never be made. Yet, within this reconnection to the Divine comes a deep peace. Ordinary life is now so fully appreciated. The motivations to succeed or the drive to do just about anything is transformed into finding the beauty, the fullness in the simplicity of our day, any day, every day. This peace is deeper than the content. It is like a river that precedes any event or external water. Perhaps that is why the Zen koan so beautifully captures daily life:

Before Enlightenment; chop wood, carry water.
After Enlightenment; chop wood, carry water.

In conclusion, I am proposing that all professionals and lay healers who work as therapists of any sort include in their training both traditional psychological training and spiritual training. The key is that spiritual training be given through someone who themselves is Enlightened. It is essential that any teacher who teaches must be Enlightened because of their ability to see deeply into the psyche, ego, needs, karma, abilities and consciousness of their student, the therapist in training.

Enlightenment, as a living consciousness, is contagious. It is passed invisibly from teacher to student. Tools are helpful yet not empowered to their fullest potential when used by the unenlightened mind. Therefore, the therapy, the healing, and the service that we can offer from the View of Enlightened Mind is far quicker and more effective than our current abilities.

Part II

Transformation

Chapter 6

Transforming Darkness into Light

In the realm of pure Enlightened Mind that abides in the Emptiness, there is only Oneness. Here there is no need to transform anything into anything because there is no anything.

There are two distinct levels within transformation. In the realm of duality, where form and formless are perceived as different, the ability to transform darkness into light is profound. This is the domain of spiritual teachers and healers of the body and mind.

These words are not mumbo jumbo. To understand each of these realms, it may help to view duality as a lower, more constricted level of consciousness and Oneness as an expanded state of consciousness. Therefore, what I want to share with you about transformation of darkness into light is a discussion on a lower level of consciousness, much as the writings on siddhis are on a lower level of consciousness.

To place this in another perspective: to win the Super Bowl, one must learn the game of football and spend endless hours of skirmish "between the forties." When you contemplate the time, money, and people—including the media and fans—involved in the sport of football, you see a great quantity of energy pouring into the physical world of duality.

How might our Universe be if comparable energy were poured into cultivating the inner experiences leading to and including Enlightenment? Consider media coverage and advertising. Consider the values instilled in our youth throughout the globe. Consider the impact on families into the future. Consider the partnership with the soul world and with the various heaven realms that all cultures—each in their own fashion—describe and yearn to enter.

This basic choice between what we know in the physical world—its values, rules and guidelines—and what we barely know in the spiritual world is the primary juncture that we each face. This node of decision and direction not only arises throughout our life during times of shock or awakening, this node occurs with each breath and nanosecond.

There are many bridges between duality and Oneness. Yet each incremental step we take strengthens our own consciousness to move from the state of consciousness that is smaller to the state that is larger.

The ability to transform from one state to another, in this sense from a negative emotion to a positive emotion, is a small example of the transformation of darkness into light. This movement that is horizontal rather than expansive is also important in the overall transformation of the psyche. Thus, incremental steps need be taken horizontally, vertically, multi-directionally, and on different fronts simultaneously. These are some arenas where transformation can occur:

- ❖ Emotional or psychological, as in therapy
- ❖ Physical illness, as in the healing and coping with a condition
- ❖ Cellular, as in yoga, qigong, chakra activation
- ❖ Dietary, as in supplements, herbs, and living foods
- ❖ Thought
- ❖ Clearing karma through offering service to others *[see Chapter 13]*
- ❖ Blessings *[see Chapter 12]*
- ❖ Transmissions *[see Chapter 12]*
- ❖ Soul wisdom, as in cultivation of our inner Divine Being

Collectively, each step moves you closer to the purity and peace that each of us needs, as our foundation to merge darkness and light into the Oneness. This is a Universal Service.

What follows here are not only examples of transformation, they are profound teachings that spontaneously happen while I am in the act of giving service to others. They are also teachings that are "far out there," foreign to my logical mind. It takes me two years to give this a name. I now recognize these teachings come from the Unknown. These examples are definitely in the realm of being unknown to me, unthinkable, and unimaginable. Because they are so far out and not familiar, I seek guidance from the Divine to know how to present this crucial discussion about transforming darkness into light and its significance on the journey.

Conversing with God on Transforming Darkness into Light

Before writing this chapter on March 13, 2003, I enter the prayer state to ask God to assist me. I receive this guidance:

"Within darkness are gradations of light.
Within light rest particles of darkness
Asking for liberation.

There is no judgment, nor blame, nor fear
Placed upon the state of Darkness.
Similarly, there is no aspiration, nor clinging, nor joy
To be placed upon the state of Light.

There is the mutual Isness of the Light and the Dark.
There is a co-existence and a balance.

They simultaneously arrive into the great Emptiness, the ultimate Creator
Out of which arises neither Time nor Space.

Who can say at what moment the Dawn becomes the Day?
Who can say at what moment the Dusk becomes the Night?

Who can say at what moment the Breath
Arising in the vastness of the Universe
Becomes human form?
Who can say at what moment
The physical rejoins the vastness?

Light, dark, goodness, negativity, universe, human—
All is seamless.

Just as God exists within you,
You, my child are the fingertips of God
Experiencing my own Creation.

Transforming Darkness into Light
Is but a step within the journey.

Transforming Darkness into Light
Is a profound service for all Souls.

Transforming Darkness into Light
Is a gift from Me.
Open to this gift."

Offering of Service Brings the Unknown

I learn in the act of giving service to others. This is why I love to teach! In the process of opening myself, entering into prayer, and requesting whatever is appropriate at the time, the Universe uses me! This has become a reoccurring phenomenon: things happen that are unexpected and quite awesome! People around me may be surprised and feel blessed. Inside, I know I am more in a state of awe than any of them!

Gorilla in the Kitchen

The journey of my soul needs neither a meditation pillow nor a charismatic guru. Sometimes, I need only the mundane.

Standing with my hands in the soapy dishwater, I carefully place the next glass onto the drain board. My head turns slightly to be sure that the glass lands safely and gently. In doing so, my eyes look now toward the sliding glass doors that lead to the outside deck of the houseboat.

A dark, eight-foot tall, hairy gorilla is in the doorway looking at me. Without missing a beat, I say, "Welcome. What do you wish?" There is no response. I begin again, "Hello. Welcome. How may I help you?"

As I patiently wait to give him the time and space to receive my welcome energy, I silently chant, "God's Light, God's Light, God's Light, God's Light." I need the blessing energy and light to wrap itself around me and to fill the space between us. I also wish him to receive this blessing.

Suddenly, within his torso of darkness, light appears as rainbow rays. I continue to chant. Instantly, there appears a naked and beautiful infant emanating rainbow light and glistening in its human form. I bow to these souls and the beauty I am witnessing. "Thank you," I say. It is gone.

There is nothing I have either read or heard described, that comes close to what I have just seen—the literal transformation of a stuck soul into a very high pure being radiating rainbow light. Awesome!

This is such a basic teaching. In allowing my heart to fill with kindness rather than terror at the sight of a gorilla, the energy is transforming. By chanting "God's Light," the energy further transforms until a new soul of light enters as an infant. I learn that darkness and light are the same.

There is something about the spontaneous nature of these events that I trust. My ego mind is not conjuring this up in fantasy. It just happens!

How To Transform Visions of Darkness into Light [1]

The guiding principles presented here are to be welcoming to ANY soul that comes to you and to be of service to that soul in a loving manner.

In the above example, I do several simple steps. First, I say, "Hello." I welcome the darkness, no matter how strange or scary. Second, I hold a centered place in my belly and begin to communicate with this soul. I ask the soul, "What do you want? How can I be of service to you?" Third, I begin to chant "God's Light" because these words are asking for transformation and healing of the light to come, now, to the soul in front of you. Remember that souls such as these are trapped and seeking light, just as you and I are seeking light and love. So, knowing this, be not afraid and be of good service.

Sam, the Harvard Graduate

One day, we are at a small gathering of people, perhaps only fifteen or sixteen, in a lovely home in Orinda. The living room has open floor to ceiling windows that look out upon a deck with a blue glistening pool and in the distance are the sun warmed hills. The living room has a beautiful white carpet, and visitors politely leave their shoes at the door. There is a sense of spaciousness and graciousness in Sam's home.

Sam has a heart of gold and a mind trained at Harvard. He is a brilliant financial executive currently in a top position in Tokyo. I mention his physical world leadership qualities because it is necessary for people to understand that the journey we have undertaken is not the journey of air-fairy fools. This is a serious and precious journey of individuals from many cultures and backgrounds.

This particular gathering occurs within the first months of meeting Master Sha. People are standing in the hallway greeting one another, waiting for the official beginning of today's teaching. A man I have never seen before turns his head and our eyes meet. His eyes are radiating. His smile is intoxicating. His energy is magnetic. "What has happened to him?" I ask myself. "This surely is something special!"

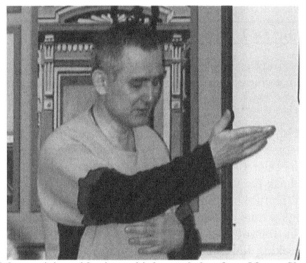

Peter Hudoba receiving a blessing to his heart chakra from Master Sha.

He is introduced as Peter, a neurosurgeon from Canada. He has come to study with Master Sha and has been spending the past two days with him. Peter is radiating unlike anyone I have ever met!

Peter and Master Sha went to the ocean the day before. Master Sha kept telling him, "Just open," and then he would twirl his body in a circle, indicating to Peter that "just open" means to open to everything, in 360 degrees! Apparently, Peter did just that. He broke through a thin veil into total Enlightenment. Peter had been a serious student of the journey of the soul for over 30 years. This breakthrough came with decades of diligent practice, commitment, pursuit, and trust.

During our morning session at Sam's home, Peter's Enlightenment experience continues to unfold. I am so honored to see this culmination and transformation before my very eyes. The prized and cherished state of Enlightenment is happening right in front of me!

It is during this day at Sam's that Peter realizes his Buddha nature. I am seated only several feet away.

Several long-standing friendships begin in this moment. One of those is between Peter and me; another is between Tom and Sam; and another is between Sam and Peter. Peter and Sam become quite close as friends in the years to follow. These early days with Master Sha are before he has a large public following. There is a particular closeness that comes from these early times, not to mention the spiritual glue of witnessing Enlightenment right in front of you! I am so deeply impressed, by Peter, by the phenomena, and by Master Sha.

PBS shoot 2002 (left to right) Sandra Sharpe, Sam Chang, Patty O'Neil.

Sam's story and his relationship with Master Sha will help you understand the pushes and pulls that happen during our spiritual journey together. This journey is often complex, riddled with moral dilemmas, and seasoned with an intense desire to transform. Sam himself has been on his spiritual quest for over 20 years, traveling to China, paying outlandish fees to sit with great masters, and always diligently being true to his own integrity. I love Sam so dearly. His story is a beautiful example of transformation.

It is now September 17th, only days after 9/11. My mother has passed away during these turbulent times. Sam comes to her memorial as the representative of Master Sha. Sam is helpful and humble. He is so kind and present in the smallest detail. I am struck by the total love and service that he offers me during the memorial. I recall his wife would often say he is too intellectual and not loving, yet the Sam who is at my side exudes a quality of love so sweet.

I also feel guilty because it is Sam who informs me of the decision to take away my role as workshop coordinator. My mother has been dead only four days and I am not in good shape. I break down in front of Sam and say, "What the fuck am I supposed to do!" Such rudeness on my part needs sincere apologies to Sam.

It is also Sam who, in his role as CEO of Master Sha's early organization, attempts to create contracts with those designated as "teachers." Money is such an issue, not only for me, but also for Master Sha. Money and spiritual relationships are such a complex tangle of human frailty.

Sam's role, however, is quite straightforward. Because Master Sha very early in our relationship told me he would pay me when I teach for him, I believed this would come about. Sam, in his role as CEO, wanted to honor this agreement. One day Sam gives me an envelope with $500 cash in it for teaching. There is no dialogue. At first, I think this is from the organization. But as time passes, I now think this is from Sam personally. It is his attempt to rein in Master Sha to more usual business practices. Sam and I have never clarified this point. It hangs in the air of the unknown and unstated.

Sam's departure from his CEO position is admirable. His behavior is a good example of practicing non-attachment in an elegant manner. His style is to graciously honor his replacement, who happens to be his close friend. I suspect that, behind the scenes, there are some clashes with Master Sha about how to conduct business in the Western world in a usual and expected manner. The clash is not cultural. They both are Chinese and educated as professionals. It is the physical world clashing with the spiritual world.

I find this dynamic of doing business in the spiritual world quite fascinating and often mystifying. And of course, some of it is the style of Master Sha.

He creates the rules, his organization attempts to follow, and then he surreptitiously breaks them! One day, Master Sha and I are sitting in my truck about to join other members of his team. He slips me several hundred dollars in cash and tells me not to tell the others. Years later, this money issue is still haunting both of us!

This kind of freewheeling unilateral manner of doing business does not sit well with Sam as the businessman. It sits quite well with him as the disciple and respectful student. It is difficult to wear both hats. Ultimately, it is the role of student that wins, for that is why each of us is here.

As Sam gradually withdraws from the group and pursues his own path, only a few of us stay in touch. A key friendship for Sam evolves with Peter. Sam has witnessed Peter's Enlightenment while in his home that weekend in October. Sam knows that Peter is the "real thing" and most likely far more evolved than any other people around Master Sha. Peter is highly educated and successful as a neurosurgeon, so the two of them share professionalism, integrity, intelligence, discriminating awareness, kind hearts, and the pursuit of Enlightenment.

One January, Peter flies from his home in Toronto to join Sam in a silent Zen meditation retreat. They sit for several days. During this retreat Sam realizes Shunyata, the Enlightenment of the Void or Emptiness. Sam's entire lifetime has been devoted to entering this state of consciousness, itself only a doorway to further openings. His dear and loyal friend Peter has helped this happen. How? This discussion reveals deep wisdom: true Enlightenment is contagious. Therefore, it is a gift to be in the presence of this energy and to receive this quality of support. Friendship of this nature is as precious as a mother to her baby. There is great excitement for all of us who know and love Sam.

Months later, Sam comes to one of my healing groups with his wife. She is beaming with love for him. "My Sam is so different now! He is so loving to me and the children!" Her story is touching as she recounts, "Every day for a year, I would go to my church and pray for Sam's mind to open. Sam's mind does open! I am so happy. I feel blessed. Love flows through Sam!"

Sam stays as my group ends. He asks me to do a healing for him. "Of course," I respond, knowing his story so well. "I am Enlightened now!" he joyously states. So, I think to myself, this will be an interesting healing/blessing session.

I face Sam with my hands in prayer position. "Dear God and Heaven's Team, and the personal guides of Sam in this life and all his lives, please be with us now." I wait for the next flow to come. Suddenly, my body is literally pulled to the left and I spin 90 degrees to face the glass sliders on the houseboat. Sam is still standing facing my right shoulder. Never, before or since, do I experience being moved physically to face a new direction. The force is strong.

I see in front of me a row of white horses mounted by soldiers in shiny armor. The first horse is so big that my eyes are directly on the level of its massive muscular chest. Its eyes flare and its veins pump vital life power. Each horse wears a chest plate of magnificent silver. The reins are tanned leather with silver ribbing on the bridle. The riders are warriors with dark olive skin and glaring brown eyes that pierce the air as sharply as their swords. The vicious, vengeful warriors and their steeds are geared for battle. They are in the room that only moments before was filled with love and light.

I am stunned by the realism of what I see. Inside, I start to look for someone to help me out. But there is no one there. Everyone else thinks I have it under control. I feel a bit like Eddie Murphy, on the spot, quick, take action! Inside I am saying, "Oh shit, now what do I do?!" This is totally new terrain. I am alone! And there is this horse's shoulder bearing down on me. "Think fast!"

"Dear souls of each soldier, welcome," I at least pretend they are welcome, when in fact I feel my own fear rising. To welcome dark forces of the spirit world is the very first step that must be done. It is important not to allow fear to arise, so I immediately shift the energy to acknowledgement and inside stay calm and centered. I can see they are not particularly impressed. They have been holding for hundreds of years, in human calendar time, their investment and their commitment to vengeance. "I see your anger," I begin in the classic therapist's mealy-mouthed response. This has no impact. It doesn't cut the mustard.

Something inside me opens into confidence and I point out what is now at this moment only the obvious. "For your souls to realize true liberation, it is imperative that you forgive Sam. Sam is asking you to forgive him. He too wants true liberation from his past," I say directly to the warrior on the first horse about to trample me. "You all need to forgive for your complete freedom!"

At this instant, in unison, all the horses turn sideways into a line into the sky. The warriors turn into souls of radiating light and in the shape of fireflies hovering in space. The leader places his hands in the prayer position at his heart and bows to me. Then in a streak of light, they are all gone.

I am flabbergasted. This is the last clearing of Sam's karma from centuries ago to give his soul the total freedom it needs. Tears are streaming down my cheeks. I turn my body to face Sam and open my eyes. Tears are streaming down his cheeks as well. I bow to Sam and he bows to me. We are complete in this healing/blessing.

Forgiveness

What am I learning here? Even a soul stuck in vindictive darkness has wisdom. This soul can instantly understand the role of forgiveness for their soul's journey. The warriors in Sam's past are vindictive and heavily vested in their emotion of darkness. We can relate to this as humans because we, too, are attached to our self-righteous positions of anger seeking pay back.

Yet the instant these warriors are offered light, they recognize how important this moment is. They too have an innate wisdom that is able to preside at this crucial opportunity and move into forgiveness. Forgiveness liberates them! The warrior who transforms into a firefly of light turns to bow to me to acknowledge what has transpired! So, I witness not only transformation, but gratitude and thanks!

Forgiveness is a willingness to let go. To cultivate this willingness means we choose, in an instant, to cast our vote for a happier and more peaceful soul. These precious moments of choice occur throughout every day. The number of times we let go and move on peacefully creates the very fabric of our lives. It is our willingness to be healthy and free and light. This is the soul's stance. With this stance our consciousness is more open and flexible. Each choice creates a cumulative fabric.

Forgiveness comes from this expanded state and not from our narrower, constricted ego state. Forgiveness comes from the soul. The soul has wisdom that time and time again will guide us well if we can just listen.

Forgiveness is healthier than attachment to anger. Forgiveness is an opportunity for the total person to move into a more clear and peaceful state.

As psychologists, we can teach this to others, helping them to let go of ego and progress on the journey of their soul.

Clearing of Karma

As a psychologist, it becomes clear our profession must address healing at the level of the soul. Family dynamics and early childhood issues are merely the tip of the iceberg. They show this life's expression of the same dynamics that have haunted the soul in prior lives. If the consciousness of the psychologist can evolve into seeing past lives of the client, this greater understanding will enable the healing process to come closer to the core issues facing that soul. Once the psychologist or healer has this understanding, they can hold the space for the client to evolve into discovering more about their own soul. If the healer does not even have the concept of soul, how can they guide their client to this core level?

A family back through generations is like a river that carries debris. The entire river needs to be cleared of its karma. By karma, I mean causality: the doing of an act, the thinking of a thought, have an effect. Over years, lifetimes, and generations, karma accumulates and repeats. This is the root of the pattern. Therefore, the entire generational lineage needs to be cleared. Family karma and family patterns need to be transformed from their darkness into the light. This is healing. This leads to Enlightenment for families.

How To Do Family Healing [2]

This is an example of multi-generational healing for families. The reason this is necessary is because the individual who comes to you for help is often reflecting both their personal karmic patterns as well as generational themes. Do this in the format of prayer only. Do it for several weeks privately. Watch your family and see where there are changes in how people relate to each other. This is a powerful prayer and will bring healing.

"Dear soul of my loved one *(name),* I recognize that you and I have struggled with deep issues that go back in time into your childhood, and how you were raised, and the pain you received. When I look at your mother's family and your grandmother, I can see this same issue also haunted them in their time. When I look back into the family tree on your father's side, I see a similar theme. Both sides of your family carry this family karma. It is now time to cut this cord of family karma. Let us call in the souls of four generations. Please be present now. Let us all together complete this pain, learn the lessons, and cleanse ourselves of this karma. May we collectively let the darkness go. May God and your personal guides and saints help us to let this darkness go. May we each and together be filled with golden light. (Chant 'God's Light' or 'Golden Liquid Light.') Thank you to all souls for this blessing. *[I learned from Dr. Ernie Pecci to ask people to look at the faces of the family members present. If you see any who are not peaceful, address them individually until they, too, are cleansed and complete. If you do not see, then sense.]* Thank you so much for coming. Thank you for this profound healing and blessing. Gong Song." (Say this four times to let all souls return from whence they came.)

Cellular to Community

Forgiveness comes from the heart, from a cultivation of compassion. Forgiveness applies to every level of transformation from cellular, to organ, to person, to family, and to community.

Cells change from the darkness of illness into the light of healthy qi flow. Medical intuitives can identify cellular darkness. Body workers can feel heat and thickness around the physical body. These practitioners are reporting two aspects of the same phenomena. Cells can be transformed from the darkness into light, and the healer can observe it.

On a social level, statistics are available in Oakland, California where a poor, violent housing project transformed into a safe, drug free community and maintained this status for five years. How? All individuals associated with this community, both the residents and the service providers, including police, were trained how to transform their negative thinking into positive thought. The approach is called Health Realization. It comes from an Enlightenment experience of Sydney Banks, who realized that our thoughts create our emotions that in turn create our actions and attitudes. In the late nineties, I spent four years in this community and its middle schools, working with this approach to social transformation. My partner was an

African American policeman, Malcolm "Jerry" Williams, recipient of the annual California Wellness Foundation Peace Prize.

The transforming of darkness into light is the work we all must do together to truly bring peace into our society, families, bodies, cells, inner spaces, and past lives. Whether we approach this as a mystic or a physicist, we each recognize that the same principles apply at each level of organism as well as in physical space. By working collectively on all levels simultaneously, we can transform our entire universe into the light of its original nature...the light of our original mind.

True healing occurs on the deepest level of our humanity, our soul. I learn I have the power to do this level of healing.

Spiritual Principles of Transformation

The key spiritual wisdom is this: The effectiveness of the healer depends upon their soul development and the presence of blessing from the Divine.

Each incremental cleansing counts: body, mind, and soul. Our thinking must be purified. Our ability to enter and sustain Enlightenment depends on the degree to which we are cleansed and purified. The transformation from darkness to light, whatever level it may occur in, IS the Journey to Enlightenment.

There are many schools of thought regarding stages of Enlightenment. They seem to agree that it is unlimited the realizations that accompany each successive opening. The school of Tibetan Buddhism identifies Emptiness as a beginning point. Zen speaks of Shunyata as a beginning point. Master Sha speaks of Soul Enlightenment due to accumulated soul virtue as a beginning point. Personally, I have found first the Emptiness and then the Luminosity as distinct stages. It is challenging to respect the constructs of these different schools while maintaining one's own truth in direct experience. Perhaps an even greater challenge is to understand how one's direct experience correlates with these differing schools. Each requires further and further transformation from the darkness into the light.

Chapter 7

Opening Spiritual Channels

To Awaken spiritually is a process of many steps. It includes purifying our karma, detaching from the grip of our egos, and activating our energy body.

Within our physical body is an energy network that closely parallels our circulatory system. This energy network is filled with a vital life force known as qi or chi. Qi runs within small pathways known as meridians and vessels. There are two primary vessels: the Conception and Governing Vessels. There is also a Central Channel, known in Tibetan Buddhism as the Oma Tube through which the Kundalini energy moves. One can conceptualize these large and small pathways in the same manner that we think of our circulatory system. Research being conducted at the New Jersey School of Medicine verifies that these energy channels, specifically the meridians, run parallel to our blood vessels and culminate in the brain.

In addition to these large and small pathways, there is also the chakra system. Chakras are physical locations within the body where intense energy accumulates into a concentrated rather small ball. The chakra system includes energy pathways and relationships. Within all of these systems, there are optimal ways to move the energy and develop it to its full potential.

Visualize yourself as a crystalline vase that needs to be clean, shiny, and empty for this energy and light to move freely through you. In time, each chakra will open with a flower or deity seated there. As one progresses to higher levels of consciousness, entire lineages of master teachers will sit within you at these points. They may enter through the top of your head. The cultivation of these stages is a subject of great depth that fills ancient texts.

Awakening the Chakras

Within the next few months, it becomes clear that I am no longer in a spiritual desert. My little red caboose takes off like a rocket ship! Powerful third eye openings continue. I begin to see saints and Buddhas when chanting. Past life experiences flood before my eyes. I begin to see into peoples' bodies as healing is being done. I actually see the fingertips of the healer extend and enter into the body of the recipient. I travel into space and enter Heaven's realms. Many of these experiences I describe in detail in later chapters. *[See Chapter 10, "Inner Vision" and Chapter 11, "Blessing and Transmissions."]* Suffice to say, for now these impressive events evoke in me a desire to learn more. What is going on here? I deeply want to understand this wisdom that is beyond healing and beyond blessing. What IS going on here?

I understand the importance and the richness in offering service to others. So, I begin assisting in as many healing and blessings sessions as I can. The offering of service is, in and of itself, a spiritual practice.

Twice a week, an ex-military barracks building is transformed. Donated flowers and fruit arrive into this hall that changes into a candle-lit sanctuary for the purpose of healing souls. Perhaps 50 to 60 people from all walks of life, all religions, and with all types of pain flood into the hall filled with hope that Master Sha will bless them and help them heal. Many suffer from conditions that Western medicine finds difficult to heal. Their motivation to heal themselves is so admirable and courageous. Unlike a workshop or seminar…this is raw and real. Much is occurring, simultaneously visible and invisible. Trying to understand is overwhelming. The vision to heal is clearly enormous because he really is taking on the task of awakening humanity!

A stage four cancer survivor sits at the front of the room telling her story. "I almost died in April." She is resisting pain medication because, to her, it means giving up. Losing touch with the pain means losing touch with energy at the cellular level. She doesn't want to mask her pain, rather she wants to know and embrace it. One night, she loses her strength and her will. She hits bottom in anguish, reaching out for the medication. "I died then." But miraculously that night, her Kundalini awakens. In her words, she is reborn. She is alive to tell her story. This gives me goosebumps. She walks her talk. There is deep teaching here in her story. Sometimes hitting bottom is the instant that the deepest transformation begins.

As I am witnessing this transformation in those that seek healing, I, too, am beginning to be affected. After only a few weeks, my cosmic orbit, so well-known in Qigong circles widens…to put it mildly! I am in deep meditation when increasingly larger arcs move up my spine, out my crown into space, circling back inside and entering up the soles of my feet. Again, this arc flows up my spine and goes even farther into the galaxy, circling back down into the soles of my feet, again and again. My heart radiates energy and my head glows golden above my crown.

As my third eye opens, a subtle energetic pulsation goes on within me. When I focus on this energy body, it becomes a doorway into my practices, a conduit of electrical power moving from the base of my spine up into my head. My chakras hang like ripening flowers on this vine. When the pressure becomes too intense, I breathe it back down my front channels, tighten my perineum, and go up my back again, as I have been doing for the past four years.

Several weeks later, my heart flower is growing. A multitude of white chrysanthemum petals is embracing ripe, golden stamen dots of pollen. Out of the center comes a small golden Buddha…he rises from my abdomen. Enlightenment must be contagious!

But not all is joy and laughter. The downward slide begins as the voices of my ego want to be heard. Just when I think there is a real possibility of realizing Enlightenment, my teacher does what good teachers do: he looks directly into my eyes and tells me I need more purification. His timing is perfect. I feel crushed, sullied in my ignorance. Perhaps I have gained no ground in my prayers and prostrations. When the first star of evening enters the sky, I always wish for the Enlightenment of all beings. I never wish for myself. I silently cry out in agony, "Perhaps this is all foolish fantasy." I review disagreements with family and friends, acts of negativity, a harshness of voice, shortcomings, with-holdings, negative and judgmental thinking, or unkindness. I crash. To the desert again.

My expectation to realize Enlightenment in this lifetime slides away. I get up at dawn to chant mantra, just because it's dawn. Om Ah Hung. I lose myself in the sound as the foghorns across the bay echo Hung. The sound is so reassuring. I love the fog. I soften inside just feeling the pulsing energy. I forget myself and the struggle. Suddenly a small golden Buddha jumps up on top of my head.

How can this be? Soul experiences come with a suddenness that I trust. My ego cannot manipulate it. Yet, that is too fast. I have doubts. I begin to consider there may be a relationship between receiving gifts of higher consciousness and the arising of doubt. I believe someone once said, "Up down. Up down. Up down. Like the stock market." I am learning about the interconnectedness of blessing and pain.

Steadily, I experience transformation in my daily life, in my cognitive understanding, in my physical body down into my cellular structure, and in my spirit. There is a seamless integration of spiritual and physical realities. I am seeing the doorway into the universe, and I am walking through it. May I be a good servant and guide for others.

Losing Ego Temporarily

In the West, a solid foundation for the expansion of consciousness may be built through psychological, mental, or physical techniques in any combination. Since the early sixties, the human potential movement has expanded into more than 50 recognized courses of study. What they have in common is the study of personality or ego and how to realize our full potential. We have talk therapy, cognitive therapy, emotional release work, muscular realignment—each addresses an aspect of the human condition.

I recommend using the Enneagram to gain insight into your own ego's characteristics. This system originates in the Sufi tradition and systematically attributes characteristics to nine personality types. These nine types further subdivide into another three for each point based upon the primary instinct of either self-preservation, social, or sexual. In studying this system, it is relatively easy to identify your own position and watch the pattern of your ego at play. The study and application of the Enneagram lays a good foundation to inner work, giving us greater understanding of our ego and showing us how to reduce the power of the ego over the soul.

Moving deeper into the body/mind is Wilhelm Reich's Body and Breath Work, an excellent sequel to the Enneagram. Reich's bodywork softens the defensive armor that rests in the musculature holding forgotten body memories. Carefully executed, this work follows the pathways of the chakra system carefully opening these primary energy centers. As the softening occurs within the muscles, the energy begins to "stream" throughout the entire body. Streaming is the flow of uninterrupted qi coupled with a heightened electrical charge. It feels rather like being rewired from 110 voltage to 220. Reich's work also increases our ability to tolerate pleasure, certainly a precursor to altered states of consciousness such as bliss. When the ego and physical cleansing have been tended to, the energy experience turns to light streaming though the body. This is a deep transformation, indicating that higher states of consciousness can now be sustained.

Deep relaxation is basic to Awakening. The Buddha himself spent six years to achieve a truly deep state of relaxation. He said of his Enlightenment, "I am Awake." As students we must first relax very deeply, right down to our nervous system. Slow down.

Second, we need both psychological and emotional clarity. This implies that our feelings are in a balanced state. There is no conflict, no push/pull, no agenda, and no intense emotion. It is a state of equilibrium and equanimity. There is no grasping, nor expectation. Clarity is also a deep quiet within the mind and heart. Clarity arises when we are not attached to the voices of our own ego. When these voices start their endless tapes and justifications, recognize the phenomena of our ego nature.

When we can BE, quiet and relaxed, then the spiritual channels automatically begin to open. We can open by ourselves using various meditation, breathing, or movement practices. We can also open in the presence of intense and powerful energy generated by a teacher. However, even though many are drawn to this particular method because it is quick and easy, the downside may result in a condition known in many traditions as "Qigong Psychosis" or the "Path of Crazy Wisdom." The Western psychiatrist Lee Sannella noted this phenomenon in his book, *Kundalini— Psychosis or Transcendence.*

Lee was one of my first teachers. His marathons go on for 24 hours without sleep. At about the 12th hour, people begin to open emotionally, usually with anger or sadness. After this catharsis, Lee administers laughing gas combined with Ritalin, the muscle relaxant. As a result of the emotional release, exhaustion, and nitrous oxide/Ritalin mixture, people open to quite awesome experiences!

One woman, the wife of a well-known physician (he later supported many of the Dalai Lama's visits to the United States) lays down on the floor next to Lee, who gives her Ritalin and nitrous oxide. She is very quiet. Suddenly, she sits bolt upright and speaks rapidly in German. This greatly shocks everyone, especially her husband, because she does not consciously know how to speak German. "What is going on here?" ask the voices in my mind. Something inside her opens. She relives her prior life in Germany. Images come to her of her death. Her voice is loud, frightened for her survival. Gradually, she comes out of this altered state, returning to the room, puzzled and shocked. She knows she has passed through some kind of threshold and returns to her current reality.

At the end of this same marathon, my first breaking of ego boundaries occurs. I am standing in the parking lot of the church where I have spent the last 24 hours. I gaze at the pale blue sky, washed with fleeting wisps of cloud. I hear cars leaving. The voices of others are distant. I am left in the stillness. I am disconnected from my own memories and habits. I cannot cognitively figure out where I am to go next. I consider calling out to someone, anyone, in this group as they get into their cars, telling them, "I don't remember where I am to go. I don't know which way is the road to my home." I feel like I am plopped down into some strange town. There is no fear or anxiety. This is such a new feeling. I patiently absorb the beauty of the sunshine and quiet.

In time, the storyline of "me" and my life—including the way home to my children—returns. At this time, I am still quite young on the inner journey. I do not yet have the concepts or the language to identify that I am without ego-identity as I stand in the parking lot. This is an experience of my consciousness being without identity and totally in the here and now.

Many of us experiment with altered states of consciousness through drugs, therapies, sleep deprivation, or samadhi tanks. These are early attempts to break free from the cultural and social constraints of our young nation so deeply steeped in the ethics of materialism and outward success. It is deeply moving to be part of this group consciousness. We have a purpose. Now I understand this is a collective movement of our souls.

We learn a great deal. We learn the limitations of peak experiences and the crash of returning home to our "regular" lives. At this time, few Caucasians have encountered Eastern religions and metaphysics. Unaware of the practices of our neighbors, the Chinese, Japanese, and other Asian immigrants, we wait for teachers like Suzuki Roshi and Alan Watts to introduce basic Eastern practices. When these early pioneers come to our awareness in the late sixties and early seventies, many of us quickly take vows and enter serious study of the inner journey of the soul. Even at that time, I can distinguish between a living transmission of consciousness and the exoteric ritual found in many established churches in the West. I seek direct experiences and masters who can provide guidance to Enlightenment.

It is necessary to prepare students gradually for the influx of energies, powerful emotions, and visions that accompany opening to Enlightenment.

Let me clarify the distinction between ego work and the soul journey. The former is what most psychotherapists do. The latter is what most spiritual teachers do. However, both are done by transpersonal psychologists or counselors who themselves are opening to expanded levels of consciousness. Spiritual masters know that the ego must be "reduced" for greater awakening to occur.

One day in the mid-nineties, I am driving to Santa Cruz with Professor Nawang Thondup Narkyid (also known as Kuno), the Dalai Lama's biographer. A kind and thoughtful man with a keen mind, Kuno had served in the Tibetan Government prior to the Chinese invasion in 1956. Kuno says to me, "I would like to learn more about the psychological techniques developed in your country. In particular, I would like to know more about how you help people to forgive their parents. In our country, we have one parent, such as a mother, and then often a second father. We call it my mother and second father. It is usual to have more than one marriage, like my mother marrying for the second time to the brother of my father. So, I feel our people need to know more about how to make peace with these different parents."

He is so free of ego that his mind can be openly curious. We begin to discuss the psychological tools found in the Fisher-Hoffman Process that postulates we both mimic and rebel against our parental role models. We must find the innocent infant or soul within each of our parents, the soul that they entered with into this lifetime. It is this soul we must forgive and come to cherish for our own freedom as well as theirs.

For the soul to truly soar, we must do the work on our ego.

Each item or memory that we cleanse, forgive, love, and understand in a deeply peaceful way gives us our freedom, gives us the internal space to progress and cultivate higher meditation practices. The real homework is done daily, hourly, and ultimately in each minute. This is the on-going purification of the mind.

No matter which high levels of consciousness we achieve, be they peak experiences or be they more sustained, there is always more work to do within the subtleties of our mind. A thought gives rise to an emotion, that in turn creates an action and an attitude. This cycle continues to another thought and becomes a self-sustaining feedback loop. When a thought is cloudy or negative, our emotions very quickly follow suit. Conversely, when a thought is peaceful or positive, emotions will be on the higher end of the tone scale— equanimity, joy, gratitude, and love.

We are a vessel that, in essence, is pure light. In the human condition, we have fallen from the state of Oneness and "think" we are separate. We become conditioned, and ego arises with a stake in its own interpretation of reality. As we attempt to awaken and to open our spiritual channels, it is not easy to maintain the opening. It is progressive with peaks and valleys, highs and lows. We are infants learning to walk. We fall many times as part of the process.

The journey of the soul is to become the purest vessel of light possible, fully realizing that this is our true nature.

Seductive Siddhis

We must open our spiritual channels to travel further on the soul journey. However, along the way there are times when we lose track of our primary purpose. In times of duress or spiritual testing, we can go astray for moments or weeks or months. We can become infatuated with inner or mystical experiences. These are examples of losing our way.

As our spiritual channels open, our physiology changes. Our parasympathetic nervous system generates qualities such as deeper relaxation, heightened senses, spontaneous creativity, and a general sense of peace and wellbeing. Since all this is most desirable, indeed quite sweet, we become greedy. We want more, and this can cause us to tighten our grip. We grasp the beautiful butterfly that sits in our hand. We need to find new ways to simultaneously open to these states while relinquishing grasping.

Another danger along the way is to become enamored with the spiritual abilities that come when the parasympathetic nervous system dominates, and our brainwaves are in the theta or delta states. These spiritual abilities are usually attributed only to high level gurus.

One of the most significant points in this entire book is that more and more serious students are demonstrating these abilities as ancient secrets of spiritual development are opened to the public in the West. To put it simply, this means that you too, dear reader, may develop these abilities.

However, these abilities are not the point, once you get there. These abilities or siddhis only indicate you are successfully moving on your journey and your spiritual channels are opening.

The moment we become attached to these siddhis, we have fallen again. When we refer to ourselves as a "this" or "that" as labels of the powers and abilities that go with these siddhis, we are caught in a back eddy and have left the mainstream of the most powerful river of our soul.

These siddhis are most seductive. People hang their shingles out saying they have these abilities and earn their living by giving these services. That is fine for them. However, if your own soul yearns for Enlightenment, becoming a titled practitioner of one or two siddhis can be your downfall.

The siddhis are seductive, not just to our ego's identity or as a label. The siddhis are seductive because of the inner spaces we enter, spaces that are like lovers, blissful, golden, euphoric, and energized. It is like the fantasy anima or animus appearing before you to seduce you and fulfill your passions. Indeed, a well-known gateway in the spiritual journey is that of the most seductive and sexual imagery and emotions arising within you to make love to the entire universe.

The most familiar of these siddhis in the West are the psychic, telepathic, clairvoyant, remote viewing, medical intuitive, healing, and astral travel abilities. When you ask what do these abilities have in common, you will find the person doing these is a) quite sensitive and intuitive by nature, and b) able to place their own body and ego aside. These are all lovely qualities. Now, it is time to go further—much further.

Siddhis are signposts. They only indicate you are on the right path. Having given these warnings about the seductive nature of spiritual abilities in that they can waylay you like Ulysses was tempted by the sirens and threatened with the breaking apart of his ship upon the rocks. The siddhis are meaningful and yet, if your ego grasps at this point, your entire journey may crash upon the rocks of your personal attachments and desire.

So, duly warned, now let us continue upon the journey of the soul. Let us learn how to further cultivate these abilities, in a state of non-attachment, and in an attitude of service. This following section presents many tools for further opening of our spiritual channels.

How to Open Our Spiritual Channels [1]

To open our spiritual channels, we need to practice the following:
- ❖ Deeply relax our body and quiet our mind.
- ❖ Place our conceptual, logical thinking to the side.
- ❖ Deeply still our nervous system through exhaling slowly, with our mouth open like a sigh, 5-6 times.
- ❖ Focus our attention upon the Conception and Governing Channels, following the orbit of their energy flow up the center of your back, over the top of your head, down the front of your forehead, the center of both eyes, to the tip of your upper lip, continuing down the center of your torso, and passing under your perineum to now rise again up the back. Circulate and move the qi.
- ❖ Focus upon the inner channel, the Oma tube that sits in front of our spine, bringing the energy upward.

Then, with this new movement of energy, much like an electrical wiring system adjusts from the old 110 watts to the new 220 watts, we maintain and sustain our new light body that is born out of this new energy. Siddhis come as our light body becomes activated. This is within and around our own bodies and minds.

The second aspect of what our spiritual channels need to open will be explored in detail in Chapter 11. For now, I'll put it simply. We need blessings and transmissions.

An Enlightened teacher who is in direct connection with the Divine can pass a living transmission to the student. This is the inner teaching and truth. It is distinctly different that any outer physical form such as an institutional facade that speaks of spirituality and has no Enlightened beings within it. When it comes to receiving truth, our physiology can directly recognize the difference. Our soul knows truth, and our physiology responds with goose bumps, tingles, heat, tears, and gratitude.

Kundalini Opening

A primary channel within us is the Oma tube, or Central Channel. As this channel opens, a most powerful energy is released. Some traditions, such as the Hindu, allow this energy to burst out the top of our head through the crown chakra. Other traditions, such as Qigong, prefer to cycle this energy up the spine and then back down the front of the body, under our feet, and up the back again. This is known as microcosmic orbit. In the Qigong tradition one wants to keep the energy for greater stamina.

There are two very important practices I want to share with you at this point. They are key to furthering your opening. The first practice is known as "OM AH HUNG."

How To Cultivate the Meditation Practice of "OM AH HUNG" [2]

Place the sound OM with the color white in your head. Place the sound AH with the color blue in your throat. Place the sound HUNG in your heart with the color red.

Chant "OM AH HUNG" in a single breath, or you may chant each sound with a single breath. Focus your mind totally upon the area of the sound and its color. As you practice you may wish to switch the color white from your head to your heart. The feeling is quite different. OM is the sound of creation of the Universe. AH is the sound of the Void or the Emptiness. HUNG is the sound of the wisdom and compassion abiding in the Heart.

By chanting these three sounds, you are also balancing these key areas in your body.

My first experience in doing this practice is most powerful: I am sitting cross-legged facing a wall about six feet away. I am chanting. Without any warning, I feel a fire at the base of my spine. It is quite intense. My body begins to jerk with sudden jolts of energy. This builds until I am trembling and shaking. I feel and see a spiraling energy going up my spine and out my head. The spiral movement is a double helix of a deep, fire-like light. A sudden energy, like lightning or electricity, literally picks me up out of my cross-legged position and tosses me like a ragdoll, upside down against the wall.

This is the kundalini energy rising and forcing open my Central Channel.

How To Cultivate the Meditation Practice of *"WENG AH HUNG"* [3]

For purposes of clarity, let me add that the Chinese version of this chant is also most powerful. The sounds and positions of the colors are different. Here the color red is placed in the head with WENG, the color white is placed in the heart with AH, and the color blue is placed in the lower abdomen with the sound HUNG. You can remember this by thinking of the American flag's colors of red, white, and blue.

Cosmic Union

The second meditation practice that changed my consciousness permanently opened my lower abdomen into an experience of the intimate connectedness between the earth and the sky. It is known as Maha Sukha or the Great Sweetness. It is chanted as a love song to the Gods and Buddhas in the Heaven Realm. The words are asking for more of the sweet nectar of the Gods, the immortal ambrosia that is so intoxicating and blissful. Whenever I want to be in the Oneness and experience my connection with all that IS, I just recall this profound state that happened at dawn years ago.

How To Cultivate the Meditation Practice of d'Tumo [4]

This begins as a breathing practice. First, we suck on our palate to bring down the sacred nectar of immortality. Then, we take a deep breath and push it down into our lower belly and hold it as long as we can. At the same time, we are visualizing fire in the belly and ice coming from the head to our heart. When the fire and ice meet in the heart, the breath in our belly is forced out in a loud sound. This powerful practice is designed to force open the Oma tube. It also stimulates our lower chakras and sexual energy. This is the food for further opening.

How To Cultivate the Meditation Practice of "Maha Sukha" [5]

Second, we chant after doing d'Tumo for several minutes. Here we focus in our hearts and sing a love song to all the Buddhas, to all the deities in the Heaven Realm. The chant is to be sung as sweetly as singing a lullaby to your newborn baby. The chant is, "Om Amrita Bindu Java Maha Sukha Soha."

Om is the sound of the Universe, so you are calling out to the entire cosmos. Amrita is the ambrosia known so well in many cultures. It is the golden nectar of immortality and infinite bliss. Bindu Java means small seed, just a beginning that will germinate and grow strong. Maha Sukha is the Great Sweetness of Great Bliss. Soha is Amen.

Rinpoche requires we do these key practices for 24 hours over a weekend. Then we are to report our experiences and pose our questions. This is what happens to me.

One morning way before the dawn light, I leave my bed without waking my family. I simply must get to the other side of San Francisco Bay, where I can see the sun rise over the water. I have never felt this way before. It is like a magnet pulling me to Marin.

I find an abandoned field filled with dirt. I lie down in the darkness with my abdomen and feet facing the eastern sky. As the sun rises, I watch the rose and golden colored fingers of dawn move across the water and enter my abdomen and belly. The rays of the sun become a lover caressing my thighs and adroitly moving toward my vagina. I begin to quiver and shake. I feel an orgasm building more powerful than intercourse. I feel my abdomen opening and pushing as if giving birth. Involuntarily, my body moves. I am simultaneously being made love to and giving birth. Then the sky and the earth begin to undulate rhythmically. Everything becomes connected in cosmic orgasm. The intimacy of the sky touches every small leaf and rock. Everything is touching everything. The cosmic union is giving birth to me. I am the little baby in the middle of their lovemaking. Everything is making love to everything. The shaking movements take over my entire being. Finally, I am exhausted. I have given birth and simultaneously I am born. It is seamless. The intimacy of the sky touching the earth, everywhere, in every small particle and leaf and rock, I will never forget.

This cosmic union with its intimacy becomes a driving force in my life. Hours pass and the sun is high in the sky. I go directly to tell Rinpoche about my belly opening. He just smiles and says, "Enjoy!"

Sexual Tantra

These first stages are like childbirth. You literally feel the pain of labor. YOU ARE GIVING BIRTH TO YOURSELF! As part of this powerful opening in my abdomen, known as the Golden Urn or Lower Dan Tian, I begin to study tantra, the union of male and female energies to realize Enlightenment.

I would like to candidly share my inner experience as a lover and as a woman having experienced my lower chakra being blasted open! I hope I have the outrageous courage, the searing knife of verbal expression, to tell you how it really is in the realm of LOVER!

Tantra has always drawn me to her bountiful promise of orgasm and Enlightenment. This must be my path says the bee to the honeysuckle bloom. The sukha, or nectar of the Gods, that runs its honeysuckle taste down our central channel is the ambrosia of the Greek gods. In the hidden practices of d'Tumo breathing rests an infant recreating a suckling on its own pallet, a drawing down from the crown chakra droplets of sukha, the taste of divine bliss.

Not the same as the milky spicy come of a man that instinctively gives him proof she loves him, adores him, succumbs to him. Nor the creamy secretion she emits as he buries himself in her blessed gardens seeking to re-enter his place of creation. For both man and woman going down is not the same as going out into the mystical universe. The first is a daunting task for many while forcing themselves to enter orgasmic release wherein rests a hint of melting and losing control. A mere shadow of a hint of the larger and boundless expansion of bliss.

How To Cultivate Sexual Spiritual Tantra [6]

A woman hunts for the right male who understands this journey. A man who uses the power of intention and focus to push her to the edge time and time again. She hunts as she ovulates.

Depending on her mate's level of awareness and cultivation of his tantric practices, she can choose from a variety of pathways. Working only internally with herself, her focus goes from the tip of his penis up her central channel to her crown. She then slithers down her forehead, eyes, and passes through her nipples on her way to her belly. Here she envelops his hot erection yet is not distracted by it and moves on to her perineum, the ultimate power base. Gathering more fire she inhales deeply, gathering up a good head of steam as she rushes through his shaft and out the slit in its mushroom cap. She heads for her cervix, the doorway to her central channel.

Now if her lover is adept, he will feel her breathing and mimic her breath cycle. This may be an invitation for the second pathway of union. She inhales, initiating a wider arc running up her spine. The energy builds until the head of the cobra wraps itself about her ears and slides over her lover's crown. They exhale. The energy runs down his back to the gateway of his perineum. They inhale and the energy jumps to her perineum and again up her spine in an undulating rhythmic current. This wider arc is microcosmic breathing as partners.

A third pathway is more internal within each partner. She follows him, coordinating with his breath and thrusting. With an inhalation, she moves the energy up her central channel, out her crown, into his crown, and exhales down his central channel until he thrusts again and the fireworks explode within her.

My hunch is that any tantric practice will take us further on two batteries than on one. Yet we can only go as far as either practitioner has cultivated. So, look for the seasoned soul! I find a blast of light in his kiss.

The mystical tantric realizations can come to the meditator without any external sexual stimulation or partners.

Opening of the Chakra System

As has been mentioned earlier, we have energy bodies that consist of quite complex pathways running parallel to our circulatory and nervous systems. We can approach greater understanding of the relationship between our energy body and our physical body through the study of yoga, Qigong, and acupuncture. Western research is still quite limited as to clarifying a medical model bridging into these more ancient traditions.

Therefore, I can only share with you a most personal integration of the relationship between our physical systems and our energy systems.

For purposes of this book, I will present our chakra system as being comprised of the crown chakra at the top of the head, the third eye in the center of the brain, the heart chakra or Message Center in the center of the chest between both nipples, the Lower Dan Tian two inches below the navel and two inches into the center of the belly, and the Snow Mountain at the tip of the inside of the spine.

Each chakra has a special purpose in the process of Awakening spiritually. As the chakra opens, we experience physiological sensations, e.g., tingling, pressure, heat, as well as emotional memories. Because chakras hold memories of our soul journey in time, past, present, and future, this unfolding process can bring us images of other lives.

As our chakras open into the beautiful flower that is contained within each center, we progressively balance and refine our spiritual abilities as transformers of energy and light and love. Within our chakras are a multitude of delicate counterparts to the ganglia of the nerves of our physical body. These are called nadis.

We have more nadis where we find our chakras. The nadis are like conduits of electrical current or antennae that can reach far out into the universe, beyond our physical body and beyond our energy body. Within the Hindu tradition these nadis that form the chakras are described as being a vortex with a spinning motion. The nadis are said to carry all forms of life energy, fluids, and even consciousness.

This entire chakra system is connected through our spiritual channels. These spiritual channels are even larger pathways that open as we transform, allowing the abilities of each chakra to be integrated into one whole and most beautiful, illuminated soul. Thus, the ability to hear with our heart can be spoken through the mouth. The ability to record images from the center of the brain may be spoken through the mouth. The pulsating heat at the base of the spine may be feed up to the brain. Each of these examples move via the spiritual channels.

Visualize a theatrical makeup mirror that is lined on both sides with a series of lightbulbs. Our chakra system is akin to this series of lightbulbs. These lightbulbs turn on, in any order, and they can randomly flash. The intensity of the lightbulb can turn higher and lower.

As a chakra begins to Awaken, there is often a sense of tremendous pressure. You feel a bursting, a ripping open of your heart. If it is your third eye, there is an aching in your head. Reach out to your spiritual community. Ask your teacher to help you rebalance your energy, ground, and move energy down to your lower belly. Feel your feet and wiggle your toes.

Each chakra brings special abilities. We open randomly. Different people may be more developed or gifted more with one ability than another. It is helpful to study with an Enlightened teacher because the Enlightened Mind is contagious, and this quality of energy will quickly stimulate your own chakras and spiritual channels to open. It is this precious quality of living transmission and its contagious nature that is the catalyst behind true transformation. This phenomenon is quite different than studying from a book compiled by an un-Enlightened author or attending exoteric rituals.

Think of the irony of this journey: I am born and I am Awake. I grow up and fall asleep. I wake up again. I die. This is the physical and spiritual life combined. Yet it is my soul that came into this body. I knew this as a two-year-old. It will be my soul that travels on after I die. This is why the Tibetan Buddhists teach the practice of Phowa, how to guide the soul during the Bardo experience. *[See Chapter 10, "Soul Travel."]*

Life is about the journey of the soul. We connect with our own soul first, and then connect with all the other souls and Enlightened Ones in the entire Universe. We must learn all the wisdom teachings we can during our human lifetime. We must learn how to maintain what we learn even when we leave our physical body. We must learn how to recognize those souls we have been with before. We must come to truly appreciate our karmic connections with those Souls and to realize completion, compassion, and forgiveness.

As we open our Spiritual Channels, all these relationships become surprisingly clear. We see and hear in unexpected ways, spontaneously, and often beyond our thinking. We see with our inner eye and we hear with our hearts.

Chapter 8

Inner Vision

As we open spiritually, our chakras begin to be activated. This has been briefly described in the section of "Opening of The Chakra System" in Chapter 7. Each chakra has a different purpose and different abilities. One of our primary chakras is the Third Eye.

This lay terminology attempts to identify the third eye as an actual physical eye that perceives through our sense of vision. This attempt is only to help people relate to the phenomena. In fact, it is quite misleading. Third eye activity does not use any of our five senses. Third eye activity is literally an inner vision that arises from our energy body, not our physical body.

Inner vision does not see like our physical pupils. Our pupils are comprised of retinal cells that react to different wavelengths of light. In turn, this sends electrical impulses into the optic nerve and then on to the brain. Once these impulses are received in the brain, they are interpreted as pictures or images based upon the visual memory of the person experiencing them. This implies that our brains will label according to our prior life experiences. No two people therefore report the same phenomena.

Conversely, inner vision is not receiving any waves of light because the ability of inner vision is located in the dead center of our brain where there is no external light. Yet, there may be electrical activity in the center of the brain. This raises an interesting question: if there is no light and therefore no stimulus as with physical seeing, how is there any vision?

Because these two processes are so different, we can surmise either one of two hypotheses: first is that the image that appears in our brain is caused by our imagination, and second is that the image that appears in our brain is caused by something other than our imagination. The latter becomes rather interesting!

What is actually experienced in inner vision is a complete image deposited in front of us. Where is it coming from? I am suggesting it is coming from either imagination or the soul world. Often people question their inner vision as real or authentic. They have doubt or skepticism and report they are imagining an image.

However, it is interesting that inner vision often will arise quickly and spontaneously. The actual images are sometimes quite new and surprising to the viewer. To me this quality of spontaneity is fresh and close to intuition as distinct from our logical minds. There is something one can trust about spontaneous phenomena. It is not labored or anguishing manufactured by our egos.

What is Inner Vision?

The phenomenon of seeing with our third eye is the gift of inner vision. The third eye is comprised of a group of cells located in the pineal gland at the center of our brain, midway between our ears and directly behind our eyebrows. This is on the physical level.

On the level of our energy body, the pineal gland contains a high density of energy. I view the relationship between the physical and energy bodies to be an interface between the ganglia of the ends of our nerve cells and an abundance of nadis which are the counterpart to ganglia on the level of our energy body. The image is like the sea anemone's tiny tentacles wiggling as it encounters another sea anemone.

These nadis are force field centers with vortices spinning like axis of the sun or any planet. These vortices are subtle matter and hold the records of all events in previous lives. They can also hold records of present and future, much like the Akashic Record or the place in the Universe where there is no time dimension. So, a vortex is like a transformer of information and energy into the soul world.

Nadis are part of a complex system of pathways and channels, our meridians and spiritual channels. This entire system works as a whole to send and receive information in direct relationship to the degree of opening and purity of our soul development.

These complex pathways have been studied for many centuries in Hindu, Chinese, and Tibetan cultures. The chakras hang like beautiful flowers off these channels, opening into the body space around us and extending out into the Universe. According to ancient Hindu tradition of the yogis, the nadis, or highly concentrated energy centers that make up the chakras carry body fluids and cosmic energy, as well as consciousness.

Inner vision is but one example of our potential brainpower. Given that we use 12% - 15% of our 15 billion brain cells, we can say there is a potential for far more activity. The interesting question then becomes, "What kind of brain activity are we capable of, and how do we begin to activate our cells and for what kind of purpose?"

We begin by activating these cells through exercises that are both ancient and modern. Many spiritual traditions teach how to stimulate the inner vision. Few people may realize that the United States Department of Defense also teaches how to activate this inner vision. They call it "remote viewing."

Children often experience seeing with this inner vision. Parents may call it fantasy. Psychotherapists may see images as their clients recount their stories. We call this intuition. The common phrases, "in my mind's eye" or "I saw a ghost" are but a few examples of inner vision. People do not realize that they are "seeing" with their inner vision, partly because of our cultural upbringing and partly because it is a foreign concept. Our logical mind does not consider seeing with something other than our eyes as part of our potential brainpower, or an innate human capability, or even a natural phenomenon.

Conversing with God on Inner Vision

I enter into the state of prayer, asking the Divine to guide me and assist me, to please help me write about inner vision. This is the response:

> *My dear children I have gifted you with Sight,*
> *Into the spirit world,*
> *Into the human body.*
>
> *Return to your inner child state of purity*
> *And you shall See again.*
> *For there are many beings surrounding you.*

They hold out their hands to touch you.

You are the one who has placed veils upon your eyes.
Look inward for the deepest wisdom
And you shall See Me.

I am the essence of pure light,
Ringed by golden waves
Carrying rainbow colors of the Infinite.

I uplift you.
I carry you to my Kingdom of Heaven.
Within every cell
Of every form
In the Universe you will find Me.

I am deeply grateful to discover such a golden vein in my connection with the Divine. You too, dear reader, can access the teachings, encouragement, and kindness that come from your own prayers.

Cultivating Inner Vision

One of the most meaningful experiences for me as a therapist and spiritual teacher is to help people recognize and claim for themselves that they are seeing. Once seeing is acknowledged, we can further cultivate this inner vision and increase accuracy. It is an ability that takes time and effort. It also requires a willingness to step into the internal space of acknowledgement of oneself, saying, "Yes, I can see."

Two qualities are required to become more accurate. First, the inner vision of the image needs to be precise and clear. Second, we need to report it without analysis and interpretation. Between seeing and speaking out loud what we see is a distinct space crucial to cultivating accuracy. We suspend our self in a distinct sense of not knowing what is coming. We just wait and are quiet. We must train our mind to move aside and be still.

For some the inner vision begins as a symbol. Congratulations! You're on your way. It is important to not analyze or attempt to attribute a meaning to this symbol. Merely report what you are seeing. Next, to move further, you become more still and this single symbol will open into the next stage where a sequence of images appears.

As images appear, the challenge is to allow yourself to suspending knowing or recognizing what you see. This means suspending the inclination to place prior experiences that are in your memory banks unto this new inner vision. You need to be willing to go beyond your logical thinking. You need to be willing to allow images without putting them into categories in your mind. This is essential because it is a doorway into the Unknown.

The Unknown is a source of profound knowledge. Spontaneous information, wisdom, teachings, experiences, all open to us in this emptiness where there is no thought. This is a pivotal idea for the cultivation of expanded states of consciousness. The Unknown is vast. Our memory and logical mind are much smaller. We know what we know, and our ego wants to continue to tell us we must place new information into this small box. However, the Unknown is beyond our logical thinking, and it is necessary to learn how to access this space and open to its knowledge.

The more you can suspend your judgment in this silence as you watch the inner image, you will quickly advance to the next stage of seeing. Here the images begin to run together until there is a movie unfolding in front of you.

All this happens before you speak. The act of placing words on the flood of images can get in the way of this inner movie. So, as you advance into this stage, it is helpful to allow the images to flow before you offer words out loud.

These movies change and evolve over a period of time such as weeks, even though externally you are viewing a similar event. For example, you may be watching a healing that is done following a certain format, yet your third eye will provide new information as time goes by. This is one of the reasons it is difficult to research and test this phenomenon because of the changing nature of inner vision. Scientific research wants to duplicate and have results that are reproducible. Yet in the soul world and our energy bodies, much is spontaneous and constantly changing.

An advanced level of inner vision is the seeing of words that come as if on a computer screen flowing in front of you like a movie.

How To Cultivate Inner Vision [1]

If you are practicing on your own, without a teacher, here are some simple tools. First, speak directly to your third eye. "Dear Soul of my Third Eye, please open and give me the gift of inner vision. Dear God *(or your personal saint or guide),* please help me to open my spiritual channels and give me the gift of inner vision. Thank you so very much." This is the invocation to the soul world to help you.

Next, place your hands at your forehead. Your left thumb is held inside your right hand's palm. Your right hand then closes over your left thumb. Now your left hand closes over the top of your right hand. This is known as the Yin Yang Hand Position. Tighten both hands, about 80% strength. Now chant the sounds, "e, e, e, e, e, e, e, e..." as short staccato sounds. Visualize white light coming into your pineal gland from 360 degrees. Do this for 10 minutes. Close by saying, "Thank you." You may wish to place your hands in front of your chest in the prayer position to be respectful.

Remember not to force these attempts to gain inner vision. If you get a headache, stop and breathe deeply, exhaling through your mouth. Your ability may suddenly come in a moment. Early experiences of inner vision can be fleeting and vague. You have to catch the moment.

A second practice that stimulates the third eye is building up the Snow Mountain Area. This powerful center is actually the source of energy needed for third eye activity. If the Snow Mountain is not strong, the third eye cannot sustain itself. You can come to the point whereby merely turning your mind to focus upon the Snow Mountain, you can feel the energy surging or pulsating upwards to your pineal gland or even to the forehead.

The Snow Mountain Area is located at the base of the spine, slightly to the inside of the tip of the tailbone. It is the size of a small ball about an inch in diameter. The Snow Mountain is the seat of power for the immune system, longevity, stamina, body strength, and sexuality. The Snow Mountain and the Lower Dan Tian (about two inches below the navel and two inches inside) are considered the foundation centers for our body energetically. *[These centers are different from the spiritual channels discussed more fully in Chapter 7, "Opening Spiritual Channels."]*

How To Cultivate Your Snow Mountain [2]

The practice for activating your Snow Mountain Area is similar to the formula given above for your third eye. First, speak directly with your Snow Mountain. "Dear Soul of my Snow Mountain, please gain power, build strength, build stamina, build my immune system. You are my foundation center. Gain power! Dear God *(or your personal saint or guide),* please help me to build my Snow Mountain. I am so appreciative. I am so honored. I thank you so very much." This is the invocation to the soul world to help you.

Next, place your hands on your back at the base of your spine. Your left thumb is held inside your right hand's palm. Your right hand then closes over your left thumb. Now your left-hand closes over the top of your right hand. This is known as the Yin Yang Hand Position. Tighten both hands to about 80% strength. Now chant the sound, "joe, joe, joe, joe..." as short staccato sound for 3-5 minutes. Next, visualize white light coming into the base of your tailbone from 360 degrees. As you visualize light you now say, "light, light, light..." for the next 2-3 minutes. Repeat this sequence several times, no more than 20 minutes total, and then rest. Close by saying, "Thank you." You may wish to place your hands in front of your chest in the prayer position to be respectful.

You may feel heat, vibration, and tingling. That is fine; do not worry. These are the physiological responses to the energy and light work we are doing. The Snow Mountain practice can be done for longer than the third eye practice.

The third practice to help you open your inner vision is to reclaim that which is inherent in each of us. As children, we are open spiritually. We close gradually because of the messages we receive from adults: "Oh, don't be silly. You are making that up." Or perhaps there is a strong incident that causes you to deny what you are seeing. These moments in our childhood progressively cause us to shut down, to minimize our potential until the ego is formed and the cognitive, logical mind attempts to guide our lives. However, in the process of Awakening spiritually, we reclaim ourselves.

How To Reconnect with Your Abilities as a Child [3]

This is a practice for psychological healing to help you reconnect with your innate childhood abilities. Find a time in your mind when you were a small child and you were given a message not to see what you were seeing. Identify the situation and the person negating your experience.

"Dear God, please come and help me heal so that I may open again spiritually. I am most appreciative. Dear my soul, please come and help me. Dear soul of my mother *(or father, or whomever caused you to shut down),* please come here now. I wish to open again all my spiritual channels and abilities I had as a child. As part of my healing, I now forgive you for what you said or did. I know you were doing the best you could at that time. I forgive you totally. I send you only love and light."

Look at their face and note their expression. Continue to speak with them with love and understanding until their expression has a smile or shows that they are receiving your words and intent. Then ask them to leave with light surrounding them. This is a great service you are giving them, for you are helping their soul be in the light.

Now you chant "God's Light" or "God's Love" for yourself. Visualize golden light pouring down upon you and surrounding you with a gossamer blanket of comfort and kindness. Now place your hands in the prayer position and give thanks.

In doing this practice you will be building your foundation energy centers, clearing some karma, and activating your third eye.

Jumping Into the Abyss

As a small child, I have many inner vision experiences. They are sporadic and often not recognized either by my parents or myself. I cannot begin to tell you how grateful I am to be reconnecting with myself and reclaiming these aspects that had been put aside. My way of showing appreciation for this gift is to present others with this same opportunity to reconnect and reclaim what is inherently there. I find people do not realize they have inner vision and in helping them identify the inner experience, they discover they do see.

I am grateful to Master Sha because he persistently puts me on the spot, demanding that I answer his questions. It is this unexpected, "Auubreeey," quality as he calls out my name that brings forth my sharing of my inner vision experience. So, when I open my mouth to speak, I haven't a clue from my logical mind as to the appropriateness of what will follow. This is often a startling experience and one of the profound teaching vehicles he brings to me: jumping into the abyss, trusting and not knowing, allowing wisdom to spring forth out of the emptiness with no chance to second guess.

For the next few years, even when I keep to the back of the room or maintain silence while others speak up, he always calls on me. I take this as a constant challenging of my mind to "let go and let God." It was and is an opportunity to relentlessly break free from my preconceptions, my doubts, or my prior experience. Each of these limits my consciousness that yearns to soar. Inside it feels like jumping off a cliff without a bottom. It is a loss of control. It cultivates trust as I allow myself to be guided. In time, I come to more deeply understand this dynamic is a profound teaching mechanism of entering the unknown.

Different Types of Inner Vision

There are many kinds of inner vision with quite varied purposes. These are only a few of the many ways one can use inner vision:

- ❖ Medical intuitives use inner vision to locate illness on the physical level. A medical intuitive may see an area of darkness or a more detailed cellular image.
- ❖ Crime investigators use psychics to help describe localities of victims, clues, and evidence.
- ❖ Psychics, such as Jeanne Dixon, use inner vision to proclaim future events.
- ❖ The US Military trains people to gather intelligence through remote viewing.
- ❖ Spiritual healers scan images in the Akashic Record for the purpose of clearing karma.
- ❖ Transpersonal psychologists view past lives to help their clients make peace with family members and recurring incidents.

❖ Spiritual masters view the Heaven Realms as part of how they receive wisdom teachings and offer blessings or transmission. *[Wisdom teachings are also received through flow. Please see Chapter 9, "Open Your Heart!"]*

❖ Adept individuals can see their spiritual guides or saints.

What I have described so far is superficial. If you go deeper, you must ask the question, "Where does inner vision come from?" Does it come from intentionally focusing your attention? Or does it come from inside yourself, outside yourself, or spontaneously arise? And what is it that we are viewing?

The Soul World

Inner vision can originate inside the viewer. You can focus your mind with a set purpose (as listed above) and watch for symbols, images, or a movie to unfold in front of you.

However, inner vision may originate from outside the viewer and quite suddenly appear without the person willing it or asking for it. When this happens, it may be quite startling. Spirits from the soul world appear in this manner.

The soul world is the realm of angels, saints, hungry ghosts, and other meandering souls of many levels of Enlightenment or non-Enlightenment. This soul world is formless and yet has some energetic coagulation or gaseous collection of atoms or intention allowing "semi-forms" to be visible.

High-level saints appear in this manner. God appears in this manner. To me, God appears as a Presence, faceless and formless yet with a distinct blue hue that is simultaneously golden light. I have also seen the heart of God as a Universe in its entirety within this profound Presence. I have seen the hands of God present to me a special gift as I am being given the Golden Healing Ball Transmission by Master Sha.

At such times, our attitude is important. We need to greet the soul in front of us by merely saying hello. We also need to ask what they want or why they have come. Be humble, compassionate, and centered.

There is a third origin that is neither inside (as in coming from the viewer's intention), nor spontaneous (arising from outside the viewer's mind). It is a more open and neutral state where you are not looking for anything in particular, and yet you are watching. You open yourself. You open your third eye. You are now an observer viewing the soul world in action.

The soul world has many aspects. There can be souls moving between forms in the physical world. There can be souls within the physical form. People are familiar with these two in that the first example can be a ghost and the second implies that every physical world entity has a soul. This aspect of the soul world is constantly doing things around you, our environment, and our planet. The soul world is busy around us.

Within the soul world, there are different heaven realms as in different spiritual traditions attribute a place in space where their special saints or angels gather. There can be heaven realms for each high Buddha in that it is the special place or kingdom for that Enlightened one. There is also Heaven with angels, archangels, Jesus, Mary, and the apostles. In my own direct experience, I have visited this last version of Heaven that is quite Christian in appearance. I have also experienced realms of different Buddhas as well as a Hell Realm with demons, fire, anguish, and lost souls.

I realize these ideas may be beyond your comfort level. Certainly, they have been for me until I began to consistently experience what I am presenting here. Entering the space of the Unknown can become an awesome moment. It is often called the abyss because from the edge it is terrifying, bottomless, and dark. In this profound letting go, experiences happen that are beyond our normal thinking and outside what I call the teacup of our mind.

To continue, in order to develop your inner vision abilities, it is now necessary to feed this system in our energy body and spiritual channels. How to do this is described in the section that follows.

How to Activate Two Energy Centers as a Unit [4]

Do the practice for the Snow Mountain and the Third Eye for a month, 20 minutes a day. Spend more time with the Snow Mountain and do it first. This will prime the pump of these two energy centers in the proper order.

Place yourself in a setting that is sacred for you. It may be in church as the organ is playing, it may be in nature where there is green and peace, it may be in the presence of an Enlightened master. As you are quietly sitting, reactivate your two energy centers by merely turning your focus upon first the base of your tailbone, then following the pumping energy up the spine, and focusing on the center of your head. Ask God and your guides to open you now to see the souls' activities that are going on in front of you. Let your mind open. Suspend doubt and analysis. Take what instantly comes to you before your ego shuts you down. Trust these initial glimpses. It is so very important to catch them and to grant them their truth.

Many of us already have some degree of inner vision. It is just that we have negated it over many years. To open again means to begin with a glimmer and allow it to be without any judgments. This glimmer will develop into full vision with encouragement. There may come a time when we think we are fantasizing. Western medicine says we are hallucinating. I say no, you are opening to your innate ability of inner vision.

Seeing Inside the Body

In this section, I offer specific examples of inner vision as it is used for healing. The latter examples are more varied.

One of the primary reasons to see inside the body, much like an X-ray machine, is to help people heal physically. I spend two years watching Master Sha do healings twice weekly for 30 or 40 people. I watch and watch so intently to learn. Many times, I do not know in advance exactly what will happen.

One night, we are at the Presidio in San Francisco. He is doing a healing while the person is sitting in a chair at the front of the room. As he places his hands upon her head and makes a, "zzzzzzzzz..." sound, I see five laser beams of bright light coming out of his fingers and going deep into her body. They are rather like light rotor-rooter drills. His fingers extend and spin like an electric drill to clean the area of sickness.

Master Sha challenges me from the front of the room to share. "Aaaubreeey! What did you see?" Initially I feel like a fool and move aside my screaming, doubting ego. "I saw your fingers like corkscrews extend and go into her body."

S,o I have no idea if what I am saying is fantasy. There is no feedback from Master Sha. However, two years later I am doing a healing in a small group. I ask people for their experience. One woman says, "I saw your fingers extend and go into her as we were doing the healing."

A few months later, Master Sha is doing a public group healing. One of the participants shares she saw his fingers extend and go into the body being healed. At this point he adds, "Yes, Aubrey has seen that." He never discusses it or what it means. It is just one of those experiences that rests on the table for future discussion.

In this manner, we find our own way and affirm ourselves in time. Be patient.

Seeing Into the Cells

I first discover this quality of X-ray vision while doing a Qigong practice of bone marrow washing. *[See Chapter 14, "Training as a Spiritual Healer," section under "How to Cultivate Medical Intuitive Abilities."]* Here, you use your palms to pass slightly above your body. You look through the center of your palm as you scan your own body. I was quite startled to see my own spine and bones after practicing this. Later, I could see on the cellular level the changes happening in my clients during a healing. Again, I thought this could be my imagination. I mentioned it to Master Sha. As he often does, there is no response at that time. His style is to respond publicly.

One day, we are at the Asilomar Retreat Center. The morning is just beginning. Master Sha opens the session by saying, "Congratulations to Aubrey. She has great third eye capabilities. She can see on the cellular level."

So, apparently this ability to see with inner vision builds and becomes more subtle and detailed. I am seeing the stage of healing in which the body is cleansed of its darkness of infection and inflammation. There is a second stage of healing—the blessing.

Seeing the Healing Light

One day, we are in San Francisco at the Unitarian Church on Geary where Master Sha is leading a healing seminar. As we are chanting "Om Mani Padme Hung," he motions to me to place my hand above a participant's crown chakra at the fontanel point, and to place my other hand in the air. He corrects me by showing how I am to cup my hand, leaving a small space above their crown chakra. Then, he places his hand on top of my hand. We are connected. I suddenly see Master Sha as a golden sheath of light. He has no body shape. In its place is a strong, solid, smooth, beam of light from heaven. This shaft is about 8 inches in width, and is golden, almost like a finely finished pillar of smooth gold.

He asks me to share this with the group. Each time as I share, it is new information. Again, I have no clue—is this correct? Each time, I feel on the edge of my own knowledge base. I am going beyond what I thought I knew. I have no words or categories to help me understand. What I am seeing, I have never heard about or read in a book. It is happening live time when Master Sha pushes me over the edge of my logical thinking.

Spiritual Chiropractic Adjustment

Two years later, Master Sha and I are in a small chiropractic clinic in San Francisco. The room is quite small and we squeeze closely together as the client stands only inches in front of us. Master Sha is introducing an entirely new kind of healing whereby he "downloads," or gives the student a permanent blessing for their healing. As he is doing this for a dislocated and ruptured disc, I suddenly see the entire spinal column replaced from white bones to golden bones. Starting at the top of the spine each disc rapidly readjusts its position and falls into perfect alignment all the way to the tailbone.

He asks me to share with the client what I see. It's another one of those moments where I may be speaking gibberish, yet I share and trust the process that is unfolding beyond my cognitive understanding. I have never heard of the notion of replacing old bones with golden bones. I have never heard of spiritual or energetic chiropractic adjustment. These are concepts beyond my ordinary thinking!

Healing at a Distance

Last April, I am called upon to do healing prayer for a close family member. I spend hours tracking the surgery, including seeing the difficulty that later turns into potentially deadly infection. While I can see remotely, I do not have the spiritual power to intervene, even if that were to be appropriate. That is a different question. *[I describe this remote healing in detail in Chapter 15, "Up Close and Personal."]*

Meeting Jesus

As a practicing Buddhist for over 30 years, I do not expect to see Jesus! This shows my narrow-opinionated mind.

One evening, I tell Master Sha I wish to realize complete Enlightenment so that I may be better able to help others. *[I mention this story in Chapter 4, "Good Teachers Hurt."]* This has been a lifetime wish and goal. It seems to me that the wisdom and the vision that comes with these highest states will enhance my healing, blessing, and teaching capabilities manifold.

Within moments of stating my vow, Jesus suddenly appears standing at the far end of the table. He is over seven feet tall and clearer than any physical form around us. He radiates warmth. He is wearing soft brown and tan hemp robes. His eyes glow with love. As he stands in front of me, a knowingness passes through me that Jesus has come to teach me true healing. He will be my guide and teacher.

A year later Master Sha, Peter, and I are in Chicago. It is Easter Sunday and the cloudy sky parts momentarily to allow piercing sunlight to enter the room. I feel a palpable presence standing in front of me. The presence takes form and I see Jesus. My tears well up until they stream down my cheeks. I feel overtaken with the directness of this contact. Master Sha asks me to come out from behind the video camera where I have been filming and to come to the front of the room. I struggle to command my body to walk, mumbling something about Jesus out loud. Staggering and in tears, I walk to the front and face the group.

Master Sha then tells me to give a blessing to the 60 people in the room. I am still inside the experience of seeing Jesus so close to me. Then the very presence of Jesus, the actual living spirit of Jesus enters my body. His love pours through my heart and out to the people in the room. His crown of thorns painfully cuts into my forehead. I physically feel the blood on my skin. His light radiates through me and enters the heart of every person in the room. I can see the rays of golden light flowing out of my heart. Like cords of light, they enter each person. I raise my hands and out of my palms comes the healing blessing light I have only seen come through Master Sha. On this day, it is coming through me.

I stay in this experience for over 45 minutes. I am still trying to understand conceptually what happened. Perhaps, "Power is given."

Seeing Karma of Others

When I am healing others emotionally as a psychologist or spiritual healer, I can now see into their past lives. Detailed images arise. I learn that these images are karmic moments or karmic actions that are continuing to haunt the person today.

In post-traumatic stress disorder—or any trauma—there is the phenomena of a "photographic image" that becomes the pivotal point of stuckness and stress. These photographic freeze frame images are repeated in the victim's mind. We know this now as psychologists or grief counselors.

A similar process occurs within the soul as we travel through numerous lifetimes. There are detailed and precise moments where either we did an action that was not right or we did not complete something that needed completion. We did not learn the lesson. These are the basis for karma.

Families can also have karma. With inner vision, I see family karma as a river moving through generations and down to the person standing in front of me. The details are often quite precise. This becomes the issue or action or emotion that needs healing.

When the healing is almost complete, I ask the person what expression they see on the face of the family member with whom they are in dialogue. Their response indicates to me whether or not we are finished on a more superficial level. How they describe the expression on the family member's face could either be a projection of my client's feelings or inner vision showing the truth of that family member's soul in another time dimension (past or present or future). We have here multiple realities, co-existing.

Most of psychology would say this is projection. That is fine, because it gives us information about the person receiving or not receiving the healing. However, when the healer has a more expanded level of consciousness, we view the same situation as a soul-to-soul dialogue with inner vision. We can also, having completed the karmic healing aspect of the session, address the question of inner vision. I ask the person what they felt or saw. This question opens the door to their inner vision being both present and affirmed. I find that reflecting back to a person their experience in a new light of higher consciousness becomes a gift to them. I tell them that they may be seeing with inner vision. This in turn opens the dialogue into the spiritual arena and leads to further spiritual Awakening. It is all perspective!

It takes me several years to accept what is happening for me as a psychologist and spiritual healer. My ability to help people opens into healing past lives and healing family karma. I understand more deeply the relationship between physical or emotional pain and past lives. The speed of this aspect of healing is far more rapid than my prior 25 years as a Western trained psychologist while using eastern meditation practices as an adjunct.

Seeing My Past Lives

Second to prayer, chanting is one of the most powerful transformation tools. If you allow yourself to focus upon the sound itself as it emerges out from your mouth, you will be carried by the soul of the chant. This soul, this consciousness will take you somewhere very special.

Dawn is breaking upon the water. I sit in the sunroom of our houseboat and immerse myself in chanting *Om Ah Hung*. In this particular version, I follow the Tibetan chant placing the Om in my head with the color red; the Ah in my throat with the color white; and the Hung in my heart with the color blue. My voice begins to take on its own timbre and intonation. A deep resonance emerges, and I hear the sound of Tibetan monks chanting in ancient multi-tonality cords coming from their throats. I am immersed in these cords when slowly an image begins to come out of the sound itself. My mouth is now emitting the sound of the monks. I am hovering above a row of monks in a cold monastery with their mouths emitting a mist. They are in robes. I seem to glide closer to them, suddenly entering in through the top of the crown chakra of a Yellow Hat. This is an ancient Gelupa monk. I am now in his body, chanting as I have for thousands of hours. Overcome with emotion, I realize this is me. This is my lineage. I am given the gift of seeing a past life through the doorway of the mantra.

Seeing My Own Buddha Nature

It seems to be difficult to admit our divinity. It has been for me. It embarrasses me and seems pretentious. Yet, that too is an ego position. So, what approach both honors our divinity and yet is not prideful? Where is the balance? We so easily project that someone else is more divine and give away our own divinity. In looking elsewhere, we are not looking inside. We all are part of the exquisite Oneness. Some might say, we are all God's children. Our divinity lives within us. We may minimize or negate it. We may exaggerate it. What matters is that we accept it, quietly, with humility and gratitude.

What I am saying here is more philosophic. However, there is a more experiential story that speaks directly to what is important for all of us: to increasingly step into our own God nature, Buddha Nature, or saint nature. We call it, "step into the hero condition."

When I first look in my lower belly to see my soul, I see a small, seated Buddha. Because it is not the image of a little girl or little boy as some report, I say nothing. I dismiss the event.

Four months later, I see a little Buddha sitting on my head while I chant, "Om Ah Hung." In my mind, I make nothing of this. I figure the Buddha moves around. Ironically—how illogical this soul journey is—seeing the Buddha on my head happens the day after Master Sha has given me a good "talking to." He informs me my past karma is not yet purified. So how can it be that while chanting, my spontaneous experience is to see a Buddha? Who am I to trust: my own experience or the words of Master Sha?

This is neither the first, nor the last, of these dilemmas I experience with my teacher.

Six months later, Peter is visiting Tom and me on our houseboat. He challenges my mind, my self-image, and my attachment to my self-image. "Are you not the Buddha?" he keeps asking me. I feel embarrassed, caught between trying to second-guess him, to give an answer that shows some degree of sophistication, and my baffled innocence. To hide this uncertainty, I rise and go to the kitchen sink. I start to wash the evening's dishes. But Peter pursues the question. "Yes," I mumble, "yes, yes, I am the Buddha...nature."

I think this admission is preposterous and laden with a prideful ego. In trying not to have an ego position, I take an ego position. In actuality, passing through the gate of self-judgment, I experience the baby steps that place me in my Buddha nature. I begin to claim my own Buddha nature. It takes another year to understand what Peter is doing with his question. There is a precious moment of Mind Enlightenment where one fully realizes one's own Buddha nature. His questions were guiding me to that breakthrough. We ALL have this Buddha nature, this Divinity.

When you look inside, how do you see your own soul? However, that is, accept your own wisdom and be willing to step into the hero condition.

Remote Viewing

I am about to tell you a story that is, because of its nature, rather long-winded. The story is about my career as a psychologist working for the State Department and hostage negotiation.

In the field of hostage negotiation, there are two distinct groups: the talkers who seek resolution without violence and the SWAT Team who seeks resolution through "surgical removal." Within both these groups, are those who have field experience working an actual incident, and those who have not had hands-on experience. Unfortunately, for our country, a few of the people teaching how to respond to terrorist incidents have not had field experience, even though they come from the FBI, which sounds good.

Anyway, to enter this field of response to disaster, terrorism, or trauma, it helps to have government clearance. This adds to one's credibility and opens doors. As a result of living in West Africa, I have both government clearance as part of my job with the State Department and subsequent hands-on experience in dealing with a terrorist incidence that has the potential to become an international incident.

In my role as regional psychologist for West Africa, I am invited to write a mental health manual for diplomats and their families living abroad. I am also invited to participate in an international medical conference dealing with counterterrorism. In the magnificent setting of Garmish nestled in the Swiss Alps, I join my host, Dr. Robert Sokol, the chair of this event. He is the chief psychiatrist of the U.S. Hospital in Germany that receives and examines all hostages who are released after being held by terrorists. This conference is also attended by several key Americans with whom I later team up and who introduce me to the man overseeing the secret intelligence project of remote viewing.

In this conference on trauma and hostage negotiation, the attending medical units of the Allied Powers are quickly gathering a body of knowledge about the mental and emotional stages hostages go through. This information becomes the guidelines for professionals in the decades to come. One of the key pieces of information that I retain is the phenomenon of "freeze frame photographic image." This means that people who go through trauma—any kind of trauma—hook their mind or recollection on a very precise moment in time. This instant becomes the foundation of subsequent stress or the inability to lead a functioning life. It therefore is also the moment that needs to be revisited, briefly and precisely, to be healed.

I now understand this freeze frame photographic image is a frozen moment in the soul's journey. Knowing this enables me to help heal victims of trauma.

Upon returning to Dakar, Senegal after this conference, I am attending a weekend baseball event where American diplomats from neighboring countries are competing. It is a big event for so many Americans who love the sport and love to be with their diplomatic colleagues. It is only 10 a.m. and the festivities are just starting. I am standing on the edge of the baseball diamond when the nurse from my medical unit runs up to me. "Aubrey, you have got to come with me! Something terrible has happened!" she says, pulling on my arm. There is no time to even ask why. We are in her car, speeding through the streets of Dakar to a house in the residential area for diplomats.

A young Georgetown student is brutally dragged through her house and left to die on the sidewalk. Her blood is splattered for all in the community to witness. Her neighbors are European and American diplomats, giving the incident the potential for international outrage. Because of my training and recent return from the conference on terrorism, I am designated as the person to handle this emergency in conjunction with the US Embassy's Chief of Security, a tough Filipino military veteran named Frank.

However, as we arrive at the designated "safehouse," Frank is a wreck. I usher him into a small room, closing the door behind us. He collapses on the bed in tears. "Why? Why does it always get harder?" he sobs. He is referring to his own pain, his cumulative exposures to trauma, bloodshed, and death. "She was so young... so beautiful... what will the Ambassador say?"

The story begins to come out. Earlier this morning, this young student was playing tennis with the Ambassador who had personally driven her home, minutes before her murder. As Frank tells me this, I understand the personal guilt the Ambassador is about to experience as he hears of these events.

I leave Frank on the couch, hiding his tears and momentary paralysis. As I return to the living room of this safehouse, women are arriving in tears. These wives of international diplomats know this young student. Now they are feeling threatened in their own homes just across the street from the victim. No one yet knows how many perpetrators are involved or where they are at this moment.

Within half a day, back in Washington, D.C., Georgetown University students are protesting the vicious murder committed by a "black man." The racial implications are building. The Chief of Security is barely able to do his job—interrogating the young African accused of the murder and restraining the local African police from murdering the prisoner during the interrogation. The situation is escalating.

For the next 24 hours, I am on duty to help the entire American community move through this trauma and to contain any international implications, basically by de-escalating the fear, panic, and pain. Later, the Ambassador gives the medical unit a commendation for a job well done. A gift from the Embassy sits on my wall today—a triptych of Jesus, Mary, and Saint George painted on cloth and wood. It is Ethiopian Coptic art... the coming of Christianity to Africa. Ironically, it had belonged to a couple who worked "in tandem" for the CIA.

It is this hands-on experience that gives me a positive reputation and gains me entry to become a team member working with trauma, hostage negotiating, and counterterrorism with law enforcement upon my return to the U.S. It takes me months to gain the respect of law enforcement. First, I am not a police officer and law enforcement personnel truly believe it is necessary to be one of them to understand their issues. Second, I am not a guy. So, to gain their respect, "I had to walk a mile in their shoes." I am invited to become a member of CAHN, the California Association of Hostage Negotiators. Thus, fortified with my commendation, some hands-on experiences, and clearance, I gain knowledge about a fascinating and little known or discussed aspect of our government training called remote viewing. This is the U.S. government's phrase to describe telepathic and audio-clairvoyant abilities used for purposes of espionage.

One day, I am standing by a window in a downtown hotel in Reno chatting with a US Army Colonel who works in the Pentagon. As a psychiatrist, he is highly respected in military and law enforcement circles. There are four of us offering a course in counterterrorism, espionage, and intelligence gathering. Dennis is speaking to me in hushed tones, yet with candor.

He begins, "There was a top-secret Army project known as Stargate that was studied by Stanford University. In this project, we selected twelve individuals and trained them in remote viewing. We did this because the Russians had quite successfully trained spies to gather intelligence using their psychic powers. We found something quite interesting. Our subjects were very accurate in what they saw. When the time came to return these twelve civilians to their normal lives, they had difficulty adjusting. Out of these twelve, only four managed to return successfully to civilian life. A number committed suicide."

"Really! Why was that?" I ask.

"Because we had introduced them into a way of life that was seductive. They had developed special abilities and truly did not have the psychological preparation for what they experienced."

While pioneers in the Human Potential Movement, such as Michael Murphy of Esalen, have known about the research experiments the Russians conduct with telepathy, many do not realize our government is also quite busy in this regard. That is why I include this story and its history. Russian and American intelligence agencies give credence to inner vision. Were I not solidly grounded in a background of dealing with trauma, Dennis would never have confided in me this story of our own country's using remote viewing for purposes of intelligence gathering and espionage.

Thus, inner vision can be applied in different settings—for remote viewing, for healing, or for spiritual growth. Regarding the latter, we know it is necessary to have a good grounding on this physical earth plane prior to moving into altered states of reality and the abilities that go with them. Unfortunately, in the case of the civilians who volunteered for the military project, they were not prepared, and this cost some of them their lives.

As fascinating, as titillating as these stories of inner vision may be, they are only "seductive siddhis." They are powers or abilities that accompany the true purpose of the inner journey. They, themselves, are not the true journey; they are signposts along the way. If you become attached to these abilities, you will lose sight of your true journey.

Chapter 9

Open Your Heart!

What is Opening Your Heart?

I give you the most exquisite multi-petaled flower, filled with a sweet golden nectar, emanating the fragrance of jasmine, reaching its delicately veined petals into the infinite edges of the Universe, touching the heart of God's Divine Love, returning to you in a golden gossamer embrace, and giving you the unconditional, limitless bliss of contentment and home.

This is the nature of your open heart seeking the golden vein of boundless compassion, emanating kindness, softness, safety, and security. Look deeply into my eyes. See yourself. As you touch me, we become the heart of this Universe, connecting in our humanity so closely, so lovingly, we find ourselves in the profundity of the Oneness, as children, as souls, throughout time and space.

Compassion moves us into the Oneness. Compassion affirms the soul's visit into the emptiness. It is compassion we emanate when we touch the heart and soul of God returning again to our human form.

I feel you. I feel for you. I feel with you. I am you. My heart pounds in my chest. I love you.

Opening Your Heart

There abides within our physical body the organ we call our heart. There also abides an energy body holding our heart chakra. One is the physical heart that pumps life into our entire body. The second pumps life into our energetic body that surrounds and contains our physical body. They are intimately connected, each reflecting the health and wellbeing of the other.

To realize our full potential of total Enlightenment, both aspects of our heart must be cleansed, healthy, balanced, and open. Similar to many other patterns of nature, the opening of our hearts follows a progression. It takes time. It is a process.

The process of opening our hearts begins on the more gross level and moves into infinite refinement of the more subtle levels. Given that this process actually unfolds in a non-linear manner where anything can occur at any time and out of sequence, it almost makes no sense to present it as a process. Yet it is a process. Like many aspects of the spiritual journey, it is non-linear, spontaneous, and unique to the individual. Yet we need to discuss it to deepen our understanding. There are pieces of the puzzle that occur over time, and it is helpful to put the total picture together.

In our physical dimension, we have a body, emotions, and physiological responses that become patterns or habits over time. Our ego and our thoughts help to create these habits. In turn, these habits impact our physiology, causing cells to contract or expand depending on the messages they receive. If our emotions are unbalanced, in distress, or exaggerated, our body begins to vibrate in an unhealthy manner. We may even feel pains in our heart. Some call this chest pains due to stress. Others sing songs about our love life, saying my heart is breaking.

Be it stress or emotional heartbreak, we do feel it in our physical hearts.

How To Cultivate the Opening of Your Heart [1]

The very first step in opening our hearts is to relax from stress and to heal our relationships. To go further on this path of Spiritual Awakening, we must make peace with those around us as well as with ourselves. From the perspective of Enlightened Mind, we will see this journey more completely. For this reason, I do not wish to dwell upon the many psychological approaches that are quite successful in dealing with personality or ego work. They are necessary as a foundation, moving beyond stress and discord. A larger perspective follows the foundation work.

For example, instead of viewing couple therapy as inter-actional or as going more deeply into the childhood of each spouse, we can take an expanded view of lifetimes and the purpose of the journey of the soul.

Instead of seeing others and their views in conflict with ourselves, we genuinely let go and allow them their own way. This letting go and allowing is born of an understanding that we each have our unique path. The object is not to convince another to pick up my path; rather it is to help others find and follow their own path. This kind of thinking goes beyond the notion that someone is doing the best they can with what they have. Know that this life is the opportune time to complete whatever we need to complete—lessons, relationships, or soul work. Within the purview of the heart, we make peace in our relationships and with the events of our lives.

By deeply understanding within ourselves that each soul has a job to complete in this lifetime, we show respect to the other person by becoming less of an obstacle or source of friction. We get out of their way, just as we get out of our own way. Our hearts begin to quiet and we are more peaceful. We call this balancing the emotions.

The second step comes as we are ready to move to the more subtle energy of the heart chakra that abides in the center of our chest.

Our heart chakra holds our emotions, our past lives, our ability to speak with all souls in the Universe, and our compassion. While our physical heart gives us life, our heart chakra governs past and present realities. Our ability to love, to forgive, to be intimate, to be touched, to be positive, to be joyous, to be grateful, and to be kind comes from our heart chakra. The potential degree of our Enlightenment is related to our heart softening and opening. As our mind stills, realizations come. Our compassion for ourselves, for humanity, and all life increases.

As the heart chakra begins to open, you may feel physiological pressure in the center of our chest. It can build to the point you feel you could burst. Tears are released sometimes for weeks or months. This emotional opening will bring a softness towards those in your life. Equanimity grows, bringing acceptance and quiet as life moves around you.

The third step in cultivating an open heart is to forget about your self. Forget the "me, me." Become less self-centered and think of others. We all can do this, be it in daily prayer or by giving healings.

Abilities of an Open Heart

The abilities of an open heart are truly boundless. Saints in many traditions reflect our ability to be compassionate. Jesus, Mary, Quan Yin, the Dalai Lama, and so many others speak of compassion as the primary virtue. When you cultivate compassion as a guiding principle, other qualities and abilities come. However, if you are merely interested in the seductive siddhis, most likely your complete unfolding will be severely hampered.

As our heart opens:

- ❖ We can hear more clearly what another person is saying, we hear their deeper meaning.
- ❖ We learn how to communicate with all souls in the universe.
- ❖ We step into the soul world with its saints and Enlightened masters, becoming them and communicating from their perspective.
- ❖ We can converse with our personal guides.
- ❖ We can speak directly with God and directly hear God's message back to us.
- ❖ We can speak in the universal language of the soul and translate that language into our native tongue.
- ❖ We shine the soul light to all souls in the entire universe, thus opening the door to our state of Luminous.

Our heart is key to the journey of the soul.

Hearing with Your Heart

We hear with our hearts.

Beneath the words, beneath the concepts, beneath the non-verbal intonations, sighs, glances, raised eyebrows, beneath the meta-message lies a more true communication. To listen with our hearts, our own mind must be still. We need to move beyond the push or sense of urgency to respond.

In this stillness of our own mind, we pause and receive the deeper communication coming to us. We move beyond the filter system and the editing process in both the speaker and the listener. It is a mutual space of soul-to-soul dialogue. It is intuitive, already poised in its wisdom.

It is not a listening of the mind, for it is not meant to be informational. It is a listening from the heart, for it has compassion, acceptance, understanding, and kindness.

When you listen to the words of your spouse, child, parent, or teacher try to listen more deeply. Listen beyond their beliefs, stories, and justifications. Listen to what they are really trying to say. Know they are doing the best they can with what they have. Everyone is here on this earth to learn what you need to learn in this lifetime. Have compassion for the journey of their soul. Listen with your heart open. Listen deeply:

We have all been everybody's mother.

Brett and Adam.

How to Hear with Your Heart [2]

Breathe and empty. Relax and be still. Focus upon the center of your chest in your heart chakra. Enter into internal silence, devoid of expectation. Open yourself; open your heart.

There is a tree in the woods that shares with me its soul. There is a squirrel whose eyes open wide and chatters at me as it runs up my pantleg. There is the person facing me speaking on so many levels. Just open and listen with your heart. They are each sharing with you the journey of their soul.

Do you know them? Have you been their sister or mother or lover? Place yourself in the prayer position and just ask. The soul that abides within everything, both physical and invisible, will speak to you when you ask and just listen deeply.

Lovingly listen and you will hear. There is an intuitive hearing within you that is the knowingness of your own soul. This is the beginning of communicating between souls.

Communicating Between Souls

What is soul communication? It is a conversation between souls. It can be done out loud in a heartfelt manner looking into the eyes of a beloved or a friend. It can be done silently in a state of Prayer. It can be done to connect with the Divine and receive guidance. It can be done as a writer receives poetry. It can be done as a physicist receives deeper understanding of the cosmology of the Universe.

Soul communication between two people in the physical world may be a conversation on a deep level that involves touching and speaking. It may even be silent between a couple, bringing new intimacy. This kind of communication has a quality of listening with compassion and gentleness. It is hearing with our hearts.

However, in a relationship where the other person will not hear what you are trying to say, an internal soul-to-soul communication may help. This is best done within the context of a prayer. This communication is quite different from the ego tapes of complaining and blaming that often haunt our mind.

Soul-to-soul communication allows for more openness. The ego does not get in the way. When there is no defending, then true listening occurs. This is also deeper than the practice of active listening that merely reflects back what the ego of the other has said. Soul communication is different. It works on a more essential and core level.

In conversation, we are most familiar with initiating when we speak. We are familiar with waiting and listening to hear from the person with whom we have just communicated. We are also familiar with interrupting and not hearing. There are many tools in the market today about how to improve this level of conversation. This is not what I am addressing.

Soul-to-soul conversation has purity and no ego. (So, we hope.) In the state of prayer, we initiate the dialogue. In a very still and receptive state we receive a response. Some of these responses are accurate and some are influenced by our ego. Accuracy seems to be related to our inner state of purity, cleanliness of karma, and gifts or abilities to intuit and receive. It is possible to be trained in our ability to hear with the heart.

Purposes of Soul Communication

There are many purposes and uses for soul communication. In Master Sha's teachings, everything has a soul that can speak and hear. Soul-to-soul communication is a powerful wavelength for communicating. Once you realize there are no secrets in the soul world, you realize every thought or pre-thought is already received. Why hide? Perhaps these thoughts arise simultaneously between us. The communication is already complete. It is received openly and lovingly. It occurs beyond physical words and is the most beautiful and effective way of communicating that I know. It is like music that moves the soul. It is like dancing that delights and expresses the soul. It is a profound communication. It is communing.

Here are a number of ways to use soul communication.

How To Begin Soul Communication [3]

To enter this deeper state, we begin in prayer. This is a non-denominational prayer. This has nothing to do with institutional religion of any kind. You can make up your own prayer, and it will be as effective as the example I am about to give. You speak from your own soul. You come into a state of compassion. You use only words that are positive and inviting and caring. You are placing yourself in your highest nature.

You begin. Call in your own soul. Stand or sit with your hands in the prayer position in front of the center of your chest. This ancient position invokes heart energy, humility, and reverence.

Perhaps you wish to speak to the soul of your husband or wife. Perhaps your spouse struggles with jealousy or possessiveness. Remember that these last two descriptive emotional words are on the ego side, or the negative side, of the coin. Because we are not having a regular conversation, we do not use these words. We address the same concerns in soul-to-soul communication without using the negative. We are actively transforming any negativity to positivity and balance. We sustain our own soul's highest interests and hold the space for the highest good for the other person.

Now that you are internally prepared, your prayer can begin.

"Dear God and Heaven's Team, please come to be with me now. Dear my own soul, please be with me now. Would the soul of my spouse please be with me now? Dear *(name)*, I request that where there is insecurity within you, this may be replaced with confidence; that where there is uncertainty about my love for you, you may feel my commitment and caring for you. Know that I love and cherish you. I ask all my Divine Protectors and Saints to help me show this love gently and effectively so that the soul of my spouse can really receive the depth of my caring. Dear all Enlightened Ones, please help me to show this love more each day and each hour. I thank you all for coming. Please now return from whence you came. Thank you."

Continue to do this prayer several times a day for several weeks. Allow enough passage of time to see the results of sending this message out into the soul world.

In working with clients now, this is what I teach. We do not spend much time discussing what is "wrong" with their spouse, parent, or friend. Rather, we speak directly to their soul.

There are many other uses of soul communication. Given that everything has a soul—rocks, trees, projects, job interviews, careers, books, events, Enlightened teachers, Jesus, Buddha, Mohammed, all saints, deceased parents, and literally anything—there are a multitude of different ways to use this form of communication.

Relationship Healing

Many years ago, I was the clinical director for a growth center where we used a therapeutic approach known as "Fisher-Hoffman" or "The Process." It was developed by Dr. Ernest Pecci, a psychiatrist, and Bob Hoffman, a psychic. While clients were going through this intense thirteen-week process, they were instructed to not be in touch with their families. We wanted to create an energetically and spiritually contained environment for this work.

During this thirteen-week period, I observed consistent phenomena. The family system of the client always went through a profound shift in how they related to each other. When our client completed the process with us, they got back in touch with their family. Almost without exception our clients reported significant changes. The very issues our clients were working to change over the last weeks of the process *were* changed. There was more love and understanding—not just in the client, but also in their family members.

How was this happening? During the last week of this process, the client created a spiritual sanctuary in their mind. In guided visualization, the client would speak with their mother and father, even would see them as an innocent baby. Over previous weeks of this process, the client had done much psychological and emotional releasing of memories and struggles from their childhood and adult life. Therefore, by the end of this clearing, there was some space and peace.

The willingness to see one's parents as innocent is an act of forgiveness. To forgive is to heal. We were working on the level of the soul without calling it that. We could see the healing power by the results in their families.

Today, I do relationship healing using some of the sanctuary work coupled with prayer.

How to do Relationship Healing [4]

Enter into the state of prayer. "Dear God and Heaven's Team, dear my personal guides, dear my soul, please be with me now. I call in the soul of my loved one *(name of spouse, child, parent, lover)*. Please be with me now. Dear guides of this soul, please be with us now. I am most grateful and appreciative of your help and your presence."

This quality of greeting and honoring sets the tone for the work that is about to take place. This tone creates a sacred space for your own soul. We want your soul to "show up" in its highest light. This is essential work for your soul's progress.

Continuing within the state of prayer, "Dear Soul of my loved one *(name)*, I love you deeply. I wish to heal completely and fully the distance that has come between us. I wish to heal our differences of opinion. I wish to regain the gentle kindness and intimacy that we can have together. I fully understand each of us sees the world differently and I promise to allow you the space and respect for you to be yourself. I understand we each have our lessons to learn and thus we must see the world in our own unique manner. Please forgive me for imposing my ideas and feelings onto you. Dear my own soul, I also forgive myself for any emotions and thoughts that are less than loving.

Dear Soul of my loved one *(name)*, I wish to ask this of you: *(any requests, only stated on the positive side of the coin)*. In my heart, this is what I am asking for, and this is what I will give to you *(your contributions)*."

Your prayer may conclude at this point if you wish. Or you can go deeper if it is necessary. Perhaps it is appropriate to do family healing *[see Chapter 12, "Karma: Causality Not Punishment"]*. As you close, say thank you and Gong Song. (This means we respectfully return the souls from whence they came.)

How To Open the Heart of a Loved One [5]

This practice is specifically to open someone's heart for their soul journey. Our motivation in seeking to open the heart of a loved one is a critical issue. It is best to wish their heart to open for the benefit of their soul and their happiness in this life. If, however, you are trying to manipulate through prayer, I suggest you change your approach to truly wishing for the wellbeing of another soul.

Several steps are necessary in this sequence. First, any physical or emotional condition needs to be addressed before coming to the opening of the heart chakra. To remove the pain and the darkness first go through the steps of physical healing, e.g., addressing the condition of headache, cancer, or whatever is causing pain. If the issue is emotional, you must first go through the steps to heal that concern.

Secondly, having created a more cleansed space, within each cell and in the spaces between the cells, transforming the cells into light, we can move to the heart chakra.

In the state of prayer, ask for all souls to forgive this person for whatever pain or anguish they may have caused in this lifetime or any lifetime. Also ask for this person to forgive any soul to whom they hold a grudge or an unmet expectation. This process of seeking forgiveness is essential to clearing the heart of darkness or emotional imbalance.

Thirdly, ask that all emotions within this soul's heart be balanced and healthy. We are ready to ask their heart chakra to open. Speak to the soul of the heart chakra directly and chant to bring a deep peace and softness into the space. Use any chant about love or loving that is familiar to you. If you do not have one, just sing "love." Be gentle in your chanting. Use words such as love, light, and peace. Close the prayer, saying thank you. I always say thank you for the opportunity to be of service. At the very end send all souls home, saying "Gong Song" four times.

A person can receive light and love only to the degree that their heart is cleansed and they are as open as possible. This is how we help them on their soul journey.

A word of caution needs to be stated here. So far, what I am suggesting to you is to ONLY use the state of prayer when seeking forgiveness and asking for the love and light to flow through another person. I am intentionally omitting any attempt to progress to the level of karma cleansing because most healers do not yet have enough virtue accumulated to do this safely in terms of their own health. If you do not have enough merit accumulated throughout all your lifetimes in your soul to carry the karma of another, it can harm you. Karma accumulates in the heart chakra and so this is a subtle and important distinction. It is fine to ask that love and light come to someone's heart while we are in prayer. That is where we stop.

Soul Marketing

Because soul communication includes speaking to all souls, and because I believe everything does indeed have a soul, this means you can have a conversation with the very essence of anything. You can converse with animate and inanimate forms. You can converse with that which does not have a form and is formless. You can converse with that in which you have placed an intention to become a form, such as a book or a project.

If you have a career and are preparing to make a presentation to a group, you can use "Soul Marketing" to help you. This is a kind of marketing within the soul world that is parallel to marketing oneself in the physical world. It is a form of prayer and public relations with the intent to manifest a positive outcome to a presentation, project, or business discussion.

How to Do Soul Marketing [6]

Enter the state of prayer: "Dear God and Heaven's Team, please come and assist me for this presentation I am about to give to this business group. I also call in the soul of the business group, and all the individual souls who will be present. I also call in the soul of this presentation. Please let my talk be well received so we can move forward into a contract and successful outcome to this business venture for all parties. I thank you very much."

What we are doing here is bringing in all souls and communicating with them what we would like to see happen. Prior to making a telephone call, you can say a prayer for a successful result because you are connecting with the soul of the person on the other end of the line. You are already speaking with them. Let me give you an example.

I receive an invitation to speak to the Marin County Prostate Cancer Group. I enter the state of prayer and ask, "Please guide me tonight as I make this Power Healing presentation to the prostate cancer group. Help me to speak with inspiration and clarity. Guide me to their hearts and souls so that I may be of service to them in their struggles." In a sense, this is a way to align my integrity and good intentions with the souls who are coming to the presentation. The key goal is to be of service.

The feedback from the head of this group, Ken Malik, a prostate cancer survivor, is that my presentation is one of their most meaningful evenings. I continue to work with one of the men in this group for the next year, a University of California, Berkeley MBA graduate who turns his life into a positive direction, a new marriage, and an opportunity to live! The depth of healing in his heart and soul is beautiful to see. Today, he sees light coming out of his own hands as he does healing prayers for other cancer survivors. Tears come to his eyes as he feels himself opening to the energies of Divine Light. He may not fully understand what is happening both to him and through him. Yet he would be the first to acknowledge its truth in his direct experience.

Because soul communication is a conversation, as distinct from unidirectional prayer, I also receive a communication back to me the night of the prostate presentation. I hear with my heart this message: "You are in my golden river of blessing, healing energies, and love. Trust that I am within you tonight." That night there were sixteen men and several women. At least half of the men were moved to tears. Yes, I felt the light and the love moving through me to them.

I will tell you frankly, dear readers, it is an awesome experience to be giving service while in a channel of light. It is an altered state. It is a blessed state. I am forever grateful. I had no idea that this could happen to me and through me. It is my wish for each of you to be able to experience this golden channel of blessing and light. I know you can. Just do it. Begin.

Divine Flow

Divine Flow is a conversation with God. To enter into this conversation, we need to be relaxed and open and then our parasympathetic nervous system is activated and our brainwaves are alpha or theta. This means our cognitive or logical mind is placed to the side. Our soul communicates with the Divine Soul of God, or you could view this as our soul reconnects with the Universe.

When we rest in the core of our being, our soul, we find within ourselves a reflection of the Divine. We reconnect and this brings us into alignment with God. From this alignment, our soul reassumes its proper place within our life: to guide us. This quality of guidance that comes from the Universe or from God to our soul is wisdom, a very deep intuition, and a profound inspiration guiding our daily life.

This conversation between our soul and God brings us closer to the experience of Oneness. The state of flow comes as a result of opening our heart chakra and opening our spiritual channels. It is a distinctly altered state of consciousness that is extremely gratifying in a number of ways—the visual space in the room becomes golden, one's voice becomes poetic, and there is a deeper sense of connection with the Divine. The more you enter this conversation, greater peace, compassion, and simplicity will come into your daily life. This conversation feels sacred. This conversation brings greater awareness of the Now. To be in direct communication with the Divine is no more than a thought away. A single thought can guide our emotions, actions, and lead us to right livelihood in any moment.

Purposes for Using the State of Flow

There are many uses for Divine Flow. Here are but a few:

- ❖ Answer personal questions
- ❖ Transform of negative thought
- ❖ Transform of negative emotion
- ❖ Enhance purity of mind
- ❖ Instant healing of relationship conflict
- ❖ Write a book
- ❖ Do healing
- ❖ Do soul reading
- ❖ Seek daily guidance

❖ Have a conversation with God
❖ Write blessings for weddings, baptisms, or other sacred events
❖ Bless others
❖ Receive wisdom teachings

Divine Flow is not channeling of higher Masters such as Saint Germain or Lazarus or people who have died. Channeling implies speaking on behalf of that saint. In channeling, there is more a quality of stepping aside and allowing a voice to come through.

Divine Flow is different in that you enter into the hero condition, becoming the saint or voice of God. The inner experience is that you step into the very being of the saint. You become that saint or the voice of God. You experience being filled with light. The words may be more poetic or profound and your voice may not have its usual tone.

While this may sound ostentatious, that is to become the saint or the voice of God, it actually is a bit intimidating. To even attempt to become a saint means letting go of our human limitations, of our mindset that cries out, "This is ridiculous!" In the journey of the soul, it is a distinct and important juncture where our ego lets go and we enter the mind of our own sainthood… even as just a momentary possibility. Entering the hero condition is a necessary step, one of many.

Entering the Hero Condition

As I have mentioned earlier in this book, we have fallen into a state of sleep, forgetting the truth of our Divinity. To reenter this Divinity and manifest its compassion and light, we need to be WILLING to do so. We need to be willing to drop this facade of our small personality and separateness and literally step into our greatness. Within the greatness, we must maintain our humility. So, we need to take, as it is said in the children's game, "one giant step" and step into our Divinity, acknowledging the beings of light and wisdom that we are. This is not only our potential, not only our birthright— it is also the truth.

On this spiritual journey, the moment we willingly, with full awareness, take this giant step, we become the voice of the Divine. In this moment we are not looking outside ourselves or up to somebody else. We are manifesting this Divine Presence by becoming it! We enter the hero condition. It requires a leap into the Unknown.

This is my inner experience as I enter the hero condition: Out of the stillness, I pause. My mouth opens. My palms are in front of my heart. A word, then another word comes. There is no effort to translate. I hear the words for the first time as they come out of my mouth. There is no internal word to be followed by a spoken word. All is simultaneous.

I can kinesthetically feel an energetic column that is focused and contained, connecting my being with the heavens. I become a spout of expression. It comes as poetry. It comes unexpectedly, without contemplation... unknown until it is spoken. Stay out of the way!

Flow as the funnel gains momentum. It is poetry of the heavens. Images flood. My voice is the voice of the spoken word. There, it is complete.
I rest. I am dazed. I open my eyes to see flickers of light flashing around me and upon the room. I am transfixed and rooted to the earth. I bow to my receiver. Dear God, I hope I have done well, have not over-spoken, have not gone beyond my bounds. Dear God, I hope there is accuracy in these messages I have spoken. I bow to you.

How to Enter the Hero Condition [7]

What are the steps into this inner experience that I have just shared? How can you, the reader, enter this space as well?

First, step up to the plate. Allow yourself the possibility of this experience. Remove your doubt or judgment. Try something new.

Second, place your hands in the prayer position in front of the center of your chest. Place your hands so that your third finder points directly under your chin. Energetically this will focus the Qi both into the center of your head and the top of your head. It feels rather like hooking up to the Universe. As Spock would say, "Beam me up!"

Third, enter the prayer state. Directly ask God for guidance. Be humble and respectful. Ask for your daily message or ask a question. Receive what comes without any editing.

Fourth, take a deep breath and exhale through your mouth. Do this several times as you quiet down. Wait and be patient. You are a conduit between the earth and the heavens.

Lastly, open your mouth. No thought. No preconception. Not waiting to first hear and then speak. Just say one single word. Let yourself be surprised by this first word. Inside the process is that your heart is listening, then sending the message to your head that, in turn, sends the word to your mouth. It is called, "borrowing the mouth." These steps will not be discernable to us as they happen so quickly.

The words will increasingly just flow out of you. It is almost as if we have been given permission to speak in a language that we long to use.

I record these words directly into a tape recorder or type them into my computer. Use whichever is comfortable for you.

Three years go by before I can truly write a book while maintaining the state of flow. The tone, the teachings, and the speed are completely different from the usual process of writing a book. In the state of flow, the entire book comes at one sitting. The Table of Contents follows. Each chapter comes in order. No editing is necessary. The state of flow has spontaneity, clarity, and accuracy.

But this took time, effort, and practice. Here is how the process of prodding, challenging, and encouraging of me by Master Sha brought me into the ability to do Divine Flow.

He has a way of suddenly giving me some command, such as "Aubrey, do a flow!" in a room filled with people. There can be no hesitation that he will accept. I learn quickly how to leap into the unknown because there is nowhere else to go.

He will continue with his lecture while I stand waiting for his attention to return. Often, this will be minutes. So, I wait patiently. I learn to empty my mind. Remove the tendency to panic, to perform, or to grab any previous experience. There is no prior experience or reference point anyway!

In the beginning, however, the process was quite slow!

I am introduced to this process in the summer of 2001, when a small group is gathered at Sam's house in Moraga. It is a hot, sunny day. The light reflects off the pool and onto the white walls and carpet. The room is open and quite modern with a sophisticated flair that is a mix of Chinese and Caucasian—as are the people in the group.

Master Sha rolls up his shirtsleeves. The butcher paper pad is moved to the side. He stands and does his classic impromptu command, "Aubrey, come here!" I never know what is about to happen. He continually catches me off guard. He has been talking about how to open the heart so that it becomes a center for communication with all souls, including with the Divine. He is saying we must not think or use our logical mind in any way. This is spontaneous. We will hear with our heart and, instantaneously, the message will go to our mind where it changes into words or sounds and then will come out our mouth.

I am standing at his side waiting. He turns and barks, "Pound your chest with your hands in the prayer position… faster… faster!!! Good. Now open your mouth and speak! No thought! Just borrow the mouth! Fast!"

His commands are new to me. I feel the push of his energy coupled with my desire to please him. All eyes in the room are upon me! Nothing comes out. Absolutely nothing. My mouth is open and inside I am at a standstill.

"Relax!" he adds in a powerful voice—far from comforting, it has the opposite effect, yet another physiological demand. I cannot second-guess my way through this!

"Just open your mouth and speak. Anything." Still nothing comes out. Then he leans behind my back and thumps me a hard bonk in the center of my back, opposite my heart chakra. "Just let it come out. Flow it out. Quick. No thought!" All these staccato commands come from his lips.

Dead silence. I physically open my mouth. One word rises from deep within my chest and through my vocal cords, "Love." That's it. One word. Love.

I feel like a two-year-old who has produced on command a very small object into the training potty. A little gift. Not much. I feel embarrassed by my meager performance.

It is not until time passes that I truly appreciate the profundity of my first flow. Love, kindness, gentleness, tenderness, and understanding are the pieces that collectively come together into compassion born of wisdom. I am grateful.

During my first year with him, Master Sha asks me to write about my Journey to Soul Enlightenment. I do so. He totally rejects my paper.

He asks me, "Why can you not write as well as you speak? You are inspirational when you speak and share your story. Do it again!" I rewrite the entire piece. I thought the original more poetic and the second less interesting.

He gives up on me saying, "This is not flow!" and tosses the pages down onto the floor. I discount his words, telling myself that he has a language barrier and does not understand my similes and analogies. He counters this by telling me he shows my writing to several others, and they do not like it either!

In the meantime, I show it to Peter, who is often so encouraging to me. Peter merely waves the pages in the air and returns them to me, "This is not flow!"

A year goes by. Along with many others, I practice hard to learn how to let go and let God. Giving up control is so difficult!

However, the next spring, Master Sha asks me to ghost write his biography to be published in *Common Ground*. I sit by my window, praying to God to help me get this one right! It comes! I am able to write in a state of flow that he accepts.

Master Sha has eight Assistant Teachers. Fortunately, we have different strengths and can help one another. Kind Anita knows how to flow quite well, so I ask her to help me. She asks me to help her see with her third eye.

Master Sha acknowledges Anita as a very pure being. She, in turn, attributes the writing of her beautiful book, *The Rainbow of Hope*, as a gift from God through her work with Master Sha. Today, her book is published as a visually rich and colorful text with carefully designed artistic paintings. In the back of her book is a CD that is her original flow. You can hear her voice is slow and has a different tone than her speaking voice. This book comes to her in a single sitting. It takes about 20 minutes to receive the original message.

Just to put things in perspective: in this state of flow Marilyn, another assistant teacher, writes five books for Master Sha on Soul Wisdom. In this state of flow, dear Joyce speaks teachings and instructions for Master Sha each morning for two years! These gifted women produce volumes in the state of flow! Finally I, too, produce a book for Master Sha while in the state of flow. The book comes out in its entirety, the final table of contents followed by each chapter and sub-section, in order, requiring minimal editing as compared to this book, which takes a couple of years and a lot of editing.

I spend one year doing flows in the morning for my personal use. During this period, I receive wisdom teachings that strengthen my direct belief in my own connection with the Divine. This pulsating energy flows out of my heart, through my fingertips, and onto the typed screen of my computer, placing words and thoughts that are not familiar to me. These flows are poetic and lyrical, unlike my usual speaking or writing style. I would like to share a few examples.

Awakening unto Enlightenment
January 14, 2003

Today I will reveal to you the changes in my creation of boundless universes. Divine light shines golden jewels in the hearts of all souls. Souls rejoice as they are each and every one uplifted to levels of brilliant suns and Enlightenments of magnificence beyond comprehension. I, as the voice of the God Enlightened One Who Gives Life in my Breath of Winds to All Souls, declare this Time of No Time, this Time of Eternity, this Time of this Moment to be NOW all be Enlightened in total Wisdom and Compassion. I declare this NOW is the full awakening for all Souls. No longer will there be souls who are not awakened to their highest in all of the Soul World.

This new level of Awakening unto Enlightenment will bring great light into the Soul World. In turn, this great light and high level of consciousness, wisdom, compassion and peace will filter down like drops of golden light falling as a rainfall into the crown chakra of all living things, both plant and animal and mineral and every atom upon the planets in all galaxies. This bindu (seed) of consciousness will grow inside the central channel of all living matter.

On Healing My Own Physical Heart
January 29, 2003

Place your left palm upon your left ventricle and your right palm upon your right ventricle. Chant Ling Zu (Chinese Buddha in charge of Buddha Realm). Deeply feel the vibration within your heart. My name will rejuvenate and cleanse your heart organ. Do this as you lie in bed every morning before rising. Time is a rolling wave of sound. Enter into the timeless for rejuvenation of youth. The essence of youth is in my Dong Qwai (Chinese herb for women to balance their menstrual cycle). *Pray before you drink tea, chant herbs in my name now.*

An Enlightened Partner is to Guide Each Soul
January 13, 2003

The change in the Soul World is their commitment to partner with each soul in the physical world. The task is to open each channel of all souls in the physical world, to give them higher teachings and wisdom, to hasten and quickly bring the entire universe to an Enlightened state.

Out of What Has God Arisen?
January 18, 2003 (full moonlight)

It is I who teaches you the Eternal Light, the highest Soul Light bringing you to Heart Enlightenment. This is the blinding total pure light of the essence of the Universe.

Tonight, I tell you there is a difference between I as the Creator and the Pure Light of the Essence of the Universe. Contemplate: out of what have I arisen?

The Great Bliss of the Golden Nectar
February 2, 2003

There is a pool of golden nectar filled from a Golden Urn of Eternal Light. Place this Golden Urn into your belly and into the bellies of those whom you teach. Help them to see clearly this Golden Urn, like a pitcher, continually flowing into the golden pond whose texture is thick like butter.

Space
February 5, 2003

You call me and I uplift you, quiet you, open you. Come with me into the Universe. Hold my hand of light as I guide you. Feast your eyes upon the beauty of the space between the planets. This is the same space as exists between healthy cells. Each planet is but a cell to a greater galaxy. This celestial body is Nothingness.

Matter turns to energy and back to matter, pulsating within each contraction and expansion between cells. The same exchange, matter to energy to matter, occurs on the level of all galaxies. Thus, both form and formless constantly change from form into formless. This is the solution to the seeming paradox of form and emptiness.

Open your mind to understand the union of form and emptiness. It is in a single breath, the in and the out, the form and the emptiness, constantly reoccurring. This is the true understanding of the teaching that everything is constantly changing. Rest well, my daughter.

Soul Travel to the Causal Realm of Emptiness in the Timeless Dimension
January 28, 2003 (2 a.m.)

In the vastness of the night sky, as far as the eye can see, there arises a sudden slit, like a knife cutting the membrane of the sky. This is the doorway beyond time. You must learn to travel here for it will bring you past and future visions.

To change events, I have placed into the story of time, enter into the new dimension I have revealed to you. Pray in this timeless dimension. This is how to affect events that have not yet occurred.

Now enter the timeless dimension—fear not for I come with thee. Enter, far distance, feel the movement of the soul, the winds, enter this holy place of eternity and emptiness.

Enter the dimension of timelessness. Pray for world peace from this dimension because here the events have not yet occurred. Pray for peace and compassion and wisdom for those souls caught in their anguish of embattled minds. This is soul travel to the Causal Realm of Emptiness in the Timeless Dimension. Pray.

By now, I am beginning to be more comfortable with allowing this state of flow to come. It brings a sense of uplifting, transforming me into greater brightness as I look out at the physical reality surrounding me. This state of flow affects my physiology. There is more light. As a psychologist, I do understand projection coming from my own mind. Yet, I must tell you quite candidly, this is not the voice I usually use. Ideas come that I have never encountered with my logical mind or read in any book. I also wish to include a more recent flow done as a baptism for a little girl.

Sacred Baptismal Blessings for the Precious Soul of Luna

As it comes to pass on this most auspicious day
In the loving presence of dear friends and family
We gather here together to welcome and to bless
Precious Luna.

Know kind souls who stand here in this circle
This day and this hour is to bless my daughter
Who comes to the planet earth
Who comes to the loving parents Patricia and Alex
Know that the soul of Luna
Comes from the Heavens directly into her infant form.

To my dearest Precious Soul of Luna
You are of the Heavens
You bring the Light and the Love
From the Moon, the mother of the tides, the oceans
The golden liquids that bless and nurture all living form.

La Luna,
La Luna,
May light surround you, enter you, bless you
May love move with you and through you
May peace be inside your heart.

Dear Patricia and Alex
Open your hearts to receive My Blessing
For I have chosen both of you to be connected
In a most special way to the Divine
As parents in this lifetime
To the special light of the Moon Child, Luna.

Luna, I bless you in the golden light of my Heart

Come inside Me now
Golden light enters every heart now
Divine Presence is here now
Precious Soul of Luna
You are Blessed,
You are blessed today and every day.

Remember Me
Remember My Light and Love.
I am with each of you.

Thank you every soul who has come today.
Thank you to all the saints and holy ones who have come today.
Thank you Divine Universe.
I Bless all of you.

Amen.

Hidden within this baptism is a special teaching. The child Luna is blessed in the golden light of the heart of God. "Come inside Me now." This infers that Luna is uplifted to receive her blessing and carried into the heart of God. It is not just a blessing where the Divine Light of God descends down from the heavens onto Luna.

Chapter 10

Soul Travel

When our soul separates from our physical body and begins to journey, no matter where or how far, we call it soul travel. This travel is distinctly different than third eye viewing where your inner eye can see something while your soul remains in your body. What are some of these differences? The experience of soul travel has a kinesthetic sucking you out through the top of your head or your mouth. You may experience winds as you travel. Your return from soul travel feels like you were dropped very rapidly back into your body. Your body, if viewed from the outside, is seen as limp, still, and in deep repose. Conversely, third eye viewing can be done with your eyes open, body standing, and your consciousness appears to still be partially present.

The most profound purpose for soul travel is not amusement; rather, it is to learn the art of navigation in six states of consciousness. The purpose within navigation is to remain longer in the desired place, have a modicum of voluntary control, and ultimately to gain soul wisdom through a highly refined sense of awareness.

As our soul travels, we accumulate experience and knowledge. Initially, these experiences seem to be disparate, although quite tasty and interesting. Over time, your internal wisdom will help you deepen and integrate these disparate moments into your own map. Perhaps as I share it with you, you will identify similar moments in your own life and thus begin your own integration. You will likely draw conclusions that are unique to you.

Our soul is presented with existential choices. We can endlessly repeat lifetimes in a blind and ignorant state, or we can learn to find true peace of mind. We can use this lifetime to gain our own freedom, or we can simply be a victim of what comes our way.

Our innate curiosity, our drive for pleasure, our confidence in feeling affirmed, our desire to understand what is happening, are all qualities that guide us toward higher states of consciousness. Although each journey appears unique, its underpinnings are universal. We build our journey in a cumulative manner, integrating life's lessons and the wisdom we gain. For our soul, it is imperative to find our way home to the Source of Oneness, Love, and Light that abides in the Emptiness.

To return home, we need to learn how to navigate in the soul world and how to retain the wisdom we find there. This means we keep in our conscious awareness the wisdom gained in prior lifetimes and carry it into our present and future lives. We need to navigate in different states of consciousness that take us out of our bodies—death, dreams, meditation, past life experiences, birth, and higher states of awareness including going into the Heaven Realms and to God.

The Pure Awareness aspect of our mind is a quality abiding in our soul. This is the navigator. This quality is beyond any sense of self.

Learning to focus our awareness in states other than our normal waking consciousness is key to the journey of our soul. There is a timeless aspect within our soul that travels from lifetime to lifetime. This same aspect within our soul travels to different realms within the Universe.

Six States of Consciousness

Given that there is no "I," there is no thought, and there is no sense of self in Pure Awareness, then what is there? In this highly refined state, there is only a subtle sense of presence, rather like suspending a breath as long as possible. Some call it Discriminating Awareness because there is recognition of the Emptiness. Learning how to enter this Emptiness and suspend one's awareness demands much study and practice. *[Please see Chapter 16, "Portals to Enlightenment."]* The deepest wisdom teachings come to us out of this Emptiness.

The six states of consciousness I am about to describe are conditions of your mind prior to entering into the Emptiness that leads to Enlightenment. These six states, also known as bardos, are gateways or Portals to Enlightenment. Yet these six states of consciousness require enough letting go of self and concepts that this initial soul travel can occur and you can also return to your body. If you go too far, then you do not return to your physical body. The Greeks taught about the "cutting of the thread" that connects your soul to your navel. Once that thread is cut, you enter the death state.

We need to learn how to navigate in different states of consciousness. Once in these states, we need to collect the information that comes and to experience fully whatever occurs. Upon returning into our bodies, we become more confined and our logical mind wants to process new information. Unfortunately, using this old way of processing will not fit as it did in the past. So, we need to process through an awareness, through new thoughts in order to deepen our understanding of what has just transpired.

There are several levels of learning here—how to navigate, how to be aware without ego, and how to bring new experiences back into your human body. It is like learning various strokes so that later you can be a long-distance swimmer or a scuba diver. And even later you can totally merge with the water in the profound state of Oneness.

Let's look further at how to maintain awareness without ego. If you fall asleep in the afternoon, the heaviness of the nap pulls you quickly into a state of almost falling off the planet. You are disorientated and feel rather thick as you awaken. When this heaviness comes on, it is difficult to maintain some modicum of awareness as you enter the sleep state. The physical body just shuts down into a deep state of repose. This is an example of how difficult it is to keep your awareness clear and pristine while changing from one state to another.

Yet this is the very task that lies in front of us: maintaining awareness as we soul travel. Sogyal Rinpoche, a Tibetan Master educated in Cambridge, England, puts it this way: "Going to sleep is similar to the bardo of dying, where the elements and thought processes dissolve, opening into the experience of the Ground Luminosity." [*The Tibetan Book of Living and Dying*, Harper San Francisco, 1992, p. 107]

It is your soul that is out traveling. Your soul has work that has nothing to do with your ego or physical body. Some soul travel is easier than others in both the going and returning. For example, if you are receiving a blessing from a teacher and you suddenly see saints, this kind of third eye vision is easy to recall as you open your eyes or return to your normal reality. This is because inner vision does not require a change of state of consciousness. It does require a change of brainwaves from beta to alpha or theta. As the soul travels further out of the physical body, we can be disoriented upon returning. We must travel many times to learn how to navigate.

I am going to describe six distinct states of consciousness: the normal waking state, the state of meditation, the state of sleep and dream, the painful state of dying, the state of death, and the state of rebirth. This is the cycle our soul will travel as we move from lifetime to lifetime. Learning to recall each state will help you find your way home through full Enlightenment. Each of these states of consciousness offers the opportunity to do practices that will greatly further your ability to travel within them and use them to realize your own Enlightenment.

How To Do Practices for Six States of Consciousness [1]

This section is only a mere introduction. Each of these states requires deep study and practice.

1. **The Normal Waking State:** positive thinking and balancing of emotions. When any negativity arises either in you or around you, chant for two minutes to transform the energies. Deal with life's issues only when you have a clear mind. Practice forgiveness. Let go of attachments. Realize life's obstacles are lessons that you must learn to move past this point. Be humble. Be of service to others. Be compassionate.

2. **The State of Meditation:** focus upon the Light, Emptiness, Oneness, your breath, the sky, and gratitude. There are meditations for specific aspects that can be further elaborated. *[See Chapter 16, "Portals to Enlightenment."]*

3. **The State of Sleep and Dream:** practice dream yoga.

4. **The Painful State of Dying**

5. **The State of Death:** practice Phowa, the Tibetan meditation on how to exit the body and travel through the after-death state.

6. **The State of Rebirth:** continue with Phowa.

Just as it has taken years of trial and error to learn how to live in the physical body, we also must apply a comparable effort to learn how to navigate in the soul world and the six states of consciousness. We must tame our minds to cultivate the ability to travel through these states with an awareness that is distinct from an ego. Why?

A comprehensive answer comes from Sogyal Rinpoche: "How your mind is in the sleep and dream state indicates how your mind will be in the corresponding bardo states (of consciousness). For example, the way in which you react to dreams, nightmares, and difficulties now shows how you might react after you die. This is why the yoga of sleep and dream plays such an important part in the preparation for death." [Ibid, p. 108.]

It is not easy to tame our mind. It is not easy to set our thoughts to one side and focus. It is not easy to be discriminating in the awareness that has no thought, no "I." As we progress through deeper states of consciousness that are increasingly removed from our normal waking reality, the ability to travel with awareness becomes more and more difficult.

This may sound like gobbledygook or riddles without points of reference. That is precisely the point—there are few points of reference. Consider this new terrain for your mind. Put aside your usual conceptual, logical mind. Walk with me into an inner, uncharted place in your mind. Open to a place of profundity, new learning, and many surprises.

A Key to Soul Travel

The crucial element in soul travel is to leave behind all ego and attachments and only maintain a bare minimal, yet pristine awareness that makes no inner commentary as you travel. Awareness has no voice, no judgment, and no position. We need to cultivate a quality of suspension and yet acute awareness to travel through these different states. What do all these different states of consciousness—waking reality, meditative visits to Heaven, death, dreams, past lives, and being born—have in common? Our soul is present in each one.

We each need this awareness to remember what we knew before and take it with us when death comes. Each state offers us the gift of total liberation. In each there is an opportunity to break free of the death and rebirth cycle that we have been undergoing for possibly thousands of years. Each state of consciousness has portals that can move us into Enlightenment where we are fully aware in the Oneness.

Deep within each of us is familiarity with what I am describing. We have already traveled this road. Now we must Awaken and Remember and practice. We each have the Enlightened Mind within us.

The Normal Waking State

In this state, the state of consciousness that you are now in while reading these words, there is much preparation you can do for soul travel. You can orient yourself to inner work, cleaning your vessel, and hearing teachings from your teacher. One such teaching from Master Sha and Master Guo is that your karma must be cleared and your virtue accumulating such that you qualify for a spiritual animal guide to carry you to the heavens. In Tibetan Buddhism, protectors for your soul are given to you through your spiritual teacher. In Christianity, we call for protection and guidance from Jesus. These are similar and yet protection, guidance, and transportation are quite distinct. It must also be said that spontaneity is a great teacher! Soul travel can happen to you suddenly. My hunch is that it often happens when you are a child or in a state of openness.

How to voluntarily prepare ourselves in this normal waking state of reality is the foundation to serious practice for soul travel. Soul travel can be to the heavens, beyond the heavens into the emptiness, astral travel, and travel outside the time dimension into the future or the past. Soul travel can be into the mind of another human being. Let us prepare.

You are familiar with a thought that grips you and continues its tenacious hold, repeating itself. The thought stirs your emotions until they form an attitude locked into our mind. This becomes your position on the point. This is an example of a karmic pattern. During our life, especially as we age, the trap becomes increasingly apparent and tenacious. Even with a plethora of self-help books available to us, we each know all too well how difficult it is to break free.

Psychology applies ego-orientated therapies causing us to continually re-experience our upset and re-trigger the very psycho-sensual roots of our trauma or conflict. I regret that I, too, spent years "helping" my patients relive trauma. While there is a definite place for this re-living, it needs to be quick, specific, and complete, not drawn out for months. Each time a person re-experiences a negative exchange or emotion, it only furthers the pattern and reinforces the result. Therefore, this is not the best road if you want to liberate your soul from these ego or karmic patterns.

In the course of our daily life, while doing the most mundane chores and activities, there are a multitude of moments when we can retrain our minds and our emotions. Mundane perception sees the endless trail of red lights of cars in front of you as a source of irritation. Retraining your perception is to look at the traffic in front of you and focus upon the light shining upon the metal, let your eyes go loose, and see a body of light with many spurts of intense light. Focus upon the light.

Retraining in the waking state also helps prepare for the time when we enter other states of consciousness over which we have even less control. If you pause to consider how difficult it is to train yourself now, you will be humbled by the job in front of you. There is not a moment to waste! Begin!

How to Train Your Mind During the Normal Waking State [2]

❖ Begin each day in prayer. Ask for guidance, pay homage, and connect with your personal guide, saint, or protector. Restate your goal for Enlightenment, offer service to all souls in the universe, and follow the path the Divine has set before you with acceptance and gratitude. Offer any merits and virtues you accumulate to the benefit of all other souls.

❖ When stress or conflict arises either from within your own mind or from someone or situation approaching you, do two things. First, exhale deeply three times and feel your feet. This will bring you into your body and into the present. Second, chant for at least two minutes. Watch and you will see the situation and the person transform in front of you. Allow time for this to occur.

❖ Recognize when your mind is thick and cloudy. This is not a time to make any decisions or to deal with life issues. Allow your mind to clear and be refreshed. A cloudy mind brings "stinking thinking;" a clear mind brings sunlight.

❖ Be willing to let go of positions, of issues, of negative exchanges, of the need to "be right." Allow a flow to move through you dissolving self-imposed blockages.

❖ Change your perspective, first in small matters. If it is raining, instead of grumbling about the weather, go outside like you did as a little kid and focus upon the mud puddles with their reflective light.

❖ Recognize that attachments are the source of your suffering. Exhale and return to the morning prayer where you are following the path the divine has placed before you. This will lead to

---

equanimity. You will see the karmic lessons and challenges that you must overcome in this lifetime.

❖ Be compassionate. Open your heart so you can hear other souls on the deepest level possible. If you wish to lead a life that is neither shallow nor based in ego—yours or theirs—then go deeper each time you can. You are the initiator of your life. Show up as you wish to be seen.

❖ Be humble. You will better perceive your place in the universe as simultaneously small and insignificant, and yet without any boundary. You will see the connectedness of all. Humility reduces ego and produces a sense of flow and connection.

❖ Be of service to others. Service loosens the grip of your ego patterns, emotions, and self-centeredness by simply turning your focus outward. It generates more virtue or good karma for your soul. It is a doorway to connecting with other souls in the universe. This last point is so very important because when cultivated it can lead to Enlightenment.

❖ Let go of your logical thinking so that your unique inner journey, with all its unexpected experiences, has a chance to unfold.

This last point is basic. Only one of six states (our normal waking state) is limited. It is further limited once our logical mind and its conceptual framework take hold—like being squeezed and constricted as one would wring out a towel.

There are fleeting moments during a day when you may glimpse an altered state of consciousness. It is so quick you barely catch it. "Oh, I feel like I have just seen a ghost!" or "I just know I have been here before. It is so familiar."

Past Lives

When I am sixteen, I had never heard of either past lives or déjà vu experiences. Yet I have a profound past life experience that convinces me that I lived before. This experience sits dormant in my philosophic and spiritual understanding for two decades. Then it begins to make sense.

I am sixteen, touring Egypt with my mother and stepfather, Luther. It is a culture that has fascinated me since I was six. One special day, we visit the great pyramids, climb some very large stones, and sit on camels that spit. Tired and yet satisfied with our adventures, we begin the drive back to Cairo. Sitting in the backseat of an old car, I am squished and hot between my parents. Mom has hired a driver and our guide is in the passenger seat. As the road gets more dusty, I get a little bored, fussy, and feel stifled by this never-ending list of places to see—the obligatory sightseeing. I hate being the American pig tourist—rich, over-privileged, self-centered, and different. People keep staring at us. Being treated this way is not a nice experience. I am more than ready to get back to the safety of the hotel.

Our guide decides to take us onto a narrow road and further off into the desert. There is a sand hill in front of us. We can see nothing but desert in every direction. Suddenly, I feel hit with a wave of emotion that throws me back into my seat. It is a wave of recognition, of coming home. I burst into tears. "I have been here before." I continue in sobs, "This is the very village where I lived." But all my family can see is sand. There are no remaining ruins or buildings or roads. There are six palm trees and sand. No people and no animals. It is empty. I describe the map of the village and its name.

Our guide is rather taken aback by this outburst. "Yes, you are right about both the village and its name. We have old maps of this village." I am overwhelmed and shocked with the newness of the feelings that are pouring out. I do not know what is happening to me. I am so used to being contained emotionally. I don't like to show any feelings in front of my parents. This is most unlike me.

Days later, I take my mother by her hand and literally lead her through the narrow pathways in the busy Cairo marketplace. I know where the jewelry booths are. I know when to turn right and when to take a few more steps to get to the next section quickly. I am like an old soul who remembers each little shortcut in this densely crowded and loud market. It is so familiar!

Seeing Past Lives of Clients and Their Ancestors

Within the normal waking state, we can enter other altered states of consciousness. Telepathy, psychic readings, healings, flows, and astral travel all seem to occur by altering our brainwaves to a quieter and slower rhythm. As distinct from spontaneously entering an altered state, we can do this intentionally.

Here is an example of deliberately entering an altered state of consciousness.

How to Connect with Clients' Past Lives [3]

Today, as I enter into the prayer state and consciously invoke the souls of my client and their family members, I am able to go back in time and even see their parents and grandparents. Often while working to resolve something within this lifetime and with a child or a parent, a client will not see or understand that the issue may be bigger than individual and may belong to an entire lineage. In the state of flow, I can hear and share with my client the issues that have haunted their family for generations. This touches upon family karma as well as individual karma.

To truly help someone may mean to go deeper than the current issue, emotion, or situation—go to the soul level. All true healing happens on the level of our soul. Once the client can see the deeper family theme, they can ask for the light to heal their family. It is almost like a river flowing from grandparent to parent to client.

Then comes the phase of forgiveness and love. By the end of the healing session, the client may offer any images they see, either of their past life or seeing the expression on the face of their parent. This projection or third eye vision that the client shares demonstrates their emotional reality at the end of this guided process. At the close of the session, I ask the client to open their eye and tell me, "How do you see this room now?" Their answers invariably include "lighter," "brighter," "colors are more vivid," "larger," "more space," and "peaceful." Each of these descriptors reveals their state change as a result of our healing session. I conclude by asking them to make an "I" statement so that they claim their new state: "I am lighter," or "I am brighter."

The State of Meditation

Meditation is one road to Enlightenment. Enlightenment, once entered, has unlimited experiences as well as boundless realizations within it. There is a foundation context, a ground if you will, that begins to describe the indescribable experience of Enlightenment. These are the three aspects of our natural mind: Emptiness, Luminosity, and a powerful undulating movement.

Sogyal Rinpoche elaborates on these, saying, "Remember now that when we looked at the nature of mind, we saw that it had these three same aspects: its empty, sky-like essence, its radiant luminous nature, and its unobstructed, all-pervasive, compassionate energy, which are all simultaneously present and interpenetrating as one within the Rigpa." [Ibid, p. 343] The Rigpa is a resting state, a quality I refer to as "suspended." It is a space between thoughts. In my early training with Tarthang Tulku, Rinpoche he always encourages us to "Look to the space between the thoughts."

The purpose of meditation is to tame the mind so that you can enter these states of Enlightenment. As you well know, there are hundreds of approaches to meditation. I will limit my discussion to what I have come to discover is the most essential and quickest road to Enlightenment and why meditation is part of that path.

Meditation trains the mind to let go into the Emptiness. Once the mind can enter the Emptiness, wisdom teachings appear.

This is how the great spiritual masters receive their gifts from the Divine. This is how spiritual teachings come to high-level spiritual masters to be spoken or written for others. YOU can realize these altered states of consciousness also! This is your innate potential. These seeds are already within each of you. You need to brush away the dust to see what is already there. Then you need to cultivate this seed into a beautiful unique flower of your own Enlightenment. The only reason I share with you my experiences is to offer hope and conviction—if I can do it, so can you!

It is one thing to enter these experiences, and it is quite another to sustain them from inside the experience. The latter is the art of soul navigation. It requires maintaining a pure awareness free from ego. Learning to navigate and maintain in the meditation state gives us a better foundation for going further into other states of consciousness such as dream, death, and rebirth.

Here are a few of my personal meditation experiences demonstrating quite different altered states of consciousness.

Past Life Experience Through Chanting

In August 2001, in the early morning hours, I am chanting Om Ah Hung and my voice changes into a timbre with a deep resonance of a Tibetan monk. I listen and listen to this deep rumbling chant. The sound carries me. Suddenly, I am back in time inside the body of a yellow hat Tibetan monk, seated chanting Om Ah Hung in a cold, dank monastery. I am the monk lifetimes ago. I have now entered, seen, and felt from the inside of the monk my past life. I now know for myself, in this direct experience, why I am a Tibetan Buddhist and how this past life has guided me over 20 years to study Vajrayana Buddhism. Suppose we could cultivate this knowledge and use it to bring back all that we knew before… not just fragments.

How to Use Sound for Soul Travel [4]

Sound is a path that will carry you. There are two aspects here. The first is allowing the progression of spontaneous sound to come up from deep inside yourself. Allow the sound to change as it wishes. The second step is to let go to the sound of the chanting, which in and of itself is another path. The sound of a chant is also the calling in of the soul of that chant to assist you. For either spontaneous sound or traditional chanting, focus upon the sound from inside your own mouth and surrender to what arises.

Emptiness Through Sky Meditation

In September 1972, I am practicing a secret advanced meditation usually reserved for those who do the traditional three-year Tibetan Buddhist retreat. Everything inside me is relaxed and quiet as I gaze upon the blue sky. Suddenly with the profound impact of powerful energy, the entire visual field of the sky changes. An almost shattering silence runs deep into space. Everything is visually still and empty, almost a quality of frozen stillness in time. This is an Emptiness of a different dimension. There is absolutely nothing—no sound, no movement, no visuals, no color—just truly void of everything.

How to Do Sky Meditation to Enter the Void [5]

Place your body in a resting position on an angle so that you can see the sky. Deeply relax and yet stay awake. I use the small rainbow colors of my quivering eyelashes as a barometer of how quiet I can make my body. When my eyelashes are quiet, then I focus on looking to the space between my thoughts. When there is no thought, then I focus on the sky. As you focus on the sky, continually cut through wherever your eyes seem to grasp. Like a sword, cut through this grasping. Go deeper and further into the sky and into the vast space. Continue cutting through until you are suddenly catapulted into the Void, the Shunyata, the Emptiness.

Luminous Changing to Energy and Movement

This Enlightenment experience (June 2002) is already described in Chapter 1, yet I include it here because it contains elements of both soul navigation and maintaining the state. In the meditation experience of Luminous, I am able to sit in the suspended perspective with awareness and no thought. For an unknown period of time, all is brilliant light in every direction. There is no I and no thought.

Then, the nature of the experience changes and enters the second aspect—a combination of undulating powerful movement and energy. There is a visual field in this aspect that is clearly undulating. There is a kinesthetic quality of undulating movement. And there is a sense of unspeakable power. This latter aspect of power is akin to a dam bursting with water that whirls and overturns and is enormous in its strength—yet a thousand-fold more powerful!

The impact or effect of these two states stays with me even though I move and speak. This characteristic of remaining with me throughout the hours of the day is more a reflection of the power or intensity of the Enlightenment experience than anything to do with my cultivation of awareness. Recall my story about Sidney Banks, where for three days he was consumed by the power of his Enlightenment experience.

How to Enter the Luminous State

There is no "how to." This is a gift from your teacher and a blessing from the Divine. All we can do is our homework and prepare.

My Soul Is in Two Realms

As I enter into the role of spiritual healer, my soul is simultaneously in two realms—soul world and physical world. Through offering service to others, I enter a state of golden light where I am guided to do whatever comes. I am connecting with healing saints in the Heaven Realm while simultaneously being present in my physical body. One of the most powerful experiences of this kind of healing happens in June 2004. *[See Chapter 14, "Training as a Spiritual Healer."]*

I am doing my weekly remote healing for Patricia, who has metastatic cancer. While I am offering a healing blessing, I see the tall figure of Jesus hovering outside my window, in the garden under the oak tree. He stretches out his hands, takes her liver out of her body, and gently caresses it, filling it with pink new cells and the rejuvenation of golden white light. Then, he places it lovingly back into her body. I am so moved I begin to tear up. I tell her of this blessing she is receiving from Jesus. She is startled by the presence of Jesus, as she believes in Goddesses. Yet she feels a tingling in her body and the light of blessing.

How to Heal While in Two Realms [6]

In every healing blessing, in every offering of service, a channel of golden light can enter the healer. This light moves to the client through the healer's whole-hearted intention. Speaking to the soul of the client, the organ, or the system; offering cleaning with light; rebalancing the energies; then chanting God's Light or any mantra—this basic healing blessing sequence will bring the golden light. Once this golden light comes, other spontaneous events can follow. Stay open and flexible. Believe in your own healing abilities. This is part of entering the hero condition—you become the Saint or Healing Buddha you invoke as you offer service.

Teaching While in Golden Light Channel

In August 2004, I am speaking to a group of 40 women at a club meeting. I enter the golden light channel and feel solid, blessed, centered in my heart. Some small voice inside questions how these older generation women in a farming community will receive my teaching about the soul. Yet I trust my heart and the words flowing out. The room is mesmerizingly silent. All eyes are riveted on me because I am speaking about the soul.

Again in November 2004, I have a similar experience in teaching 50 alternative health practitioners. As I enter the golden light channel to teach about the soul, the room falls into a magnetic, mesmerizing silence.

How To Teach in the Golden Channel [7]

First, enter the hero condition. I allow my mouth to flow. My logical mind has set the topic. Yet once in front of the groups, I enter into prayer and ask for help in touching the hearts and souls of everyone present. This connection to the souls of the people in the room and to the Divine sets the first step of alignment. The second alignment is to be requesting, in a whole-hearted manner, to be of service. These two qualities allow my soul to travel simultaneously into the hearts of those present and into the soul world.

This is sub-divided soul work. As a healer, I am entering a state of consciousness that is meditative and quiet, moving my sense of self aside, and surrendering to the energy, light, or inspiration that directs me.

These last examples are meditative states through the offering of service. I experience the same state while offering a blessing at a wedding. Brainwave studies suggest this quality of meditation could well be an alpha state. However, what is so different from most alpha states is that it is golden. I am coming to understand that the golden light quality is the spiritual link. On one side is our understanding of physiology and brainwaves that belongs to psychology. On the other side is our newly acquired skill to enter the Soul world. The golden link comes through offering service.

Out From the Emptiness

In September 1972, through practicing the Sky Meditation I am suddenly in the Void, Shunyata, or Emptiness. I have been resting for some time in this Emptiness—I have no concept of how long because there is no time dimension. It is long enough to drink deeply.

Suddenly, the whole experience changes. Where there has been infinite emptiness, there is now the image of Guru Padmasambhava filling the entire sky! This being literally fills the sky! He comes swiftly almost as if the force of his presence popped out with a push into my awareness. It has a quality of being thrown at me from within the Emptiness. He comes from the vastness of the Emptiness. I have never heard of anyone being thrown into my awareness out of the sky!

I return to my Vajrayana teacher, Tarthang Tulku, to tell him this amazing experience. He merely smiles and says, "I wish I had that connection." I dismiss the "connection" implication instead focus, ignorantly as I later learn, upon my perspective that all this happens through his channel and connection with Padmasambhava. Cognitively, I have no seed idea that a direct connection can be a conferring, a formal introduction with an Enlightened and powerful saint. I simply do not know that such a saint or buddha chooses you.

Years pass and I begin to learn about what this connection is and what it can do for the journey of your soul. In October 2005, Master Sha confirms that in his teaching, Padmasambhava is my Shi Fu, protector saint. Sometimes, these affirmations take time.

> ## How To Receive Saints Coming Out from The Emptiness [8]
>
> The instructions given above for the Sky Meditation will open you to the Emptiness. What happens after you enter the Emptiness will be completely your own experience. Your training, spiritual connections, personal karma, and natural affinities will shape what arises.
>
> This meditation is key to learning how to navigate in the bardo states.
>
> Perhaps there is no "how to" other than surrendering to the experience and trusting that what arises out of the unknown is, in and of itself, a great teaching. The further I go, the more I learn that the Unknown is the greatest teacher of all.
>
> The Unknown is the Emptiness that can be entered instantaneously. The wisdom teachings come to us out of the Emptiness. This is great wisdom.

The State of Sleep and Dream

I am no older than two. I flee to my mother's bed, seeking comfort from the wicked witch who is terrifying me in my dream. Mother imparts a piece of wisdom that becomes the backbone of a lifelong study of the dream state. I am eternally grateful for this information. She tells me, "You are the boss of your dream. If you want to stop the witch, you have the power to do that. It's like a play and you're the director." Armed with this idea, I begin to change my dreams from inside the dream. The next time the wicked witch comes to chase me, I climb to the top of a tree and fly away.

Flying in my dreams takes long practice. At first, I am not very good. Years later, I can navigate over hilltops, trees, and even cities. I can land where I want to land. I can soar when I jump or merely spread my wings.

When I am 30, Tarthang Tulku, Rinpoche tells me there is a large body of wisdom called dream yoga. Many of us who meditate and study with him discover that he is an adept at this yoga. During our summer training program in 1972, he enters our dreams. We learn this as we begin to chat during the day and share our experiences. I begin to notice that when he enters my dreams, there is a significantly different quality. The visual field of the dream is quite clear. It is clearer than my normal waking state. Another quality of these dreams is that I may suddenly wake up and find myself bolt upright in bed. I record all these dreams in my journal. Two years later when I tell him I am moving to Mt. Shasta, Rinpoche is quite upset with me. I thank him for all the teachings he has given me in the dream state. He thunders at me, "And there will be no more!" He cuts me off in a manner that still brings me pain.

What is significant is that Tarthang Tulku has mastered the role of sender in the dream state. Many of us know how to receive, but few know how to send. He sends me one last message a few months later, but he sends it through a total stranger. He enters the dream state of a young man who is to attend a public talk on dreams that we give in the town of Mt. Shasta. I ask the audience to volunteer a dream. One young man stands up and says, "Last night I had the strangest dream. A man in orange and purple robes came to me. He said his name was…something like 'Tartag Tulke Rinpo' or something close to that." I ask him, "Was it Tarthang Tulku, Rinpoche?" "Yes! Yes! That was it! Who is that?"

For 30 years, I puzzle over this ability. Now, I am beginning to understand the power of Rinpoche's ability to navigate with his soul. Through this ability, I can begin to glimpse the power of his consciousness and how deeply he has cultivated his Enlightenment. As Sogyal Rinpoche says, "Dreaming is akin to the bardo of becoming, the intermediate state where you have a clairvoyant and highly mobile 'mental body' that goes through all kinds of experiences. In the dream state too we have a similar kind of body, the dream body, in which we undergo all the experiences of dream life." [Ibid, p. 107.]

The practice of dream yoga is so important, for here we can begin to control our experiences. As we get better, we will be more equipped to handle the other bardo states that are further removed from our minds as we know them.

There are two distinct categories of dreams. Those in the first category range from personal dreams that may be either processing and integrating the activities of our daily lives or plummeting deeper into the collective unconscious. The field of psychology primarily studies this category.

Awakening Dreams

Soul travel can happen in the dream state. It can also be outside the dimension of time, such as into the future. In recent years, enough literature has been written on "lucid dreaming" that psychology now includes this new tilt on dreams. But even lucid dreaming only touches the surface of true dream yoga, an ancient body of wisdom with specific practices. I call this latter group Awakening Dreams because they are about Spiritual Awakening. Their visual field is clear, pristine, precise, and brilliant. They may be prophetic. They may be teaching dreams where you receive wisdom. They may be astral projection dreams. These kinds of dreams are a spiritual ability within the dream bardo consciousness. Here are two examples of my spiritual awakening dreams.

The Assassination of President Kennedy

When I am 23, I have a prophetic dream that so shocks me I write it down and put it in a sealed envelope, hidden at the back of my linen closet. I didn't know what to do. Months later, I am interviewed by the journalist Jess Stearn for his book, *Adventures into the Psychic*. This dream experience becomes a cornerstone in my conscious understanding and pursuit of Dream Yoga. Here is what Stearn writes:

> In an equally singular case, a beautiful undergraduate at Berkeley's University of California was particularly drawn to the youthful President who had a special charisma for the young. She had even involved herself in the Kennedy election campaign, having made a pre-election poll of the Berkeley-Oakland area which gave Kennedy a hairline margin. As a crusading liberal, whose family was associated with the pro-Kennedy Americans for Democratic Action, Aubrey Degnan's shiny-eyed partisanship for the charmer in the White House never faltered.
>
> Before the dream in which she was to see her hero hospitalized, Aubrey, like Jackie Joyce, had a number of psychic experiences, establishing her subconscious as a better than average channel. Once, while touring Egypt with her mother, she was haunted by a strange familiarity as she strode through a Cairo marketplace and correctly anticipated the scene as she turned a corner—a bazaar never consciously seen before, in a city she had never been in before.
>
> She had many dreams in color, and kept a pencil and pad at her bedside to record them the moment she got up. On the night of November 2, 1963, in New York City, where she was then living, Aubrey had the most upsetting

dream of her life. In the dream, a voice told her to warn the President of his imminent danger. The nature of the danger was not clear, but as the voice faded out Aubrey saw herself turning into the White House. And there in a corridor, in a building she had actually never been in, she encountered a guard with nondescript features. He seemed to be patrolling the hallway. The voice now returned to her dream, describing the guard as "Kennedy's timekeeper," and then "Kennedy's watchman." She had the hazy impression that he was really a Secret Service operator. He was carrying a gold watch, clock size, which read 2PM. "He wanted to stop me, but somehow I pushed past him," she recalled, "and then I passed through a series of corridors, doors and smaller hallways, into a large rectangular room—much of it covered in yellow."

Aubrey had been a hospital aid, and her father was a doctor, so she was familiar with hospital procedures. "As I saw the President for the first time," she recalled, "he was lying on what appeared to be a hospital bed; it was iron-framed and had a thick mattress. He was lying on his back, his body tilted at the angle at which a person is normally placed in shock. His head was tilted up, his knees were hunched up by the tilt of the lower part of the bed. His bed was surrounded by chairs, perhaps two dozen of them, with people sitting in them." She recognized none of these people, but all appeared worried.

An oxygen tent, of plastic, transparent design, was hanging over the upper frame of the bed, but had not been placed over his face, though this appeared to be imminent. The atmosphere in the room deepened to one of great alarm. And then the timekeeper appeared. He announced somebody had stolen his way into the White House and had to be gotten out.

In her dream, Aubrey suddenly found herself sitting in a chair around the President's bed. As she looked about apprehensively, the President turned his head and regarded her blankly.

At this point, most of the people got up to leave, and Aubrey saw the President was going to be left alone. He had obviously been injured and was receiving treatment for shock, but she saw no wound or blood. That ended the dream. When Aubrey awoke that morning at about 8 o'clock, she felt strangely troubled. She kept seeing that sloping hospital bed, with the President on it, and the big watch at 2 P.M.

Nearly two weeks later, on November 14, after flying from New York to the Bahamas for a holiday with her parents, she was still brooding oppressively over the dream. She told her mother about it, also some others–her aunt and uncle, and a friend, all of New York. Then listened without, of course, having any suggestions. Oddly, even then, she did not realize the full significance of her dream.

All that week her dark mood prevailed. On the day of the assassination, at
1:30 P.M., she was walking down to the docks when she saw some people
clustered intently around an outside radio, but she did not stop to inquire.
She got home a half-hour later, and the phone rang. It was a friend saying
that Kennedy had been killed. Her eye happened to fall on the clock. It was
2 P.M. exactly.

She felt curiously empty. A warning had been given her, and she had done
nothing with it. "I felt personally responsible," she said, "because I did not
fully recognize the purport of my dream. Obviously, I could not have stopped
the President from going to Dallas, but I would have felt better for the effort."

Ironically, the day before the assassination she had picked up The Door to
the Future but stopped reading just before the chapter dealing with the Jeanne
Dixon prediction. The night of the assassination, rather sadly, she returned
to the book. She read on a few pages, and then bolted upright in her chair.
There it was on page 28: "A Democrat in 1960 with the aid of labor, and he
will die or be assassinated in office."

Had she read this twenty-four hours earlier, it would have crystallized her
own fears – and she would have acted." [Adventures into the Psychic, Jess
Stearn, Coward-McCann, Inc., New York, 1969, pp.30-32.]

It is true that morning I had stopped reading on the left side of the page. I
still feel the guilt and anguish with the question, "Could I have done
something to stop this action?" I was so young and did not understand these
phenomena.

This is an example of what I mean by the gifts given to us from God. Often
people receive information that they do not know how to handle. This
happened to me. I felt guilt, because I was unable to save his life. Today as
a spiritual healer, I feel guilt when I cannot save someone's life. Part of my
own training is to more deeply understand and accept the role of karma. I
have seen the Lord of Karma, and he is not a pretty sight. Part of my own
training is to cultivate compassion and service while in the state of non-
attachment.

Blessings in the Dream State

This is a short, yet significant blessing dream. I am kneeling in front of Quan
Yin as she is blessing me. I am receiving her compassion to use while
healing others. She is in flowing robes with a pale blue light from within all
her body. I physically awaken quickly.

This image from the dream state is the same as the image I saw on the day of Peter's Enlightenment two years prior. Sometimes the blue light appears without any figure.

How To Enter Dream Yoga [9]

Do this practice just as you begin to sleep.

1. Focus on your throat chakra, placing a blue light in it. Follow this blue light as you fall asleep.
2. Focus on the Emptiness and go further into the Emptiness in the blue light.
3. Place a request for the kind of dream you wish to have this night.
4. Try to remember inside the dream state that you are dreaming. Try to direct your dream or to ask the questions you may have.
5. Upon awakening, even if it is the middle of the night, write down briefly what glimpse you have of the dream. The very act of writing allows more of the dream state to return to you. Just begin to write and the rest will follow.

Stay with doing this practice for a number of weeks and your abilities within the dream state will increase.

The State of Dying

To approach the inevitable process of dying, it is helpful to be prepared for this as a time of potential liberation, of freedom from the on-going wheel of life and reincarnation.

In assisting others as they make this inevitable transition, my experience shows me to help them ease their minds and hearts. People want to express what is on their mind, unresolved relationships, personal shortcomings, giving final "I love you" messages to family or friends, or fear of letting go and losing control. People want to feel heard, truly and deeply listened to. This will help them to relax. People usually have some personal connection with their spiritual nature, some favored guide who comforts them. By chanting the name of this spiritual guide, saint, or even God, you help the dying person in this transition. You can further encourage them to go into the light, to let go and depart on their journey, go in peace, and go with love.

Holding their hand, chanting, being kind will further the peacefulness to come.

Yet, going deeper than these words is to realize that death is **the optimal** moment for your potential liberation. You need to be aware that this is the moment and to be as fully present in the light as you can.

The clearest explanation of death and dying is to be found in *The Tibetan Book of Living and Dying*, by Sogyal Rinpoche. Here, Sogyal Rinpoche gives these simple instructions to help others and to help your self during the precious moments of dying.

❖ Be comfortable and, if possible, sit in a meditative position or you can lay down. Relax.

❖ Place the vast sky in front of you and into this sky place whatever spiritual guide or Divine being you feel close to. Or just imagine a being of pure golden light. Know these are the beings of compassion, wisdom, and truth.

❖ Pray to this light or this being with all your heart.
"May all my negative karma, destructive emotions, obscurations, and blockages be purified and removed,
May I know myself forgiven for all the harm I may have thought and done,
May I accomplish this profound practice of phowa, and die a good and peaceful death,
And through the triumph of my death, may I be able to benefit all other beings, living or dead."

❖ Now the presence of the light sends love, compassion in streams of light to you, cleansing you and purifying you, removing your suffering.

❖ You become immersed in light.

❖ Now your body dissolves completely into this light and soars up into the sky becoming one with this light. *(The Tibetan Book of Living and Dying,* Sogyal Rinpoche, HarperSan Francisco, pg.215)

This simple practice is so profound. The preparation that the Buddhist Phowa practice offers is essential to do as one is approaching the final breath of life. The moment of death itself is one of the most opportune times to realize total liberation.

The State of Death

If there is no awareness or memory when you take a nap, imagine how difficult it will be to cultivate awareness at the moment of your death. Winds blow, lights flash, sounds pierce, and there is no foundation of familiarity such as a physical body. Yet, in this moment of death is the potential of total liberation, IF, and only if, you can recognize and have awareness about what is happening. And know how to navigate in these precious nanoseconds.

Death is a moment of truth in two directions: reflection upon our lives and removal of that which has obscured our Enlightened Mind. Death offers the "dawning of the Ground Luminosity, or 'Clear Light,' where consciousness itself dissolves into the all-encompassing space of truth." (Ibid, pg. 259) The Tibetan Book of the Dead continues to state, "The nature of everything is open, empty and naked like the sky. Luminous emptiness, without center or circumference: the pure, naked Rigpa dawns." (Ibid, pg. 259) Why is it called luminosity? "The masters say…it expresses the radiant clarity of the nature of mind, its total freedom from darkness or obscuration."

This moment of death that reveals to us the Clear Light Luminosity is also known as the Mother Luminosity. This initial luminosity leads into another experience called the Child Luminosity, the nature of our mind. It is here that one of the highest Tibetan Buddhist practices, Dzogchen, comes to fruition. When studying under a realized master, you have the potential to stabilize your mind within the death state. It takes a high-level meditation practitioner to cultivate the fruits of this practice.

In my own life, I have met three great masters who maintained either their seated meditation posture for three days following their physical death or some other demonstration of the power of their practice post death. Their ability to stabilize their minds continued even though they were technically dead. They were the 16th Karmapa, the 17th Karmapa, and Sister Palmo. These three have a significant relationship with one another and hence with this practice.

In the summer of 1976, Sister Palmo comes to my land in Mount Shasta for what is to be her final retreat prior to her death. During this retreat, she kindly gives many teachings to those to come to the wilderness of our land to see her. During her life, she was a Professor of English at Cambridge and then renounced her career to become the translator for the 16th Karmapa. When she died the next year, she maintained her seated posture of meditation for several days.

Gyalwang, the 16th Karmapa, comes to San Francisco in 1976 to perform the ancient Tibetan Black Hat Ceremony. His vow to all present is that upon the moment of our death, we are to remember his placing of this 14th century hat made of angel hair and he will come to help us go through the Bardo. Upon the death of the 16th Karmapa in 1981 in the United States, his American doctor reported that the area around Karmapa's heart was still warm 36 hours after he died.

During the days of the Black Hat Ceremony, our family has the occasion to spend time with Karmapa and his monks. Karmapa calls my son, Adam to his side, identifying him as a reincarnated Tulku. Karmapa gives him a special gift of a wooden dorje (symbolizing wisdom) with five rings around it. He wishes Adam to return to their monastery in India for training.

(left) His Holiness the 16th Karmapa in San Francisco, 1976, performing the Black Hat Ceremony. (right) His Holiness the 17th Karmapa at age nine in Tibet, staring at Adam.

At the time, Adam is six years old. It is his decision to remain in the West. Yet when Adam is a young man of 22, we visit Tibet together to pay our respects to the 17th Karmapa, the living reincarnation of the 16th Karmapa. We are most curious as to whether or not this nine-year-old boy will show any recognition or memory of the wooden dorje that he gave my son years earlier.

Because this young Karmapa is carefully guarded by the Chinese, we are unable to have a private interview. We join a line of other tourists who one at a time bow in front of the 17th Karmapa receiving his blessing. As the moment comes for Adam to be directly in front of him, Karmapa scrutinizes Adam, somewhat puzzled and highly focused. Adam holds up the dorje. Karmapa blesses him, and the dorje. The guards push us to continue walking. Karmapa's gaze continues to follow Adam as he slowly moves away...all the way to the other side of the receiving hall.

So many questions arise. How much awareness has this young Karmapa retained from his prior incarnation? It is an amazing time to be able to personally witness and participate in the tradition of the transfer of consciousness from one generation to another.

The 17th Karmapa with His Holiness the Dalai Lama in Dharmasala.

Adam and I travel out of Tibet during the August monsoon season. It is one of the most harrowing journeys I have ever made. It gives me a small taste of the courage and fortitude of the young 17th Karmapa as he fled his Chinese captors five years later and escapes to Dharmasala.

The third great and highly respected master was His Eminence Kalu Rinpoche, sent to the West in 1971 by the 16th Karmapa. During the next years, Kalu gave Refuge Vows and Buddhist names to thousands in both the United States and Europe. He gave me my Tibetan name, "Karma Llamo

Yangtso" (Goddess of the Ocean of Plenty, hence the photo on the cover of this book.)

Kalu Rinpoche in Northern California in 1976.
Adam as a young boy is directly behind him.

Kalu is purported to have also mastered the state of dying while maintaining his seated posture post physical death, as was witnessed by a doctor and nurse at his monastery in the Himalayas.

These are remarkable testimonials to the power of the mind to attain and then to rest in the luminosity experience of death.

These teachings continue into the duration of the Bardo experience that may go on for up to 48 days before our rebirth.

The State of Rebirth or Coming In

Listen carefully to the "fantasies" and stories that small children tell you. My grandson Ethan, when he had just started to speak, would tell us about how Tom came to get him in his airplane. Whenever Ethan became scared, he would say Tom will come now and get me. I often wonder what their relationship was before Ethan was born, because Tom was a pilot in Laos and did rescue military personnel.

When I am about two years old, I feel myself soaring through the towers of the Golden Gate Bridge and heading down into the bay in a rush of white and golden light. I head down into one sailboat in particular. My mother, years later, tells me she got stuck in the hatch of their sailboat while out on the bay because she was so pregnant and close to delivery.

In writing this book, I found a similar experience in these lines written by Sogyal Rinpoche, "In between the bardo of dying and the bardo of becoming is a very special state of luminosity or Clear Light called, as I have said, 'the bardo of dharmata.' This is an experience that occurs to everyone, but there are very few who can even notice it, let alone experience it completely, as it can only be recognized by a trained practitioner. This bardo of dharmata corresponds to the period after falling asleep and before dreams begin." [Ibid, p. 108.]

Master Sha's teachings echo as aspect of this stage before rebirth. As he puts it, "You should know what is your spiritual purpose. The purpose for every being is to uplift your spiritual standing! You have a Shi Fu (personal saint). Most important is that your Shi Fu is committed to reincarnate with you! This is a very important point. Your Shi Fu will meld with you when you are reborn."

"Keeping" Our Wisdom

In conclusion, to progress on the path to Enlightenment, we aspire to keep whatever wisdom we gain as we move through our life, our death, our birth, our dreams, our past lives, and our expanded states of awareness. If we cannot somehow retain the wisdom of these experiences, we will forever be in ignorance, constantly beginning again and again.

How do we "keep" our wisdoms? We "keep" nothing. We only open, cultivating a discriminating awareness that glides through these experiences without the contamination of ego and attachment. This quality of awareness will tell us when something is familiar when you can almost, but not quite, place it.

That is why you must trust yourselves. Do everything you can to align with your own truth. Learn how to listen to yourself, to your soul, and hear the wisdoms you already know. Study with an Enlightened teacher who can help you quickly grow.

Part III

Spiritual Training

Chapter 11

Blessings and Transmissions

Introducing the Divine through Blessings and Transmissions

A Divine Blessing is a washing with golden light that simultaneously cleanses, purifies, and transforms the recipient. A Divine Blessing is a gift from the Heavens directly into your soul to protect you, support you, uplift you, ease your burdens, and strengthen your connection with the Source of all Creation. A Divine Transmission is the passing on of an ability or a wisdom that empowers the student or disciple. Power is given. Power is passed on to the student through a spiritual teacher, through a direct connect with a saint or buddha, or by God directly. Blessings and transmissions are both generous gifts. Blessings and transmissions are one of the means through which there is a transformation from darkness to light. *[See Chapter 6, "Transforming Darkness into Light."]* The higher is the consciousness or divinity of the giver, the greater is the impact on the receiver, providing the latter is in a state of clarity and balance. Yet, keep in mind there is no higher or lower—as you really go "higher," it all dissolves.

Blessings and transmissions are a means of introducing the Divine into the temple of our humanity.

The living essence of an Enlightened Master's consciousness can also be passed to students through both blessings and transmissions, as well as in invisible ways. This contact has an inseminating quality. It is rather like a flower's pollen carrying potential reproduction. It is contagious. Years may pass before the recipient fully manifests the impact of these blessings and transmissions.

Conversely, in many exoteric, institutionalized church settings, the living essence may not be present or realized within the priest or minister. They may be compassionate and highly schooled, having wonderful emotional attributes and ethics. However, the actual Enlightenment realization may not be present in the giver and therefore the living transmission, that is contagious, fertile, and inseminating in nature is lacking.

Transmissions are empowerments such as the ability to heal, to do Divine flow, or to manifest. For both blessings and transmissions, the giver must have realized a higher state of consciousness than the receiver for there to be an impact. As is the case with blessings, transmissions can be given spontaneously and directly by the Divine to an Enlightened being. This is how termas are given.

Termas are the teachings that have been hidden for safekeeping in the rivers, caves, mountains, and even the minds that emerge out of the Emptiness. This means that, when you enter the emptiness, teachings that have been hidden for hundreds of years may be revealed to you as a transmission, knowledge, and empowerment.

First, we will talk about blessings in some depth. What are they? What is their purpose? What is the role of purification in blessings? What are the various vessels through which blessings come?

What are Divine Blessings?

Blessing is in the *giving* and the *receiving* of Divine Grace. Blessings come from the Heavens. Divine Blessings are a living connection between our self and the Divine. The reason I say blessing is also in the giving is because as the giver you:

❖   Cultivate your own soul and gain more merit or virtue
❖   The state you experience is golden and beautiful

To fully receive a blessing, and for maximum effect, the recipient needs to be:

❖   Open
❖   Clear in their mind
❖   Relaxed
❖   Peaceful
❖   Pure of heart

It is also necessary for maximum effect to not be in a period of spiritual testing. In this sense, blessings are a Divine Communication, a two-way street.

Thus, there are two distinct qualifications about the effectiveness of blessings. The first has to do with the spiritual power and level of realization of the giver, and the second has to do with the qualities of the recipient. Greater power equals greater effect. Greater openness and readiness equals greater effect.

Is your soul receiving the blessings that are continually present? Are you aware of them?

How to Receive a Divine Blessing from Nature [1]

Each day at dawn, there is such beauty in the skies. If you but pause to look, to receive, to feel awe as the heavens flood the sky with raspberry, turquoise, and golden light, announcing the arrival of the magnificent sun that nurtures us and helps us grow. Each morning, we are blessed by nature.

At dawn, Divine Blessings are omnipresent. It is you who may be absent. Literally, you are spiritually asleep. Emotionally, you may be asleep. The effect of receiving Divine Blessings varies upon the openness of the recipient. This receiving follows a process. First, you need to deeply open, to look, to breathe, to take time and be present, living in the Now, and then you will indeed recognize this precious blessing. Deeply drink in the beauty and a sense of awe about Creation will follow. You will feel profound gratitude. You will simultaneously experience your significance within this Creation and your minuteness within this Oneness.

As the receiver of Divine Blessings, the door opens inside us, allowing our soul to partake of Divine Nourishment. Our soul grows and sings for joy. We may even cry with tears of relief at the profundity of feeling connected, once again, with the Divine.

Purpose of Divine Blessings

There are a number of purposes that Divine Blessings can fulfill:

❖ **Cosmic Hug.** In this cosmic hug, the light and the boundless love of the Heavens wrap around you, holding you tenderly as a precious infant. It is a gossamer blanket surrounding you, enveloping you as your mother held you when you were born. This tender hug reassures you on the deepest level of your connection. The love and light continue to pour into you, your heart, and the very marrow of your bones. The sense of being held safely and securely is present. Blessing is loving. Light is healing.

❖ **Soul Food.** An invisible process is taking place as each blessing is received. You are nourished deep inside and feel peaceful and content. You become more aware of the qualities developing within you that directly reflect the Divine. This is soul food. A blessing brings peace.

❖ **Compassion.** There is a cumulative effect when receiving blessings. In receiving the cosmic hug and feeling more loved yourself, you are now able to give more love to others. With this love, you will transform into a more loving being, reflecting the love that is poured into you. Your heart is opening and compassion is growing. You become more kind and gentle with others

❖ **Your "cup runneth over."** This Biblical phrase eloquently describes the quality of fullness that accompanies cumulative blessings. Fullness brings gratitude.

❖ **Transformation.** If you think of Divine blessings as small droplets of golden light, you gradually collect a cupful, transforming your body, mind, and soul. This is the golden washing of liquid light, the yin aspect of God's Light.

❖ **Removing Obstacles.** There is often a cloudy, muddy quality within our minds and emotions. It is part of our karmic pattern and perspective on life. Spiritual testing is karma cleansing. Blessings assist us in removing these obstacles and our karma in this life. Thus, as obstacles are removed, our commitment to service is strengthened.

❖ **Return to Grace.** Part of our human condition is that we have fallen asleep to our true nature. We struggle through our childhoods. As a result, we grow further and further away from our original of purity. So as the blessings pour upon us, we are washed by a golden rain in preparation for the return into grace.

Blessings are crucial to this inner journey. They uplift us, transform us, and enable us to be kinder to others in our lives. Blessings open our spiritual channels, heal us physically, emotionally, and mentally. Blessings feed our soul.

Purification Leads to Cultivation

There is a progression on this inner journey of the soul through the many stages or levels of Enlightenment. Purification on all levels of our being, physical, mental, emotional, and karmic is one of the first requirements. Without going through this purification, we cannot begin our cultivation for compassion, peace, joy, and harmony. This is why blessings are so helpful, speeding our journey, and cleansing of our inner vessel. In order to become increasingly pure light beings, we must be committed to unconditional Universal Service. Then we begin to gain spiritual capabilities and spiritual standing.

What is it that needs purification? Our physical body needs healing anywhere there is darkness or illness. Our minds need to produce a quality of thinking that reflects our highest nature. Our emotions need to be positive, uplifting, and filled with inspiration. In purifying these key aspects of our humanity, our lives will transform. We will know joy, purpose, and have a sense of wellbeing. This is where and how darkness is transformed into light.

Let us deepen our understanding. We wish to be a clear vessel radiating infinite light. Picture yourself as a glass vase gracefully curving outward at the top. This vase is clear and laced with reflective golden and white light crystals. This is your soul, open and pure. It radiates out to the entire universe and receives back from all souls, never-ending rays of rainbow light.

Physical Purification. Often, illness is the initial reason that people seek healing and the blessings that accompany healing. When people become ill, they are motivated to seek cures and answers. Western Medicine becomes an adjunct as more and more people seek alternative forms of healing. People are coming to recognize the obvious: the body and mind must heal together. Recently, many people seek healing on the level of their soul. For any of these to heal, purification must take place first.

Those of us involved in healing have come to understand that true healing happens on the deepest level of the human psyche: the soul.

On the gross level of the physical body, the process of purification cleans the cells and the spaces between the cells. Many energy healers and medical intuitives can see the darkness that accompanies physical illness. Many lay people can feel the heat outside a person's body where there is infection or inflammation. Many others can feel the thickness in the energy field about two or three inches outside the body of the ill person. These are all examples of what we mean by darkness that accompanies physical illness.

In the subtle energy body that surrounds the physical form, there is also a need for cleansing. This energy body reflects what is occurring in the physical body. Tibetan medicine deals with healing and purification within this energy body. Eventually, as this energy body becomes more pure and more healthy, it will reflect more golden to white light within the aura.

Mind Purification. This subject fills hundreds of books and thousands of hours of meditation practice. Western Psychology, in particular Transpersonal Psychology, has come to acknowledge this subject as essential to true healing, harmony, and quality of life.

Mind purification occurs in two ways: reducing negative thinking and increasing the space between thoughts. Purification occurs within the content of a single thought or sequence of thoughts. Purification occurs in the absence of any thought or in the space between a thought finishing and a new thought beginning. The latter is a key portal to enter Emptiness— essential to cultivating Enlightenment.

The process of purifying our thinking includes moving beyond our habitual, never-ending tapes; letting go of our blame, shame, judgments; and finally, being able to forgive.

Emotional Purification. To purify on the emotional level means cultivating positive emotions, balanced emotions, and forgiveness of oneself and others.

How To Cultivate Positive Emotions [2]

In daily life, whenever there is an arising of fear, irritability, doubt, jealousy, or any emotional negativity, try to catch it immediately before it gains momentum and power. Do not spend time trying to justify the emotion or to tell your story about why it is necessary. Simply begin to chant. Personally, I encourage clients to chant, "God's Light." It could be any chant. Within two minutes, the emotion will quiet and you will be in a more balanced state.

Balanced emotions do not have extreme highs or lows. Balance implies a quality of equanimity, of acceptance, of perceiving God's will rather than our will. Seeing God's will helps us to be connected with the Divine. This is a blessing in itself!

We need to forgive ourselves and others. This is in our best interests. It has a greater impact than hanging on to vindictiveness and vengeance. Why? Because it furthers the journey of our soul to learn whatever lesson is before us. If we don't get it this time round, we will have to repeat it endlessly in future lifetimes. This understanding seems to motivate even the most vindictive ego to forgive.

How to Cultivate Forgiveness [3]

First, recognize you have an attachment to a position of judgment, incrimination, and blame. You are playing good guy/bad guy, and the other person is the bad guy. These are not qualities that will further your soul journey. Having recognized this trap, look more introspectively at yourself. The other person's behavior is not your business. Look to the origin of your knee-jerk response. Where is the lesson for *you?* This will touch upon the karma in the situation or between you. *[See Chapter 12, "Karma: Causality not Punishment."]* Specifically, if someone has wronged you, perhaps you wronged them in a prior life. Identifying the lesson precedes letting go. To let go and forgive, enter into the state of prayer. Next, bring in the soul of this person and have a soul-to-soul communication with them. Tell their soul clearly that you forgive them and yourself. Wish only the best for this soul. Thank them for coming and close the prayer.

As we forgive ourselves for our own shortcomings and ignorance, we are being more loving to ourselves. Once we increase our ability to love ourselves, we have greater capacity to love others, way beyond what we can do now.

Purification of Karma. This aspect of purification will be covered in the next chapter. It bears a direct impact on how deeply we can receive both blessings and transmissions.

In studying under an Enlightened Master, the blessings will be the passage of light and love from the heart of your teacher directly into your body. In passing in front of an Enlightened Master in a large crowd of people, you receive the blessings from their heart through their hand and into your crown chakra or the fontanel location in the center of your skull.

Vessels of Divine Blessings

Blessings are given through many vessels. Blessings are given through chanting, prayer, a touch on the crown chakra, a glance of the eye, and intention. They may be given through a teacher, a hymn, a saint, a wafer, or a book. Blessings are also given through an experience that may be invisible and spontaneous. Blessings may come to you directly from Heaven.

I would like to tell you two stories about Divine Blessings. The first occurred in the early seventies, and the second occurred in 2001. In between were 30 years of incubating the Divine Presence until it could come to fruition, to the experience of Luminous, and to this book.

Inner Experience of Receiving Divine Blessings

People have varied responses to receiving Divine Blessings. For some, nothing happens; for others, they get sick; and for others, their life changes. One of the initial responses is kinesthetic, a sense of heat, pins and needles, internal movement, dizziness, elation, or exhaustion. A second response may be one of inner vision, a "seeing" of images or symbols. These images are spontaneous and often new to the person experiencing them. A third response is hearing messages or sounds. These are progressive stages of receptivity. Often, people feel profoundly moved in a manner they cannot describe. People cry and they do not know why. They just know that something profound has happened.

What happens to me over 30 years ago changes my life. It also changes the lives of many of those who are present this particular afternoon.

Baraka

I am sitting cross-legged on the grass in the backyard of Dr. Claudio Naranjo's home in Berkeley. I am here because of my dream several nights before telling me to visit Claudio, a man I have never met. I call him the next morning to discover he is beginning a group that will study esoteric Sufi teachings. He invites me to join on this particular afternoon.

30 people are sitting on the ground in a circle. The gentle sounds of a Mozart concerto waft over us. Claudio places himself in the center of the circle. We are all silent, momentarily suspended in time, and transfixed by his gaze. Claudio's deep brown eyes fix themselves upon each of us. He pauses for a minute or two, gazing into the eyes of the person in front of him and then moves on.

As he faces me, I initially see his pupils, warm and expressive that change to piercing like lasers. He holds my gaze, unmoving. Our eyes are locked together for this precious, timeless exchange. For the very first time in my conscious memory, I feel energy moving inside, tingles, heat, an impregnation of each cell with a droplet of blessing. He moves to the next person and my eyes gaze up into the trees above me. Falling from the blue sky are droplets of golden mist that sprinkle down upon us.

What has transpired is an ancient Sufi ritual of Transpasso, or the passing of Divine Blessing by the Enlightened teacher to the student. The actual blessing carries within it the seed for future Enlightenment. This seed is known as Baraka (in Arabic, baraka means blessing) because it carries a special energy of Divine Grace. The golden mist was an aspect of the baraka. At the time of this holy ritual, I do not have the words or a concept of this remarkable event other than to know inside something most special has just happened. Those of us present were impregnated with this spiritual energy, the baraka, that in time comes to fruition. In the years to come, several people in this group realize Enlightenment and go on to be teachers in their own right.

Claudio's blessing is also a transmission, in that he passes something to us that empowers us. What he passes is a living pollination for which he pays dearly. For when he gives this to us, he later becomes depleted and falls from the state of Divine Grace. Apparently, this energy is limited.

I will always honor this gift. Without this blessing and living transmission that plants the seed for my Enlightenment, I may not have been ready for my work with Master Sha. I will always honor both my teachers and the connection between these events that were 30 years apart in human time.

Between these events, I spend years in the desert of the inner journey—a period of dryness and slow spiritual growth. I continue my studies. I have peak experiences. But it is not until I meet Master Sha that my full Awakening continues.

Eighty-Seven Buddhas

The following story is about a blessing so powerful that it changes the course of my life, literally taking me in a new direction. I have only known Master Sha three months when I receive this blessing. By the end of the evening, both Tom and I are accompanying Master Sha out of the event and he is discussing with us our new jobs with him! I am to teach, and Tom is to build the database.

It is July 2001, and we are in a downtown hotel in San Francisco where Master Sha is giving a presentation. 20 rows of chairs are squeezed into a most sterile room. I sit down in one of many cold metal chairs that fill this tight and unattractive room. The ceiling is low. The windows are closed, locked, and covered with aluminum blinds.

There is such an incongruity between the sterile conference room and this Chinese gentleman chanting mantra in a pinstriped suit. It is not only a culture clash, it is a time warp moving between ancient China and modern US society.

He begins a long mantra, a blessing to the Eighty-Seven Buddhas. This sense of incongruity continues to build as Master Sha's chanting takes me beyond these external physical surroundings.

He is invoking the Eighty-Seven Buddhas to come to us now. I enter the mesmerizing sound, forgetting about myself. Suddenly, I am uplifted in a whoosh of energy. A line of eighty-seven golden, glistening Buddhas are sitting attentively in front of me! I have never seen so many Buddhas! They may be there all the time, but I am the one who is blind until my third eye opens momentarily.

Master Sha asks the people in the room to share what they experience. I raise my hand and he calls upon me. I have brought two therapists with me and momentarily pause, "What if they think I'm crazy?" However, the beauty and impact of what I actually see so moves me, my mouth opens, and words tumble out.

I share out loud, with tears in my eyes and my voice trembling. The profound impact of this blessing, set in this incongruous location in a downtown hotel room, returns me to the path that works for me. I enter the role of disciple to Master Sha.

Entering the Unknown

Entering the unknown has many levels of meaning on the spiritual path. In our cognitive world, and in our world of prior experience, there is much we know. We try to cling to this knowledge and to these experiences as we enter any new terrain. We always think in the box of our prior knowing.

The next level that is deeper inside us has to do with our belief system. Often, we are not conscious of the different principles that guide us in our daily lives—our choices about where and how to live, who to be friends with and why, what to set as a goal and why. These choices are based upon what we believe about the world and life. Again, this level of belief is based upon prior experience and knowledge. This, too, is in the box of our prior knowing.

The next level of entering the Unknown has to do with letting go. Letting go of concepts, beliefs, prior worldly experience, and being willing to go into new terrain.

Perhaps the deepest level of entering the Unknown comes through the meditative experience of going into the Emptiness where there is no I, no anything, just a vast empty without distinctions.

These then are various levels of the Unknown. I submit to you, dear reader, that these levels are progressive as we ascend or descend into our selves, and therefore into the Universe.

I am learning the Unknown is a teacher. Getting out of the teacup of our prior knowing is essential to truly expanding our consciousness and cultivating our relationship with the Divine.

Part of what is so fascinating about this inner spiritual journey is that things happen we have never heard of before! It is such new terrain! And it is always changing! I am **entering the Unknown.** This is an inner place that offers deep wisdom. It takes me several years to even be able to share with you this concept of the Unknown as a place or space of deep teaching. I step into the emptiness, go beyond my self, enter a place of no concepts. The Unknown opens to me.

After 30 years of leading groups in the West, some of which were in their own right quite outrageous, I become part of a totally new and different group dynamic. What I am about to describe takes place over the next three years in a continual unfolding. I am witnessing an inner epic. This three-year epic integrates seeing with inner vision, opening my heart, and receiving blessings. Master Sha brings all of these abilities or phenomena together into a single experience that is a group blessing.

It is summer of 2001 in San Francisco. We meet in the Presidio twice a week. This carefully preserved yet barren ex-military barrack fills with donated flowers and fruit, becoming a candlelit sanctuary for the purpose of healing souls. In these early Power Healing sessions, people come with many conditions of illness. They bring their children and their pets. They drag in spouses. They introduce friends. Master Sha brings blessings. Although externally, each class repeats the same dynamic, I see an internal scene evolving, shifting each time like a movie playing.

He asks those in the front to place their palm upon the center of his chest, his heart chakra. The lines fan out around him. As the lines of the fan spread out, sometimes there are more than 20 people each placing their palm upon the back of the person in front them. People push in next to each other, bodies sweat, and the room heats up.

"Close your eyes and receive the blessings of the Universe. 'Dear Every Soul of the Universe, could you chant with me?' Now chant, 'God's Light.'" For a half hour at a time, all hands connect into his chest.

Because I am videotaping these sessions, I often stand in the back, watching the expressions, the tears, the joy, the release, and the sound of humanity touching so many hearts.

This group dynamic, this blessing becomes a cross-cultural ritual, embracing ancient Chinese hidden secrets with African rhythms, Chinese chanting, and timid Caucasians, all sweating and crying and touching one another. People of all ages, all classes, and all backgrounds gather around him to freely open their souls to his blessings. It is wild!

Spiritual United Nations Convening in His Heart

My inner eye sees another sequence. I am finding that, while I have my physical eyes open to do the videotaping, I can simultaneously see with my third eye. I look into Master Sha's chest where all palms are touching. Let me remind you, just one more time, that what I am about to report I have never heard of before. This is what I see.

The scene inside his heart opens into a round hall filled with tiered benches in a circle like an amphitheater. Guests, Enlightened Masters, and saints are filing in through an aisle on my right. They come in groups, circumspectly staying close together. They are dressed in robes of different fabrics and colors, clearly indicating their spiritual tradition. There is a sense of curiosity mixed with a proper respect that one would bring to a spiritual United Nations meeting.

On my right, and twelve feet above the aisle, is a raised platform with a gilded chair. Master Sha is seated in this chair, presiding over the many traditions that are arriving for this meeting. I am viewing this from above the entry aisle and behind the tiers of benches.

People cluster within their own tradition, energetically containing themselves in a cautious manner. There is subtle distrust for this new convening. The spiritual groups are not open to each other at this point. They are poised to claim their own way as the only way. Here, a new soul presides and dares to proclaim this spiritual United Nations meeting. The groups fill the benches, waiting for whatever is to transpire.

I hear no words. I only see this movie. I do not know that inner vision has stages of cultivation. Because of this, I have no understanding of the phenomenon that is occurring inside me. The movie continues in a similar fashion for many weeks. One day, the movie changes. For my conscious mind, all of what I am describing is without precedent. I also have no concept that what I see will change.

During these practices, Master Sha calls on me in his booming voice, "Aubrey! What do you see? Tell people!" Obeying his prompting, I blurt out my inner experience. I have to jump over my doubt, my fear of looking like a fool, my inner voices suggesting this is group hypnosis, and my uncertainty. In short, I had to jump into the abyss of the unknown.

Master Sha asking me to tell people what pictures I see in his heart chakra.

One day during a team meeting, I am physically standing by Master Sha's right shoulder with my hand on his back, just opposite his heart chakra. Others are placing their hands on his chest. For some reason, I feel it is important today to directly touch his shirt and physical body. On the left side of his body is a woman, also a member of this team, guiding Master Sha's organization. She spontaneously is in the same position that I am. This becomes important, because we proceed to have identical third eye viewing.

We instantly become gatekeepers to the backside of his heart chakra. Usually, there is a golden funnel opening from the front of his chest to the back. However, this time it is the backside that suddenly is flooded with souls flying in from all over the universe.

Somehow, Master Sha has gained the confidence of these high-level Enlightened Beings and they come in droves, excited to attend the spiritual UN meeting. Whatever doubts or questions were present before are now replaced with a camaraderie and sense of mutually shared mission. There is work to be done in the spiritual realm, and all traditions must now be unified.

Within a few months, this movie again shifts during a class. By now, I am myself seated toward the front of the tiers, down close to the ground level. I turn to see the room is filled. Souls are standing in the back, pushing to get closer. They are eager to hear the teaching coming from Master Sha. They accept his position as spiritual leader within the Soul World. The groups no longer are sitting within their own tradition. Instead, these Enlightened Souls and Masters are mingling and laughing joyously.

"Finally, there is one who can bring all of us together," are the words I am hearing.

Another few months go by and my image again shifts. This large hall within Master Sha's heart, the convening amphitheater itself, now dissolves into vast, deep blue, infinite space without any form. The Universe now pours into his heart so there is a simultaneous outward and inward direction of movement. It has a pouring quality, like the winds in the sky moving outward on the edges and inward in the center. I now see the Universe within his heart. Only there is no physical form to contain this Universe.

We enter the infinite Soul World. Through this blessing of the heart chakra, he has somehow hooked each of us up so that our spiritual channel is open and connected to the Source of the Universe.

Now we are ready to receive the cherished holy transmissions.

Ancient Ritual of Transmission

In the physical world, we are familiar with "the passing of the mantle" such as a presidential inauguration or the appointing of a judge. We are familiar with the marriage ceremony that joins two people in the holy state of matrimony. These recognized ceremonies are highly ritualized. Once they occur, the person is quite changed and is seen by others quite differently.

A similar ceremony occurs within many spiritual traditions. In this setting, there is both a physical world shift and a soul world shift. Because the latter is invisible to many of us, we question the phenomenon's authenticity.

In the West over the past 40 years, there has been an increasing interest and participation in Eastern traditions. More than 100,000 people have received Eastern empowerments or transmissions. The last appearance of the Dalai Lama in Vancouver (2004) drew 30,000 people for the Kalachakra initiation. A lesser number remained for the full five-day retreat.

Often, empowerments are offered in two tiers. The first is a short version given to any member of the public who shows up that day. It is a transmission of sorts, a blessing to enter and begin a practice. Often, these practices consist of repeating a mantra 108,000 times with the proper visualization.

The second tier is for more dedicated students and requires diligent practice and a deeper commitment. Some of us have also observed a third tier, in which the full transmission of a lineage or saint or power is given in an instant. This is highly cherished and reserved only for a very few of the highest disciples within that tradition.

"Power is given," is a frequent statement made by Master Sha as he speaks of empowerments or transmissions. Which student is chosen to receive higher transmissions is a secret process having to do with how the teacher views the readiness of their student. In a sense, they read the soul of their student, their progress or cultivation over the time spent together.

The process that Master Sha uses is based upon tossing the I Ching coins. It is an old Chinese tradition that, to Westerners, seems rather arbitrary and certainly non-linear. These choices can cause internal uproar and the pain of rejection or judgment. It may seem unfair. If his guidance tells him no, the student will not receive that transmission and will have to wait.

The process starts with the student asking for a transmission that Master Sha is now making available. I have found that if you are attached to receiving this transmission, you quite likely will not receive approval. Attachment implies your ego wants something. Like a knife through butter, the answer may be "No!" If this triggers pain or rejection, then the smart student seizes the opportunity to lessen the grip of their ego, purify, and let go.

Within this process of rejection, approval, pain, or elation, one begins to see the ego at play. Many masters use this teaching tool. *[See Chapter 14, "Spiritual Testing."]* If you are accepted for a transmission and you feel pride, competition, or any form of one-upmanship, your ego will actually rob your soul of the full impact of the transmission. When we are clouded emotionally, whether the emotion be negative or positive, we will receive only a portion of the transmission. The full power simply does not come through.

Given that the ultimate purpose of transmissions is to empower you spiritually, it is so very important to receive them in a state of equanimity. Again and again, we must transform ourselves from darkness into light.

We need to change perspective here for a moment. What I have just described to you may make sense in the linear, material world. However, in the non-linear dimension of no time or space and absolute Oneness, our soul is going through an invisible evolution. Each of us needs to trust more deeply that this evolution is occurring in absolute perfection. We need to relax and trust. We need to hear and follow our own wisdom. Let me tell you a story that illustrates this evolution.

My precious daughter Brett is with me in the early seventies as the monks and spiritual lineage holders of Tibetan Buddhism are beginning to pass empowerments to the public. We attended many of these. One is for the Blue Medicine Buddha, who has great healing powers. My daughter receives this empowerment. She believes in what she receives. So, when her little puppy becomes quite ill, she diligently chants and chants. The puppy recovers. Today, some 30 years later, my daughter is still practicing diligently as a devoted Vajrayana Buddhist. I have the utmost respect for her devotion.

I share this with you because it makes such perfect sense from the perspective of the soul. She knew as a child her direction in life that was yet to unfold in the dimension of time. Years later, she became a chiropractor, devoted to healing, service, and to her Dharma teachings. This kind of wisdom is within each of us. We need but allow ourselves to hear and to follow our hearts. We need to know we each have a mission to fulfill this time in our lives. The Sufis call it, "Follow your nose."

Different Kinds of Transmissions

Master Sha gives different kinds of transmissions. He continues to add new categories as he receives his inspirations and guidance from the Divine. Spiritual Masters continue to grow just as we do. They enter the Emptiness and receive new teachings. This is part of the phenomena I refer to as Entering the Unknown. However, if you are studying under a more traditional lineage, the kinds of empowerments that are given may be more predictable.

At this time, Master Sha gives these transmissions:

❖ **Transmission of Soul Software for Healing.** These transmissions are open to the general public. The soul software is a permanent gift or transmission for the healing of an organ, physical system, or condition. These are practices designed for healing, rejuvenation, boosting stamina, and increasing immunity.

❖ **Transmission of Soul Software for Blessings.** This group addresses quality of life issues, such as world peace and financial success.

❖ **Transmission of Healing Abilities.** This is to help the lay or professional practitioner have the spiritual power to be a more effective healer. There are nine levels, and each gives a different, increasingly more powerful ability.

❖ **Transmission of Soul Capabilities.** These transmissions reflect the level of the soul's cultivation and readiness to receive higher capabilities. They help the recipient become a better Universal Servant. Examples are the capability to open the heart of another person for their soul journey, the capability to write an entire book in a month (part of the process of flow), and the capability to give soul software for healing specific conditions.

❖ **Transmission of Kai Quan.** This is a Divine Blessing that places light directly into an object so that it can be used as a healing and blessing tool. An example would be a book, CD, or prayer beads. (Prayer beads are used in many cultures: the Greeks call them kumbaloi, the Catholics call them rosary beads, and the Buddhists call them malas. They are used to say mantras or prayers as a means of keeping track of the number of repetitions.)

Inner Experience of Receiving Transmissions

There is a selection process that everyone must go through to receive a transmission from Master Sha. In the beginning, I receive a "no." Quite simply, when I WANT a transmission, when I feel it is somehow my due because I heal others, or because I am committed, then I am turned down. I am *publicly* turned down. It is not pretty. It is not something we accept in the West where we are more private. But in this work, it is public and humiliating. Yet, I must ask myself, "Just who is it inside me is hurt and humiliated?"

The answer is obvious. It can only be my ego. My ego is something I wish to lessen and perhaps even wash away. Recall all my years of therapy, of working with the Enneagram, and of deep Reichian work. I have to talk to myself in this way.

This inner talk is not new to me. What is new is to so directly observe HOW to change the situation. I learn quickly how to let go and let God. I learn to truly accept God's will and, with this humility and equanimity, things begin to change. In accepting I go deeper to contemplate two issues: what is readiness, and what needs to occur in me to be ready?

The second issue leads me to go deeper in my trust in God's plan for me to unfold. **This last thought, more than any other in my journey, is the bottom line that guides me. I do not know and yet, I trust.**

Before I recount for you the inner experience of receiving a transmission, I wish to share with you when I do not receive my initial approval. I am turned down to receive the first level transmission of Power Healing. This hurts. I do not understand this is a test. Either I am not ready, or my mind is filled with negative thinking and doubt. I go through weeks of trying to understand why this is happening and why other, more recent students are chosen. All I come up with is confusion and ignorance of what to do and where to turn. I am all ego—thrashing, writhing like a snake.

Patience, I tell myself. Three months go by. At the conclusion of a long retreat, we are exhausted. Master Sha calls me. "Get ready. Do not drive home tonight. Come to see me. I will give you two transmissions." I wait outside his door for hours while others are speaking with him. Gradually, they all leave and the deep quiet of night comes.

Soul Wisdom Transmission

It is midnight, June 23rd at the Land of Medicine Buddha in Soquel, California when I receive the Transmission for Soul Wisdom.

The retreat participants have left to return to their homes. Only the steadfast assistant teachers (Anita, Marilyn, Patricia, Shu Chin, and I) remain. Because Master Sha loves to throw the unexpected at me, he decides to give me a second transmission immediately following the first. For others, he separates them because the energy is so intense.

The room holds the shadows of the night with only a silhouette image of Master Sha, backlit by a bedside lamp. He sits half lotus on his bed, shirtsleeves rolled up, his back to the wall. I lay on the bed, face up, my head near his knees. A specially placed white towel covers a pillow for my head and feet. The atmosphere holds a sacred quality of ancient traditions transpiring in the quiet of the night. Master Sha places his right hand on my head such that his palm rests on my crown and his fingers curve down onto my forehead. I feel soothed by ancient rivers that cradle me and guide me to somehow arrive at this moment.

As he begins the invocation of God, Heavenly Saints, and Enlightened Ones of all times, I settle down, melting and allowing myself to open. My mind wants to create something, so I breathe out through my mouth to further relax and quiet. I wait. I feel my soul directly connecting with Master Sha's heart. My soul enters a curving tube and links through his hands and his belly, up into his heart. He is opening his consciousness to me so that I can travel, see, and understand what his consciousness knows. Then this tube continues up through his head and out into God. As this connection is established, a gentle coming, a subtle arising of an image begins. As it became stronger, there is a mist of gentle light in a large round shape directly in front of me. Behind this increasing light is the Divine presence of God.

Faces seen for the first time begin moving in front of my eyes. Images that are indescribable and unfamiliar begin coming from behind my ears and head until they are in front of me and pass through my body. There is a sense of eons. Other kinds of existence are showing themselves to me, like entering a deep river revealing the wisdom teachings of all times and spaces. A large stone tablet, perhaps 20 by 40 feet, holds hieroglyphs in many rows. A four-armed Hindu deity comes dancing. Tibetan Tantric deities come with gemstones in their hands and flames about their bodies. The gemstones turn into jewels that radiate colors from each prism. Intense light and color pulsate from the jewels. The jewels are alive.

Master Sha begins to call, "God, God, God," in a voice so sweet, so pure. It goes back so far into the universe. A Tantric deity becomes a shaft of light on first the inside, then the outside, and next merges into me. I am the Tantric deity looking outward. I dance with one leg up. The jewels are radiating.

Suddenly, a jolt of electric light comes into me through Master Sha's hands, catapulting me further into a space of infinite expansion. Then all is empty space—quiet, light, pale powder blue, gentle sweet space. Empty expansion glides and slides, opening further. I slide and open simultaneously into the space until all is deep quiet and peace. "Gate gate paragate parasamgate." Gone, gone, gone beyond.

His voice is calling to me from so very far away, calling me back and raising my body to sit up. I am willing, yet not able. My eyes open to gaze upon this man in a white shirt, his sleeves rolled up and his trousers trim. He is familiar, yet still so far away. He asks me to speak. I try, but it is not coming. I feel the effects of the empty space now lighting each cell of my body into beautiful light. My cells shine light like candles with a golden white flame. From the formless beauty of the space, I gather myself back into some smaller form.

"What did you see?" I cannot separate myself from this oneness to articulate words. Again, he asks, "What did you see?"

"Master Sha, this is beyond anything I could have ever imagined. I saw God."

The night is still outside this room. Only the beetles are awake. The air is suspended. I am blessed with the presence of four assistant teachers witnessing this powerful and profound transmission. They are tired, yet their bodies quiver with the energy in the room. They each give a flow, their versions of direct communication with God, each contributing to deepening my inner experience, helping me integrate what transpired this memorable midnight.

Master Sha tells me to go first. "Aubrey, do a flow!" He has a way of catapulting me into an altered state of consciousness and then bringing me back to share. I think it must be a test of my ability to soar and then return to articulate a non-verbal state.

I flow:

> *"I have entered into you directly through my son and beyond my son. My son is my light. That blessed light enters into you. You are transformed. You are the Goddess with the Gods. You are one of the Beings of Light. The wisdoms are multitudes, multitudes coming to you rapidly. Receive these gifts, draw from all these books, draw from all these sources as you teach, as you love, as you guide. All of this that you see, touch, the complexities, the brilliance, the emptiness, the light, the calling of my name, are within you to teach. Guide and assist all sentient beings who suffer and long to be in the stream which has been opened to you. Guide them back to me as you have been shown this path. I live within every cell of your being. You are transformed. I am in you."*

Next, dear Marilyn is told to do a flow. Marilyn is a Christian nun. Of all of us, she has become one of the most accurate in her flows. Each morning before she goes to her daytime job, she does a flow for Master Sha. Her flows now fill books with the teachings that pour through her. Her service is continual. Her purity is seen by all of us. Two years ago, I film Marilyn in a state of prayer where the light is streaming in through the afternoon window behind her. Her profile is illuminated. Her true nature is visually revealed in purity, service, and light.

This is her flow:

> *"My dear daughter Aubrey has entered into my presence and I into her in a unique and infinite way through your dear Master, my beloved son Zhi Gang Sha. This transmission of Soul Wisdom is in fact exactly that. My dear daughter will be able to live this wisdom because every part of her being has been transformed and charged with divine light and love. Much that has been a struggle for her has also been transformed. There will be a new way of walking upon the*

earth, of being present, of being Presence. Because in fact that is the gift that has been given this night. This is another holy night. It is another occasion when a person, a human being, has been brought to a level beyond human, so that the mission [Universal Enlightenment for all sentient beings] *can be served. This is an indescribable blessing and privilege. With it is an indescribable responsibility. This is your gift. This is your blessing. Amen. Amen. Amen."*

Next, Master Sha turns to Anita. This is her flow:

"In this deep and endless transmission, her soul is now united with God and she is holding the Golden Urn. This urn is now filled with the light of God. As though the urn is a part of her whole being, she is now an overflowing, ever filling vessel for God's Light. We feel this is a blessing that will serve Aubrey for her deep dedication to healing others. One which will carry her very far. We see she will be lifted up into the highest level of energy transmission. She will be able to heal others at a distance and in large gatherings. We see her speaking before large groups of audiences, and she will be able to project this Light of God out to many who are gathered there. She will be at the right hand of Master Sha. She will be offering this gift of service. The other disciples will also be seated at the right hand of Master Sha, and they too will have these gifts. We see this as a blessing for all the disciples who are gathered here tonight. Your beloved Aubrey has been the first to receive such a high blessing. We feel you will all rise in turn each in your own way, as you are as individual as the stars in the sky. Each of you will carry a sacred gift and a special blessing from God. We feel each one of you will be a missionary, will fulfill this mission and your Master will feel joy. We honor each of you. God's Light. God's Love."

Master Sha now turns to Patricia, who is lying on the carpet with a blanket wrapped around her. Dear Patricia, who works so hard preparing participants for the retreat just completed. She and I go through so much together before studying with Master Sha. We practice and teach Qigong often in this very retreat center. We take the first Refuge Vows given in this country by a Chinese Rinpoche who is the 68th generation lineage holder of the original Sakyamuni Buddha. I sponsor Rinpoche to come to the U.S. I am deeply honored to have him stay in my home for his first three months in this country.

The third close connection I share with Patricia occurs as she is driving her car to do a PBS shoot on Power Healing. Suddenly, out of nowhere, her car is struck and careens across the street. Master Sha does an immediate healing blessing as Patricia faints to the ground. I spend the next six hours with her in the hospital chanting "Guru Padmasambhava." It is a long and difficult recovery for her.

Patricia is a soul sister to me. I felt greatly honored as she makes the physical effort to do a flow. Although exhausted, she straightens her back and with visible sincerity places her hands in the prayer position.

This is her flow:

> *"This is an auspicious night. Our dear Aubrey is the first of the Assistant Teachers to receive this special blessing. This transmission will elevate you to very high levels, ones you could not have gone to alone or unassisted. This is an important point to remember. The guidance, the work, the pain, and the testing are all necessary parts of following this precious representative of the Holy and Highest Being on Earth. The reason you are going through the suffering is that your light and your mission will be the same as his* [our teacher], *brilliant and difficult. You must be strong. You must be made very, very strong. Never hesitate. Never look back. You cannot imagine how blessed all of you are. To our dear Aubrey, we send much love and congratulations. Thank you so very much."*

As the night concludes, I know deep within that I am further opening to connections beyond what I have ever dreamed possible. I am forever changed. I return home the next morning, more loving, gentle, and appreciative of my life.

Chapter 12

Karma: Causality not Punishment

Connie

In times of crisis, turmoil, illness, and death we are such fragile creatures. Our facades, our power, health, youth, vitality, convictions, and even our belief systems come crashing down. The shell we create, our roles and our postures, crumble and shatter before us.

In these vulnerable moments, the nakedness of our soul reaches out for guidance, stripping us to our core. "Dear God!" we cry out. Even the non-believers cry out. Help me. Show me the way through. Help me find the Light. Guide me through the darkened tunnel. Please take my hand and comfort me. Bring me hope as I cling to my life and loved ones. And indeed, if this is the time to go, forgive me for all my shortcomings for I was ignorant, non-caring, and non-seeing of others. Dear God, there is much I do not know. I have never been very good at praying or believing in you. Yet I ask you now to help me.

This is the position many find themselves in during these vulnerable times. This is the truth that faces Connie, my mother-in-law. It is a truth that many of us will come to face.

The steel door closes behind me and we are left alone together. Connie is lying flat on the hospital bed. She is suffering from a brain tumor. Often, we go together to her medical appointments. It is hard for her sons and daughters to be with her. With her children, she always saves face taking the role of the Grande Dame, with her Irish flair for love of life and vitality. With me, it is not the same. There is no history, and she is able to show her human frailties and vulnerabilities.

Only a week ago, her doctor tells her she has a tumor that is aggressive and they cannot operate. She looks him dead in the eye and says, "You have just taken away my hope." I will never forget the impact of what he did. Hope. There is so little acknowledgement about the importance of hope. Hope engages us in our dreams, our aspirations for our lives. When that hope is cavalierly severed, the pathway into our goals, our life force is blocked and shuts in seconds. Now Connie accepts she is dying.

It is this day in the hospital room as she is resting from some procedure that she initiates for the first, and actually the only time, any discussion about her imminent death. She gives me a teaching calmly stating, "I hope I did well in the Good Book."

This is the only indication I have that she believes deeds are recorded and goodness will be rewarded. I confess to her that I honestly don't know how these matters work, but I know she has been a good person in her life.

I ask her to let me know what it is like after she dies. She agrees to contact me. The day of her memorial service, I am downstairs in her house preparing to leave for the church. Suddenly, a ceiling tile falls out of its place and hits me on the head just as I am putting on one of her fabulous hats.

Karma

Karma is causality. An action causes a reaction. A pebble in the pond causes ripples. Given that we are all in the oneness, a movement in one aspect will cause a movement or reverberation in another. Hence, an emotion or a thought can cause a reaction. There need not be judgment attached to causality, although many believe some actions are good and others are bad. Certainly, I agree that grossly unkind actions are not appropriate. Yet somehow in the larger picture, in that place in your consciousness where there is no duality, it is important to avoid judgmental thinking that separates "good and bad."

Key Principles of Karma

To deepen our understanding of the concept that karma is causality, let me present some key principles:

❖ **Karma is the legacy of your soul.** As you move from lifetime to lifetime, your karmic legacy moves with you. You may lose your body and your ego or personality as you know yourself today. Yet, within your soul is a storehouse of history, past relationships, unresolved lessons, talents, and abilities. These qualities go with you when you die. There are those who diligently meditate to be able to retain their awareness of what they have gained in this lifetime, to take it with them through the death experience and into their next lifetime. They do this believing they will not need to begin all over again from a place of ignorance.

❖ **Often a karmic issue is the root cause of any illness, emotional imbalance, or life struggle.** Negative karma can haunt your soul from lifetime to lifetime. It can haunt a family and a lineage. Because as a culture we tend to constantly complain, we often spend hours missing the appropriate appreciation of our abundance. And in the missing, in the focus upon the half empty glass, we generate more negative karma for ourselves. It is your choice where and how you train your mind, moment to moment. How you train your mind has implications into future lifetimes.

❖ **The blockages that continually plague us as human beings are often issues from past lives as well as this life.** The film *Groundhog Day* beautifully depicts the repetitious nature of spiritual testing. The main character wakes up, day after day, to the very same unpleasant events. However, each day he makes a little progress in becoming more compassionate. Each day, he transforms a little, until finally he truly moves into unselfishness. The blockage is removed, and he is allowed to go forward with the rest of his life.

❖ **Blockages, also known as obstacles, are the struggles we encounter on a daily level.** They may occur in finances, relationships, health, career, project, house, or spirituality. The suffering of the human condition touches each and every one of us. Do not think that anyone escapes this condition, for we do not. Realizing this brings compassion for our shared humanness. This direct deepening of compassion is like sweet golden nectar that brings smoothness and fluidity into the areas of blockage. By opening our minds to new concepts and our hearts to new feelings, we literally become uplifted. Our karma loosens its hold upon the very life issue that has been a struggle and we begin to glide. We rise out of the mud.

❖ **Anger burns up your good karma.** You can realize that when another speaks to you in anger, you are really hearing their pain. As you recognize their pain, you now see their suffering. If you do not take their anger personally and do not pick up the dirty end of the stick, then this interaction and realization is a moment of potential freedom for you. How is this freedom? It is both emotional and karmic freedom because you did not get angry back. You did not get hooked in a familiar, repetitive manner.

❖ **If you cling to the struggle, you are making it harder on yourself!** When you recognize the suffering of the person in front of you, then you are less likely to blame them and point the finger to their faults. When you stop the blame and finger-pointing, you also can turn the mirror inward and ask, "What is my blockage in this moment?" This is an opportunity to resolve, make peace, gain insight and move through whatever has been tripping you up in this pattern or issue. Once you have clarity, step into either non-attachment or forgiveness.

❖ **Move beyond psychological lingo of "my issue, button, or trigger."** Enter the spiritual domain to see my karma. This is work on the soul level. The soul needs to be cleansed of karma accumulated through lifetimes.

❖ **Negative thinking and negative emotions create more negative karma in current time.** This means that, whatever you may be doing to help rid yourself of past negative karma, you are now replenishing with current negative karma.

❖ **The legacy of positive karma is seen by the smoothness and abundance that is in your life.** You enter a new life that is built upon the merits of your past life. Thus, a person who appears to be happy, with gracious surroundings of the material world, who is well liked, and leading successful intimate relationships is an example of past life positive karma.

❖ **Positive karma may also run in a family, originating with the grandparents.** In this case, the grandparents have accumulated enough merit that the fruits of their virtues are passed down to the grandchildren's lives. The impact from the maternal side is greater, and therefore the cultivation of a grandmother's soul will enter into the lives of future generations.

❖ **Positive karma builds within a family when one member is Enlightened.** The merits of the person who realizes this level of consciousness are then passed to all family members. Thus, the entire family benefits, in past, present, and future lives.

❖ **"In the physical world money talks. In the soul world, virtue talks,"** states Master Sha. The most profound service to be offered in the boundless Universe is the transformation of darkness into light. In the offering of this service, good karma abounds. To offer this service quietly and without recognition brings even more good karma. This is virtue.

Now that you clearly know karma is caused by thoughts, deeds, emotions, unresolved lessons, and relationships throughout many lifetimes, how are you going to lead this precious life? How are you going to transform darkness into light for the benefit of your soul journey, your family, and your children's children?

Clearing of Negative Karma

Connie had the innate wisdom to know that, at the end of her life, there is a balance sheet where good deeds and not so good deeds are placed side by side. One side will be higher than the other. This sets the stage for your future life.

How can this balancing be shifted to our favor so that our future is more peaceful, harmonious, and conscious? We need to increase our virtue, clear our negative karma, resolve unlearned lessons, and complete relationships.

How can one do this? One key method is to offer service wherever you can, humbly, silently, and constantly through prayer, chanting, and actions. When spiritual obstacles come to you, it is a moment to clear karma. People question whether a high-level teacher can clear the karma for another. Many healers, who are also Enlightened teachers, say that they can. Some struggle physically following any form of karma clearing when they do a healing for another. Master Sha takes a different approach. He is the only teacher I have met who overtly teaches virtue can be given from the Master to the student to help them heal and clear karma.

How to Clear Karma Through Offering Yin Service [1]

If you are lying in bed and sick or depleted, you can still offer a prayer to the entire Universe each morning and evening. You can offer healing prayers to loved ones or those with whom you struggle. You can give money, food, clothes, or assistance where it is need. You can give coins to the homeless. You can release animals scheduled to die, such as small goldfish or worms. You can place small insects carefully outside, so they are not stepped upon. You can tithe. You can give free workshops or demonstrations. You can chant, "Om Mani Padme Hung," when you pass an animal killed on the freeway.

These are examples of Yin Service. This means that you do not tell others what you are doing. These are private acts. Because of this, the value of the service is higher than public demonstrations or actions you discuss with your friends or even your teacher.

How to Clear Karma Through Offering Yang Service [2]

Yang Service is public service in the sense that it is made public. Our society demonstrates financial gifts to institutions by placing plaques upon a wall listing Donors. In Africa, if you have given coins to a leper or hungry person that day, you can say to the next one requesting alms that you have already made your contribution. It is then accepted that you have given your due for the day. It is further viewed that the blessings will return to you.

Yang Service has only one distinction from Yin Service. Yang receives public acknowledgement. You can do any of the Yin Services examples, but once you tell others or make a public announcement, the Yin becomes Yang. There is less virtue acquired by the Yang Service than the Yin Service.

How to Clear Karma Through Spiritual Testing [3]

As you successfully move through spiritual obstacles and tests, *[see Chapter 14, "Training as a Spiritual Healer"]* your karma is being cleared. You are building the necessary virtue by understanding the issue facing you, doing the service, and letting it go in order to move on. You are extracting the lesson inherent in the test. There is a dual purpose for each spiritual test: karma clearing and learning the lesson.

How to Clear Karma Through Prayer [4]

By offering prayers that focus on others, you are building virtue—a primary antidote to karma. These prayers may be the Universal Prayer for peace, love, harmony, healing, love, forgiveness, and Enlightenment. The prayer done before meals inviting all souls to eat first is one of the most powerful invocations of the day.

How to Clear Karma Through Forgiveness [5]

Western psychology has an understanding of the importance of forgiving both oneself and others within the paradigm of this lifetime. Forgiveness must extend into events as well, because in the soul world whatever is being done to us in this life we may well have done to others. Once our scope of understanding goes beyond our current existence and into countless other lifetimes in countless different forms, it is highly likely we have been both victim and perpetrator. Forgiveness, therefore, is all encompassing. It is letting go with love.

How to Clear Karma Through Taking on of Karma by Your Healer [6]

Many practitioners in the healing arts are attempting to do a version of karma removal. Massage therapists and chiropractors can feel the heat and thickness of the energy field that surrounds the body. They use their hands to clear the field until the heat is gone.

Psychotherapists attempt to remove negative emotions that are linked to karma by helping their patients vent or discuss traumatic events and relationships. Often these professionals will come to me for guidance to help them replenish or heal their own physical bodies.

What has happened here is that the healer is taking on the pain, negativity, and literally the darkness of the karma. It hurts the healer. It also hurts the client or patient because the healer has taken the client's opportunity to remove negative karma on their own through facing their spiritual pain, testing, and realization of the lesson. Further down the line, the patients may be revisited by a similar condition until they resolve it themselves. Most high-level teachers and healers I personally know become exhausted and depleted in this process, called "taking on your karma." It is a very high act of service.

Master Sha is an exception. Note the following sequence: First, he removes the blockage in the area of the cancer. Then, he begins the process of the clearing of karma that is located in the heart chakra and ends with a group blessing to her heart.

Removing the blockage.

Clearing of karma.

Pulling out the darkness.

Blessing of light.

However, I do not recommend that healers and health practitioners continue to do this without themselves having adequate strength, spiritual standing, or virtue.

How to Clear Karma Through the Giving of Virtue [7]

As distinct from the healer who takes on the karma of their client, there are Masters who offer their virtue to their student or client. A teacher of this ilk must have acquired great virtue throughout his or her lifetimes to be able to give without becoming ill.

These few methods of clearing of one's karma remove major obstacles and difficulties. One's karma can be cleansed to the point of being a "karma free being," and yet there are obstacles and struggle within your life. How can both these ideas co-exist? Being karma free is not being without struggle. Struggle is due to attachment—any form of attachment. Attachment and non-attachment are reflections of our humanity and our consciousness. When we are in a more human mode, attachment and suffering are ready to be present. When we are in an expanded state of consciousness, there automatically is less attachment, less suffering, and therefore our perspective seems to be more flexible without obstacles or impediments. In this latter state, we are quite content living in the Now.

There is a second, equally strong principle underlying why some people experience pain and suffering even after they are "karma free beings." It is because they are accruing new negative karma due to their present emotions, thoughts, or even actions. This underlying condition leads the serious student to be ever vigilant as to one's motivations and the purity of one's thinking.

Inner Experience of Karma Cleansing

For two years, I do not pay much attention to receiving the direct karma cleansing abilities of my teacher. He gives me several over many months. He places his hand upon my chest and literally pulls the darkness from my heart chakra. His fingers often leave red marks for days where the pressure of contact touches my skin. It hurts. It feels as if he has entered into my very core and pulled out sinews and blood and images of twisted souls. It has a sucking and tugging quality. Then it is quiet.

Master Sha asks me to describe the inner experience of multiple karma cleansings.

A year ago, one of the most painful public pronouncements caught me as its scapegoat. The group was on board, witnessing and reveling in the unfolding of my karmic record. It raises the question as to the ethics of telling people, when they are open and vulnerable, terrible things about themselves that are allegedly true. I do mean allegedly.

I speak from my heart about Tom's illness, the surgeries, the constant practice of healing and focus. I speak about the isolation from my spiritual community, as Tom did not want anyone to know what he was going through. He was containing the energy and wished there to be no negativity in thought or emotion expressed to him or about him. I deeply honored his request. Together, we embarked on this difficult test.

Master Sha later tells me, "It hurts my feelings to not be told."

"I feel that my challenge during Tom's illness was for me to be steadfast in the healing practices you have taught me, and also to honor Tom's wishes. I feel so much more compassion for the condition of our humanity. I have seen the death of three friends during this time. I am learning that where there is joy for a newborn infant and where there is sadness for the dying, are they both merely points on the pendulum of continual recycling between birth, death, and rebirth. Why then attach the emotions of joy and sadness? Why not just accept with equanimity the birth/death recycling? This is part of what I learned, Master Sha."

My teacher and I often converse in public. It is our dance. It is one of the few opportunities to get a word in edgewise. The comments may be oblique. One has to be listening carefully to hear the real conversations that are buried in innuendoes and stories.

Although this may appear to be an entertaining tangent, he is going somewhere that ultimately will reconnect with spiritual testing.

This quality of microscopic examination of one's behavior through the eyes of your teacher most likely will produce shortcomings. I know I face many moments of spiritual testing wherein old patterns come through many lifetimes and replay today. These are the karmic issues. Spiritual testing is but one way to cleanse these karmic patterns. Karma going back lifetimes can block you, your career, finances, relationships, and health.

A core dilemma is to whom do you listen? Do you listen to your own guidance or does your teacher have the final word? I gently suggest to my teacher not to polarize positions, because these dilemmas are potential teaching moments. These are deep questions—food for contemplation and discussion.

Now, I just allow the questions to be present.

To be able to do what I have just described is a deep wisdom. I come to this process through months and years of trying different postures. Now, I realize to just BE with the inquiry and the questions that are being posed is the process to follow. It is an opportunity to look deeply into oneself. It is a time for contemplation. It is rather Zen-like. Be a good warrior! Be brave and honest as you look inward! The layers of the onion are being peeled away. Within the layers are the sting that causes pain and my tears to flow. The peace and the clarity come in time. We cannot push the river.

When Karma Cleansing Goes the Wrong Direction

Thus far, I have only told you about the clearing of karma. It is also quite possible for a dedicated student who practices with great diligence to encounter a serious obstacle. The most difficult obstacles show themselves as blockages in the path. These blockages are often the exact point where we were blocked in a prior life. For this reason, they are quite tenacious blockages. This is a great challenge for the disciple.

Part of what may occur is that the disciple is now convinced that their opinion is the correct one, and that the teacher's interpretation of the matter is wrong. This then becomes a battle of wills with quite serious implications. These are the moral dilemmas that haunt our minds because they hit such core issues. Am I to believe myself? Am I to believe my teacher?

In many ancient texts, this juncture between a high-level disciple and the teacher is described. It is also a challenge for the teacher to be able to honor and recognize a new peer, the very disciple whom he or she has taught so carefully. At the same time, it is also a challenge for the disciple, because it is essential to always honor one's teacher.

By failing to fulfill the task the teacher gives at this crucial point, the disciple can fall backwards into recreating negative karma. The disciple's mind becomes clouded and confused. The pain is enormous. It seems the higher one's soul evolves, the greater is the fall at this crucial point.

This is the spiritual teaching that is applied to the disciple who is blocked in writing a book. The writing of this book was never completed in a prior lifetime. Thus, the teacher is giving his disciple both a task and an opportunity to complete something from a prior life. The struggle that ensures, the depth of the misunderstanding is a good example of the tenacity of the karma from a prior life.

From the perspective of the disciple in this lifetime, the writing was done and presented—left on a table for his teacher to review. But he does not find the writing. This is part of the power of karmic patterns. Both are caught. There is no simple resolution.

The teacher says, "I gave you a task to complete." The disciple says, "I left the writing for you to review." The gulf widens and pain ensues on both sides. It is of great significance that, if you were blocked completing a task in a prior life, you can be blocked again on the same point. Perhaps the only way through such dilemmas is the acknowledgement of love. The love between a teacher and a disciple is special, beyond the usual quality of love experienced in our lives.

Karma, Blessings, Spiritual Testing, and Transmissions

These four key spiritual principles—karma, blessings, spiritual testing, and transmissions—are interwoven and must now be integrated into a clear space in your mind. It is helpful to understand their relationship with one another.

Karma is the legacy of your soul. Spiritual testing consists of obstacles and struggles that are placed in front of you. Blessings are gifts from God. Transmissions are the direct passing of spiritual abilities and power from God through the teacher's spiritual channel to the student.

These key spiritual principles are rather like a family. There are many cross-relationships, some stronger than others, with many emotions and varying degrees of communication. If you view these four spiritual principles as a family system, you will begin to understand their complex dance.

Karma moves with you throughout many lifetimes. You can clear your karma and you can accumulate more. One of the ways to clear your karma is through the process of spiritual testing. This testing will offer you struggles. Yet the struggles are opportunities to move further than you have before. You have the opportunity to learn a lesson or to complete a task. If you fail to rise to the occasion, there will be a repetitious nature to your theme of spiritual testing.

Spiritual testing is a form of karma cleansing. When you are in the middle of a spiritual testing that can go on for months, you are not able to fully receive transmissions. You simply are not open or quiet inside. The effect of the transmission will not be as powerful as it potentially can be.

Blessings are the grace from the Divine, helping us to move through difficult karma, spiritual testing, and open us to receive the full potential of the transmissions. Blessings help us glide more smoothly and gently through the turmoil. Blessings bring us continual light that helps us to remove the obstacles, known as clearing the karma. When we are in a clear state, not in a spiritual testing state, we feel the blessings even more deeply. We allow them to touch our hearts and we are moved to tears. Conversely, when the mind is in turmoil, even though the blessings are cumulative, they are not felt as profoundly.

Therefore, as it is said in many ways and in many spiritual traditions, we must strive to maintain a clear and healthy mind. We must watch our thinking, for it is thought that gives rise to emotions, and then to actions and beliefs.

On this journey of the soul, first we must clear our thinking. Then we can move quickly through the portal of the space between thoughts and enter the Emptiness.

Chapter 13

Expansion Follows Constriction: Spiritual Testing

S piritual Testing is a difficult discussion. It is important to be frank and disclosing. The spiritual journey can bring us to profound bliss. It can also bring us to pain, struggle, ethical dilemmas, emotional imbalance, and separation from our family. It is not easy. It is not all pretty.

I ask God for guidance about what to say. This is what comes.

> *"You go to the heights and depths, to the light and to the darkened caves of the mind. You study. You teach. You are in the human form and you are a special spiritual soul. Write of this journey, the greater journey, in such a manner that it will be of service to the soul traveler. Help them to identify the states of mind, the ego mind, and the Enlightened Mind. Help to guide them, to strengthen them. This is your task."*

My teacher asks me to write, openly and honestly, about my struggles on this journey. As he puts it, "You go through so much. People need to know. People need to understand spiritual testing. I go through so much… much more than you do." As time passes over these years, I have learned more about his struggles as we grow closer, and he trusts me more.

What is Spiritual Testing?

We all experience struggle, pain, and suffering. It is part of the human condition. No one escapes it. No matter how wonderful on the surface someone's life may appear, they too experience suffering. The only difference between this condition of human suffering and spiritual testing is that, when you are on the spiritual journey, you choose to view suffering as "testing." You choose to move beyond the "poor me" syndrome and step into a more purposeful approach to life. You choose to learn the lessons often presented through pain.

This is a big step. It is a path that will bring great rewards, and also bring separation from old friends and an old way of living. You will simultaneously feel more connected with all souls and yet feel more profoundly alone on your path. You must embrace this paradox.

I distinctly remember the moment I stepped consciously onto this path and knew it would become more rarified in terms of friendships and lovers. I was 22 and in a therapy session with a psychiatrist named Lee Sannella. It was one of those moments when the world stops and you feel hit over the head. I even remember the color of the wallpaper behind his chair. Thank you, Lee. You just smiled. Lee is on the cutting edge of psychiatry. He is a gifted medical doctor, inventor of an electrically propelled car, a dedicated teacher of the spiritual journey, and author of *Kundalini: Psychosis or Transcendence*. I thank you for your guidance.

You must consciously and courageously embark on this journey.

Once you choose to view suffering as challenges and lessons, then when the obstacles come, you have a mindset to learn rather than complain. Why on the spiritual journey are there many such moments? Because, in addition to the innate suffering of the human condition, you are pushing yourself beyond your conceptual limitations and challenging your ego to give up control. These last two dynamics completely change the terrain of the struggle. It intensifies it.

The first dynamic of pushing oneself beyond conceptual limitations is an enormous task. You cannot do it by your will or your intention. Nor can it be done through any conscious decision that has a push or force within it. To go beyond our conceptual framework requires a softening, a melting of mental and emotional boundaries. There needs to be a genuine willingness to explore that which you do not yet know, let alone understand.

Logically, your mind knows that everything you understand to be reality is made from your intellect combined with your intuition. You know there is an aspect of your mind, and of the greater Mind, that you do not yet understand or perhaps have never experienced. You acknowledge there is something beyond your present understanding. You are comfortable with this quality of not knowing everything.

Yet, to have the courage to allow this unknown to come into your personal life is like jumping off a cliff into the abyss. It requires placing your belief system temporarily aside and opening in a new way. It may not be easy to read ideas presented in this book that are foreign to you. In fact, if I go too far, your mind wants to go to sleep and put the book down, dismissing its truths. Reading this book is a challenge because it introduces new ideas and experiences. Imagine how difficult it is to open into the rest of your personal life and allow these new experiences to come.

It is in the Unknown that the deeper spiritual truths will come to you. This requires jumping into the abyss again and again. Gradually, the terror transforms into a freeform flight and you gain new abilities and sensitivities that help you travel in this unknown terrain or space.

The second dynamic, giving up ego's control over your life, builds upon the first described above. Again, the choice must be conscious to view suffering as challenges and lessons to be learned. These concepts are directly contrary to our cultural values that state success is something we make through hard work, and we have the power to do it.

This same can-do attitude does apply to the spiritual journey, yet needs to be guided by our soul, with humility, obedience, and compassion. Conversely, our ego is formed through setting goals established by our parents or rebelliously going in our own direction, flaunting our independence. Neither the mimicking nor the rebelling attitudes of ego work in the spiritual journey. Why?

Because when our ego is the boss and runs things as they work in the physical world, none of this is appropriate in the spiritual world. The rules are quite different. This creates a BIG struggle. We wish to be successful spiritually and try to apply our worldly success or modus operandi, and time and time again come up against a wall. This is an example of spiritual testing, because we carry our ego expectations into the spiritual domain that by its very nature is beyond, and other than, our conceptual framework.

Some esoteric schools refer to the letting go of ego as ego reduction. This is part of the purpose of the Sufi Enneagram. You identify your ego and its characteristics and methodically grind it down until it loosens control of your life. In the Zen tradition, this is done through "peeling away the layers of the onion." In the tradition of Master Sha, it is called spiritual testing.

Spiritual testing is a process of confronting and successfully resolving repetitive themes or issues within your life. Spiritual testing IS karma cleansing. Spiritual testing means that an old issue from a past life continues to haunt you until you successfully resolve it and learn the lesson. Then you will move on.

Spiritual Testing in Ancient Cultures: Hercules, Abraham, and Milarepa

Spiritual testing is recognized historically throughout many cultures. This is an ancient journey. In ancient Greek culture, there existed Gods and Goddesses as well as demigods and demigoddesses. I was always fascinated by these tales as a child because each God had a human failing or weakness. Zeus was a notorious womanizer and his wife, Hera, was hopelessly jealous. And so it went.

Hercules, a mere mortal, wanted to become a demigod and requested this of Zeus. Zeus gave him a task. Hercules had a powerful physique and highly sculpted musculature. He looked like a modern-day athletic club buff. To pass this spiritual test, he had to successfully complete twelve tasks. They were time limited.

One task was to clean the Aegean stables in 24 hours. It was a perfect task for someone who had made his way with his physically strong body because he had to use his mind to figure out this problem. There were many stables in the barn, each filled with decades of horse manure. Nearby was a river. Hercules had to step outside the box of his own mind and his old way of doing things to perceive the river as a possible solution. He rerouted the flow of the river to go through each stable and thereby successfully passed this test.

In the Christian Biblical tradition, Abraham had to be willing to offer up his son in sacrifice to God. God allowed this test to go to the very last moment, when it was clear that Abraham was willing to obey God's words. Then God provided a lamb for sacrifice and let Abraham's son be saved.

In the Tibetan Buddhist tradition, Marpa was a high-level spiritual master. He had a very devoted disciple. Teachers are often the most demanding of the disciples that hold the greatest potential. So Marpa seriously tested Milarepa. Marpa gave Milarepa the task of building a house. When Milarepa completed the house, Marpa had him tear it down. Milarepa tore it down. For many of us, this hard work that is then torn down is enough to cause us to leave and be critical of our teacher. Not so for Milarepa, because he knew this was a test.

A second time, Marpa asked him to rebuild the house. Milarepa rebuilt the house. Marpa, again, asked him to tear it down. Milarepa, again, tore it down.

The same sequence happened a third time and a fourth time. Marpa continued to have him build the house and tear it down. Milarepa was a smart student and did not complain or question. He simply obeyed his master. This is a deep spiritual teaching. Suddenly, Milarepa realized Enlightenment. This was what his teacher intended. The building and tearing down, that appears on the surface to be testing the patience and obedience of the student, is what we call spiritual testing. The deeper purpose was to help his student realize Enlightenment.

These three stories carry deep teachings about thinking outside the box of your logical mind to find a solution and move through the test. This is a teaching about a key spiritual principle: obedience to God. A second teaching is that things are not what they appear to be.

Karma creates the obstacle. Spiritual testing is an opportunity to cleanse the karma. A task is a test. Be not attached. The deeper goal is to prepare your soul to realize the highest level of Enlightenment possible in this lifetime. Keep your eye on the ball.

Characteristics of Spiritual Testing

Perhaps these characteristics of spiritual testing will help you remember what is happening to you, even in the midst of your storm.

Spiritual tests
- ❖ Are perfectly tailored to your life, e.g., appear in your individual situation with a painful irony
- ❖ Have an up/down quality, e.g., life is great and suddenly you get hit
- ❖ Have a repetitive nature, e.g., same relationship issue with different people

❖ May originate from outside you, e.g., financial hardship, career issue, car accident

❖ May originate from inside you, e.g., emotion, illness, thought

❖ May last for a split second, hours, days, weeks, or months

❖ Challenge your core belief systems

❖ Trigger your psychological resistance, e.g., "this is just too much" or "no"

❖ Originate not just in this lifetime, but rather are karmic patterns of the mind over many lifetimes

❖ Are painful

❖ Are draining

❖ Are intense

❖ Create confusion and doubt

Hopefully, this list will help you move more quickly through each successive challenge. Remember, spiritual testing is a doorway to freedom.

Belief Systems

Here are four different examples of spiritual testing common to us all. They are issues relating to our belief systems, our emotions, our family relationships, and our friends.

Sometimes, the external conditions in our lives quiet down. Then the deeper internal struggles arise. This is our mind. This period allows us to watch our habitual way of thinking. As we progress along the path, it is the quality of our thinking that displays our internal landscape. We learn a great deal about ourselves as we learn how to quiet down. It is here that a spiritual test can be most difficult.

As you progress along this path of the journey of the soul, your boundaries will be pushed. Your sense of what is "correct" or "how things are done" will be challenged. These phrases come from our prior experience in life and what we have chosen to integrate along the way as part of our belief system. These are our guiding principles.

But the spiritual journey is not like life. Yet it is paradoxically life. The guiding principles are often on the far end of the pendulum from where we usually operate. Because we are thoughtful and introspective people, when we come up against our own principles, we can quickly slip like a car on black ice into a moral dilemma. We experience the very basis of our belief system or our values being torn apart. Perhaps a moral dilemma takes place in our minds, causing our inner voices to rage into a cacophony so loud we lose perspective. We cannot identify it as a test. The dilemmas may be what choices to make or how to be pure or honorable. This can happen in an instant.

The very nature of being inside this chaos is that we are blind. We thrash about in our negativity and turmoil. We forget we must break through our conceptual thinking. We justify our own positions and the noose of attachment tightens.

Our mind plays endlessly like a broken record. "This is just too much!" "This is too difficult!" We complain. This is a victim position filled with blame and finger-pointing. This mindset is self-fulfilling. In this state, there is no recognition we are in a spiritual test. We don't even care about spiritual testing!

How to Move Through Testing of Your Belief System [1]

As you catch your mind using words such as "should or ought" or phrases that complain, blame, or judge, start to chant immediately. "Should" and "ought" show your own attachment. Complaining and blaming show judgment. These qualities are impure, disrespectful, and born out of ignorance. These are positions of an entrenched ego.

To lessen the grip these words and emotions hold on you, quickly chant for at least two minutes. If you do this quickly, your mind will not have had time to really build up steam to support its case. Whatever is going on externally is truly not your business. Your business is to cultivate your own purity. Turn the mirror inward and look at yourself. That is your business. That is how you use the situation rather than it using you.

At the same time, there is deep wisdom within you. Tap into your own wisdom. Be balanced. The Sufis put it beautifully saying, "Trust in God and tie your camel."

Emotions

In Western psychology, emotions are accepted as part and parcel of life. Experiencing great passion such as joy, happiness, fury, or terror is seen as simply very strong emotion. Yet many Eastern masters warn that extreme expression of the emotions creates an imbalance that, by its very nature, must come crashing down. A little wave has a little tide. A big wave is a tsunami. So, to avoid this crash, they suggest we temper ourselves and reach 80% of any given emotional state and not reach the 100%, or peak, of that emotion. In this way, we will lead a more serene and healthy emotional existence.

How To Address Anger in Spiritual Testing [2]

Anger is an obstacle. It tells you many things about yourself. On the surface, the physical level, constant irritation that bursts into flares of anger is your liver in a state of excess energy. On the emotional level, anger is an imbalance in your heart chakra.

This imbalance psychologically may be due to "events" in this life. Yet it may also be a causal result of unresolved karma in this life or past lives. Anger of this sort is part of a habitual response of your ego that is carried from lifetime to lifetime. If you go to this level, you will see anger is an emotional state and you are its victim. Why do I call it "victim"? Because you have not broken free from your own habits or learned the lessons that are present. If you could but gain the clarity necessary to undo this response, you would feel lighter and liberated.

Often, cancer patients will have an imbalance of too much anger or irritation. Spiritual testing asks us to go deeper into the very root of the problem. Why am I angry? How long have I been angry? What happened before? What are my hidden expectations that I have unconsciously placed upon this person or situation? As you discover the answers to these questions, you will then have the opportunity to forgive, to cleanse the karma between yourself and other souls, and lastly to heal the physical and emotional conditions.

Under anger is often a quality of lack of love, such as not feeling appreciated or seen. To heal this emotional deficit, begin to actively listen to the little voice inside that is asking for some small kindness in this day, some little act of gentleness to oneself. Take action and give to yourself. A loving nature begins at home inside your heart and to yourself.

Once you heal in this manner, you will see you do not respond to situations with anger. You can catch yourself and stop this response. That is successfully moving through a spiritual test. The test comes up into your face, and you do not have the old response anymore.

Family Conditions

We are each aware that certain predicaments in our families occur time and time again. Unfortunately, family and close friends frequently make judgments about your spiritual path. Either they insist you do what they do, or they find what you do is outrageous or wrong. Families who lack tolerance often have extreme reactions. Sometimes, they enter periods of protracted silence or ostracize you from family events. These set opinions are obstacles, created by your karma and their karma and the entire family's karma. When these obstacles flare up in front of you, because of their opinions, intolerance, or desires for you, your ego also responds in its habitual pattern. This is a tough cycle to break.

How to Move Through Family Disagreements in Spiritual Testing [3]

It is very sad, because the souls of your family members back through many generations are stuck in how they relate to you, and you are stuck in it as well. The patterns of intolerance and judgment are passed down through our lineages. You, because of the journey of your soul and your commitment to heal, are now in a position to say, "The buck stops here. I will change this family pattern." So, you make every effort to help your family heal.

It is most important to heal these separations. If you cannot do so on the external level, then do so soul-to-soul in your prayers. Soul prayer work needs to be kind and patient. Use loving words. Work on this for weeks or months. Remember to turn the mirror inward and you show up in the most pure light possible. Some call this "taking the high road." Be forgiving. Know that the situation is cyclical and that you are committed to move beyond this particular pattern that is a spiritual test. Otherwise, next time round in your next life, it will play out again.

On the deepest level, remember the purpose of this lifetime for you is to realize Enlightenment. In so doing, you will automatically help all family members move through their positions and family relationships will improve.

Although my mother met many of my teachers, she never really allowed herself to be vulnerable, trusting, or personally disclosing. She would not have passed the spiritual test of "obedience" because a) she was unsure there is a "God," and b) she would not allow another to have control over her. In the last years of her life, she had frequent third eye visions of souls coming into her home. She saw herself seated upon the knee of a gigantic Buddha who filled the heavens. She sat there and gazed at the lake in the center of his lap. She felt peace.

She acknowledged her past lives by giving me a watercolor she painted inscribed with "our lives as sisters in 1580."

Our final healing was a gift of respect for my spiritual journey. In her mind, she could now see the commonality within our family: her brother, the poet; and her cousin, the physicist; and now her daughter, the mystic. All three have much in common yet use different languages to access the essence of the universe.

In contrast, on my father's side, while I am quite close spiritually with Andree, my stepmother, there is silence with my siblings. On the passing of my father, she and I dared to chant, "Om Mani Padme Hum," much to their disapproval. I am working on it. It is still painful. Yet whenever my mind goes to this place, I let go, again and again. We may need to meet again in a future life to achieve a trusting and close connection.

Friendship

Friends, even the more spiritual ones, can disagree with your path and may even feel competitive or judgmental, thus causing separation and disagreement. I had a dear friend for over 30 years, a woman quite accomplished in her own journey. The week I experienced the Great Luminosity, I tried to share with her. I was blocked by her anger and attacks on my character. This kind of interaction was unusual. In all the years I had known her, we never had any difficulty. I am unable to share, to discuss, or to celebrate with her.

I interpret this kind of obstacle as a blocking. Perhaps I am not meant to share. There are teachings that strongly suggest one not share inner milestones. The danger is that we brag, thereby feeding our ego rather than dissolving it for further cultivation.

These two stories, the one about my father's side of the family and the one about my friend, are examples where I must continue to work, to gently re-approach, and to hold forgiveness in my heart.

How To Move Through Disagreements with Friends [4]

Recognize that each one of us has a unique soul journey. Allow for differences. Be compassionate where others may be judgmental. Practice forgiveness.

The Shale of Mount Shasta

Spiritual testing has a counterpart in Western psychotherapy. It is resistance. As the student or client gets closer to breaking through an issue or an ego pattern, the resistance builds. It is not unusual for a client to bolt out of therapy at this point. The more intense this struggle, the greater the results can be. It is like a rubber band stretched to its limit and then allowed to spring forward. This is a potential quantum leap into a new way of viewing life.

If one is a serious student of the inner journey, be they a medical client, psychotherapy client, student, adept, or disciple, there is a commitment to look inward and ask, "What can I learn here?"

I guarantee you, the ego will fight for its existence. The ego seeks self-justification every step of the way. An internal cacophony of "yes" and "no" escalates.

Just as the dynamic of resistance has its story, defenses, self-justification, and rigidity, so does the tenacity of spiritual testing. In the latter, you will find doubt or criticism about new learning, requests, or tasks. You may have expectations as to how things ought to be. When old expectations are applied as a prerequisite to your spiritual growth, you set yourself up for a conflict.

I recall an advanced student who tenaciously held on to her expectations that her spiritual master would answer all her questions and enter into dialogues. When these expectations were not fulfilled, the student felt hurt and unloved. She kept setting herself up for something that the teacher was not going to give her and then being hurt. She blamed her teacher for not answering her questions, as if there was something wrong with her teacher. Blame and expectations are traps.

It is quite possible that the teacher was testing her and, each time the student took the bait, the teacher upped the ante. Finally, when the student no longer has any response to the same repetitive issue, the teacher will move on as well. Good teachers are tough.

For me, the spiritual tests are challenging and difficult. They can last for months on end. I learn to live with the feeling that every 30 seconds I am out the door. I don't know if any of you have ever climbed a mountain with shale near the peak. The atmosphere is thin from rarified oxygen. Each step up the mountain has an almost equal slide backwards. This is a wonderful analogy to the spiritual tests that come as we get close to breaking through.

It has taken three years for me to see how tests work and, most importantly, the pathway through the struggle. When I break through, I feel so light and clear! There may also be a distinct sense of uplifting, not of the cloud of confusion, but rather like a jump up in total perception. Sometimes, that which I am convinced is true turns out to be made up by my own mind. In fact, it is not true, and I am wrong. This is like flipping to the opposite side of the coin where everything looks different. Suddenly, there is space in my head. The voices are silent. There is a peace. I am solid and clear.

In the Chinese Buddhist tradition and in the Taoist tradition, spiritual testing is a means of clearing karma. Successfully resolving a period of spiritual testing is certainly a means of arriving into a more open, clear, and peaceful inner state of consciousness.

The good news is that Enlightenment is possible in this lifetime. The bad news is that you must suffer to get through this! It is hard work.

The Art of Testing

Good teachers give you tasks. Great teachers give you tests! A task is a job. It may be demanding and hard work to succeed. A test places you against your own ego right down to its very depths. God, the Universal Source of all energy and light, is the ultimate taskmaster.

Testing is an art. It is an art for both the teacher and the student. It is an art to survive and learn. It is a dance of the highest form. Many philosophies and schools of psychology study the role of ego. Many higher esoteric spiritual schools study HOW to cut through ego. In Tibetan Buddhist thangkas (the spiritual cloth paintings), the cutting through of ego is depicted as dancing figures of women with swords.

The further we progress on the path, the tougher become the tests. For indeed, these are the tests of many lifetimes, culminating as we move closer to Divine Bliss. It is painful. It is difficult. Ego complains. The complaints are justified from one perspective. From another perspective, they are merely the driving forces of the storm coming at you, piercing through the armor of your skin, your sense of justice and fairness, and your very sense of yourself. It is a key meditation to be able to use this form for your own benefit rather than fight against it. This is another mastery over your mind.

Who is this self anyway? There is no self as we merge with the Universe. Therein lies the freedom. So, who is this one complaining? Go to the very root and find the very first moment you felt wronged. Ask yourself to undo this negative thought and transmute it into a voice of self-mastery, of confidence, and of choice. As the ego voice is quieted, you find the entrance into light.

What I have just shared here has taken me decades to learn. In Western Psychology, one can spend years of therapy and growth-oriented pursuits to gain this wisdom. While the words may be quickly stated, to do the actions takes two qualities. The first quality is a genuine willingness—a genuine willingness to let go, to come off it, and to gain insight. The second quality is entering into the appropriate attitudes that allow for serious study with a teacher. It is possible to move through these obstacles more easily with proper guidance and support.

Tasks and Tests

It gives Master Sha great delight each time he asks me to stand up in front of a group and share my stories of spiritual testing. He takes pride in how hard he can train. He thinks a great teacher produces great disciples. And the bigger the job he has planned for with his key students, the more effort he puts into training them. Spiritual testing is a large part of his training.

In August 2001, he gives me the task of writing about my experiences with him over the first six months. For me, it is a wonderful story of unfolding and transformation. Although I cannot yet use Enlightenment because I am not there, I must somehow find a way to convey the progress being made. I spend days and hours pulling together notes from my journal and present "On the Road to Soul Enlightenment with Master Sha." *[See Appendix]*

He says, "You speak and you inspire people. You speak from the heart. Write like this. Do it again."

"My goodness," I say to myself, "I worked so hard. Maybe his language barrier has trouble understanding my similes." This is a good example of how my mind made HIM the problem. I had not yet been exposed to the practice of flow. So I am in ignorance. I am blaming. This is my mindset.

In this blind state, I try again. Two weeks later, I present a rewrite with a letter to him. In this letter, I question his judgment. In retrospect, I am horrifyingly disrespectful raising issues to a possible language barrier.

My second attempt is rejected! I am using my logical mind to attempt to make sense out of what is going on. And it simply does not work. When I next see Peter, I ask him to read these pages and help me. Even Peter does not read it! He merely takes the four pages, places them on his palm for a spiritual evaluation, then waves it in the air, and states, "No, this does not have it!" So, what the heck is "IT"?

"So, I am being tested. I am set up to do something. I write my precious little story as best I can and he still rejects me," says the voice of ego. Then, to make matters worse, Peter merely waves it in the air. He knows something I do not, so now I feel ignorant. This rattles on my ego. The four pages disappear into the great void of nothingness.

It takes time to understand that my first lesson is one of attachment and ignorance: the logical mind cannot understand the spiritual mind. At my level of consciousness, I cannot perceive a higher level because I am not yet there. I do not know what I do not know.

I struggle in my ignorance because I have no clue as what they are both are telling me. They are referring to "writing while in the state of flow." I do not know what flow is. I can only do the best I can with the tools that I have. My attitude is poor.

The Haunting Darkness in Growing an Organization

When people are aspiring to spiritual growth, there is frequent conflict around organizational issues. The mix of spiritual values and organizational power shows the dark side of different institutions. Where do you trust the authority and where do you trust yourself? Personality failings coupled with positions of authority make it hard to distinguish between a person making guided choices or supporting their personal weaknesses. Issues of delegation, lines of communication, decision-making authority, and short or long term strategies are key concerns of every organization. However, when these concerns are overridden by a spiritual vision that is "higher" or more "accurate" than our physical world knowledge, conflict and confusion abound.

I have never seen spiritual organizations deal with the dynamics of their process because the foundation belief system is not in agreement or in accord with the best or most successful businesses in the physical realm. In organizational development, it is recognized that a business reflects its leader. If the personality of that CEO is authoritarian, then the business under them will be run by those values. If the CEO is more egalitarian and hires people for their expertise and listens to their advice, then the entire organization will reflect listening and valuing individuals and their creativity.

Early team meeting on Tom and my houseboat, 2001.
(left to right) Master Sha, Shu Chin Su, Anita Eubank, Allan Chuck,
myself, Mimi Chuck, and Sam Chang.

Master Sha is attempting to have a physical world organization run by soul world principles. This creates massive conflict both organizationally and personally.

It takes a long time for me to see these two dichotomies. Initially, I am quite personally attached to working for the organization in some capacity that reflects my prior life experiences. Each time I attempt to share my knowledge of the physical world with my teacher, I get in trouble. I irritate him when I suggest the organizational ideas that have worked in other human potential start-up organizations. It takes months before it no longer irritates him and negatively impacts our teacher/student rapport. I learn to keep my mouth shut and quiet my internal voices.

I watch others try to do the same, to use their professional talents and experience, only to be rebuffed. I watch consultants come and go because of these differences.

I begin to perceive a fascinating duality of diametrically opposing truths. In the laws of physics, there are forces and counter forces. For Master Sha's organization, the positive force shows its forward movement of touching more people seeking healing or spiritual opening. The counter force is equally strong and shows itself through obstacles encountered, e.g., negative feedback about marketing, selling, testing, and money. Talented people come into his organization and then leave because of how he is running it. The very magnet that brings people in also pushes them away. This push/pull seems to settle into two distinct camps: the purity of Master Sha as a teacher, and the negativity and darkness around the business.

He would be the first to state that he views his spiritual task as integrating both dark and light forces. It is therefore not surprising that this position plays out within his organization and teachings. It takes time for me to understand this balancing and to stay clear of its backlash when I get attached to a role or position.

Again, my own expectations based upon my Western and psychological organizational skills anticipate team building, group participation, brainstorming, round-table discussion, and consensus. Wrong. The tone of many meetings is dominated by my teacher alternating between inspiring spiritual teachings and unilateral decision-making through tossing of the coins. These differences cause people to leave, be replaced, or even friendships to be broken.

However, some of us just hang in, retreating to the background. To survive, I revert to my core question, "Why am I here?" I am here for truly one reason only: to realize Enlightenment so that I may be of better service to others. I offer this as a suggestion for moving through spiritual testing: return to the essential reason that you are doing the spiritual journey. Let this be your unwavering focus. Let all other matters be moved aside. Be true to your purpose. Cut through all other obstacles.

When I am asked any question about the organization, I can feel the subtle energies of conflict, negative emotions coming towards me in this dialogue. I have been hurt so many times in this kind of conversation that now I just chant inside myself as I listen to the person in front of me. I do not wish to go there with them in this discussion. I will now only teach when I am asked. I will travel with him and teach. I love this work. Keep it simple. Wait to be asked. Be patient. Be peaceful. Be in equanimity. These are the qualities to cultivate.

As my consciousness evolves, I am more able to learn from the soul world. I can see into my teacher's heart chakra and watch what he is doing over a two-year period. I now see and understand the nature of backlash or counter force. It is rather like the ocean tides. The more powerful is the tsunami, the more powerfully waters both rush in and rush out.

Three years later, in a hushed conversation with Master Sha, he privately shares with me his ambivalence about the very organization he has empowered. Now they are dictating to him. He, by nature, is much more freewheeling. He wants to do what the moment presents, and he cannot. The rules that an organization needs to follow, that they have created by consensus and commitment, now get in his way. Even though I am beholden to follow these rules, I can feel the tear in his heart.

I can feel when the storms are coming, and I get out of the way. He is brilliant at remembering hundreds of details and being clear about where he is heading. Because by nature he is inspirational, continuity is not what runs his vision. He can create chaos through rapid change and yet demands perfection and precision down to the smallest detail. He embraces the light and the dark within his own organization just as he teaches this on the spiritual plane. Not all his staff can do the same and this is part of the struggle and challenge.

Bottom Line: Toss the Coins

The *I Ching* is the ancient Eastern tradition of divination through tossing 64 yarrow sticks. Today's simplified version is tossing blessed coins. This toss, accompanied by prayer, is seen as an authentic connection with the will of God. It is an act of surrender to the Divine. A question is posed and the first toss gives the direction one is to face. The primary question on one's mind is then carefully worded and asked. This second toss gives a yes or no answer. If the question involves quantities, the numbers are slightly shifted until a yes is received.

All decisions in Master Sha's life are done in this fashion. Where he travels, where he teaches, and how he runs his business. His spiritual and physical lives are seamlessly governed by the toss of the coins. This is one of the difficulties that his consultants have with how business decisions are made.

As his student, and in matters of my relationship with my teacher, my life is also governed by the toss of the coins.

At first (and truly for quite a while), this coin toss is hard to swallow. While I have tossed the coins as part of using the *I Ching* for the past 30 years, I have viewed each reading as a reflection of my mind during the process. I understand the *I Ching* to be more like a mirror than a final decision.

Beginning in September of 2001, within months of meeting my teacher, this tossing of the coins removes me from the role of registrar during his workshops. The tossing of the coins selects 20 new people for new roles. The level of my soul is lower than half the new team members. This is publicly announced during a team meeting and I am so embarrassed. Within months, the first transmissions for healing are being given to selected students. New students are receiving this coveted blessing. Again, publicly, he announces even some of his teachers are not approved. So painful—I cannot begin to tell you the hurt in my heart. Other disciples and advanced students pass me by in the hierarchy that begins to emerge. Promises are broken. Why do I stay?

In expanded states of consciousness, it is clear that ANY perception is already in the realm of duality, ignorance, and ego. It is no longer pure. How then can the toss of the coins, influenced by both the question and the perception of the person tossing the coins, be anything other than individual separation from the Oneness into impurity?

However, my dear friend Peter, whom I endlessly respect, used his coins to help him escape from communist Czechoslovakia in the darkness of the night. It worked for him!

In my mind, this is most incredulous. I am amazed at Peter's escape.

Conversely, when the toss of the coins becomes a decision that Master Sha makes on my behalf, such as I am not to travel with him to a particular city or to receive a special transmission, my ego goes wild!

In fact, my teacher is quite proud of the fact that he has been harder on me, given me more spiritual testing than many others. One day, he tells me that God had rebuked me five times in a row through the tossing of the coins. He continues to say, "I am concerned. You have some funny thinking! You cannot go that way!" So, I am being evaluated even when I know nothing about it. This is a shock.

I feel saddened when others shine in his eyes and I am in the doghouse. I feel the unfairness and misunderstanding. I bow down in the privacy of my home to the Divinity of God and the Universe to purify my mind and my thoughts. It is true that my thoughts think all this is crazy. My thoughts also acknowledge that my direct experiences are awesome and blessed. This is my pendulum swinging. Craziness and bliss!

I stay recalling the story of Milarepa who realizes Enlightenment when his ego has been ground down to a state of nothingness. I stay because I am here to realize Enlightenment in this lifetime and with this teacher. This is unshakable.

Obedience and Guidance

"I bring you to the door. You walk through." These words are Master Sha's way of saying he opens you spiritually to your own Enlightenment. Then it is up to you. Yet, he challenges you saying, "In matters where we conflict, you must always check with me before you follow your own guidance because I am the Master."

This dance between high-level disciples and their spiritual teacher is classic and recorded in texts on transformation. In some Buddhist teachings, the final or third stage is when the disciple's consciousness matches that of his or her teacher. At this point, the teacher also faces a spiritual test: how will they handle this? The teacher may acknowledge the level and equality of the disciple, paying his respects to his successful student, or the two will part company. It is said a high teacher is pushed further by his own students' growth. It is challenging for the teacher to answer questions that the high-level disciple now poses. It is always appropriate to remain respectful and honor your teacher, even if you grow beyond your teacher in some of your abilities or realizations.

I have personally witnessed disciples challenge my teacher. They wish to believe their own guidance as truth. He teaches that his word is the final word because his connection with the Divine carries greater accuracy.

There are different spiritual tests in this discussion. The first test is how both disciple and teacher handle the moment of equality. The second test is how a teacher handles students coming to the spot where they wish to believe in themselves and stand on their own. The third test is how a student handles their own guidance when it conflicts with the issue of obedience to one's teacher. Walk carefully through this maze.

Fruits of Spiritual Testing

The sticky quality of anguish present in each of the above stories is itself the darkness of karma and negativity. It is this very quality that we must avoid or transmute. If you have the ability to transmute darkness into light, this is definitely a big service. However, usually the stickiness attaches to you. Before you can blink an eye, you are trapped in the negativity. We do get better and quicker at recognizing the instant this process begins.

Going through this process is the peeling of the layers of the onion described in many Zen tales. Each layer brings tears, and yet, each layer that is removed also brings a more clear light inside the body and mind of the student. You can even see the light in their eyes. I see the light in my own eyes when I look in the mirror. And I know how dark was the sadness of so many years. In this way, you can bear witness to your own transformation.

As I realize the fruits of my testing, my goodness, how I am opening! My teacher is a powerful spiritual catalyst. Through his many challenges, my abilities to see, to flow, to heal, to see past lives, and to see karma assist me as I work with others. The speed of work is many times more rapid than the past 25 years working with just western therapies and meditation.

On the other side of a spiritual test is the potential breakthrough into a more clear, expanded, and even luminous state of consciousness. When our perspective is no longer clouded from attachment or resentment, our mind literally jumps up to a higher level. From this vantage point, the world looks different. Peacefulness is consistent!

Successfully Moving Through Spiritual Testing

To move through a difficult phase in one's life requires a certain wisdom that seems, unfortunately, to be gained through experience. In black belt circles, those with the highest belt have taken the most falls. A difficult situation can come suddenly. It takes so much longer to live it out.

One key characteristic of a test is that it grabs you. It consumes you. My mind thinks about it constantly. My emotions rage. My energy is drained. My perspective narrows. My mood drops. It is a familiar space because my patterns of feeling and thinking, my very perspective about life is repeating yet again in full-blown regalia.

A second key characteristic of a spiritual test rests in a deeper dynamic. The process may be circular, a feedback loop. Or the process can become a spiral, allowing you to jump to a higher level of understanding. This jump does not eradicate fully the issues. However, each jump of the spiral brings some freedom. It is also known as a quantum leap.

To successfully move through spiritual testing, you must enter the spiral dynamic. This phenomenon was recently portrayed quite well in the film *Groundhog Day.* As a new test grabs you, it is crucial to recognize "Aha, this is a test." Then ask yourself how you can use this situation. Turn the mirror inward and look at yourself. At the same time, look to your own personal goal in life. Both of these require focus. The moment you shift your focus from the negative feedback loop to looking in these two other directions, the inward and your future (life purpose), you automatically break into the spiral into greater freedom.

Looking towards one's goal is filled with hope. Hope is the least sung of many virtues. While love is on the tongue of many people, few refer to hope. Hope is so profound. Without hope, how can we reach our goal? Hope immediately comes into our energy field when we focus towards our goal. Hope is essential food for the soul.

To look inward is to utilize your own commitment as a student of the journey of the soul. What is it that I have to learn in this situation? I see my old patterns. Frankly, they bore even me! What can I do that is different NOW? Learn the lesson so that you can move forward.

In addition to looking in these two directions that are still within the physical world and within the human condition, we must focus further. The third ingredient is the essential role of the soul. Focus totally upon a chant. Any chant that has meaning to you or any hymn such as "Amazing Grace." I teach people to chant "God's Light."

What is happening in this chanting? On the physical plane, the focus of our mind is now outside ourselves. In forgetting yourself, states of peace and comfort have an opportunity to enter you. On the spiritual plane, this chant is doing a twofold task. First, it directly invokes of the presence of God to bless you and assist you. Secondly, it sends the Divine Light onto the situation of your struggle. Here you are asking for blessing of others involved in the situation as well as for yourself.

You are now being of Service by asking God's Light to come and bless the entire situation, the issues, the people, the interactions, the lessons, and, most importantly, all the souls involved. This is Service.

When we focus upon others in this manner, we are, without even thinking about it, detaching from our ego. This is now a practice of non-attachment. This is now a practice of focus. This is now a practice of forgetting about our drama and replacing it with Service and Light for others.

Chapter 14

Training as a Spiritual Healer

I am an apprentice, training in the traditional manner under a Master Healer. I spend two years at his side and another two years applying what he teaches while still under his careful eye. Throughout these four years, we travel together as I assist him during his workshops. I attend his teleclasses and retreats. I teach some of these classes for him. I lead my own groups and seminars, practicing what he has taught me.

During these years with Master Sha, I am fortunate to have direct contact with him, observing him, being tested by him, receiving his empowering transmissions, writing for him, and coming to know both the Master and the man. At first, I am mystified by what he is doing! I watch him very carefully for hours and months. In time, I begin to comprehend a body of knowledge so very new to me.

Training as an apprentice is deeper than hand positions, chants, and other external practices. The true training is in my heart. Training in this traditional manner means being available to your teacher whenever he asks you. I always feel honored when he calls me on the phone to ask if I can travel with him. When we are together, he is constantly teaching me, telling me ancient wisdoms, challenging me, and giving me the opportunity to teach.

Being able to teach is the fastest path to your own transformation, because when you teach, you hear your teachers' words coming through your own mouth. Being able to teach and being able to heal is a gift to the healer, because you directly feel the golden light running through you. To be able to be of service is a gift. Therefore, his training of me is a profound gift on a multitude of levels.

These gifts include high-level empowerments and transmissions. These last two, in addition to my apprenticeship, help me purify. In this process, my healing abilities also grow. During this apprenticeship, I feel a continuum of emotions. I feel joy witnessing the faces of people as they recover from an illness that has plagued them for years. It is wonderful to see them realize they have the power to heal themselves!

I feel sorrow when I witness death. One day on a street corner in Illinois, I tell Master Sha it is hard for me to watch people die. He gives me a teaching. I have a wrong attitude because it is their time, because we have many lives, because God sets the time, not us. I contemplate his teaching and my consciousness opens to be at peace with this gigantic recycling. I find the place in my heart where I feel neither great joy in the birth of an infant nor grief in the passing of an elder. I find equanimity. I assist others as they enter the transition of death, for our work is with the journey of the soul.

Transforming from Psychologist into Spiritual Healer

A psychologist helps people with their pain. A spiritual healer brings joy and Enlightenment. Which role would you rather have?

This chapter is about the transformation of the healer. While this chapter will touch upon healing, self-healing, group healing, and remote healing, it is not about the techniques and tools used for healing. There is a body of knowledge omitted that has been part of my training. This is a rich and precise field originating in Traditional Chinese Medicine and Zhi Neng Medicine, as developed by Master Guo, M.D., the teacher of Master Sha. Please refer to their work on Body Space Medicine.

While the external training, certification, and understanding of healing, are demanding, the requirements of the internal transformation are the most rigorous.

Twice, I have been examined on the points of Power Healing. I am certified as a Divine Healer Level One and Level Two. The latter are for Power Healing and Soul Healing. Truly, they are mere entry points to Master Sha's transmissions. I have received other transmissions as well, all of which are applied when I give healings.

The internal requirements are to further one's purity, commitment, and love as a preliminary to truly be of service to others. My compassion comes from personal pain and witnessing the pain of others. It is a compassion born of understanding the very nature of the human dilemma—a condition of suffering combined with aspirations of Light. The ability to love deepens as empathy grows into compassion. Tolerance grows into patience. Understanding grows into forgiveness. Peace follows the upheavals of the mind. My outer surroundings reflect this life transformation.

The Healing Format

The basic format for any healing—of self, of other, remote or in person—always follows this progression:

❖ As I enter into the sacred space of offering healings and blessings, I empty and begin my prayer to the Divine.

❖ Next, I request my healing empowerments to come and assist me.

❖ I ask the personal guides of the soul before me to come and be present.

❖ I ask the soul of the person to tell me, within this sacred space of this moment, how may I best support him or her.

❖ The healing begins by first focusing upon the area of pain, conflict, inflammation, degeneration, or whatever is the primary issue. I ask for light to assist me. I cleanse the area of excess energy, darkness, or blockage.

❖ The light regenerates inside of the cells and around the cells.

❖ The light flows between all the cells like a golden liquid, caressing and soothing.

❖ Once this level of cleansing is complete, the second stage of blessing follows. Here, I focus upon the heart, opening the person to space and peace.

❖ Then the golden light flows from their head to their feet as love surrounds them in a gossamer blanket. The presence of love is profound.

This is the essential format. It varies with the particular empowerment and its visualization. Words, song, and sound flow through me, always resonating with the soul in front of me. Mantra becomes soul communication as song. The mantras come as love songs for the wounded. The words come as poetry and prayer. Sounds become a vibration of a tuning fork that rises into the heavens and returns into those before me. I surrender to the highest Enlightened Master Teachers and Master Healers. I am becoming One with the Divine to be of service to others. I open myself as I enter the hero condition and the unknown. I experience the golden light. I, too, am in a state of awe, watching those around me blossom in their own Awakening. I feel blessed as they are touched by God. This is Love and Light Healing.

I tell you my story because you, too, may be inspired to pursue your dreams to become a healer. You may also be inspired to heal yourself.

How Does Healing Happen?

Healing happens because you are willing to hold the space, the possibility, the conviction, or the hope that healing will occur. It is not a blind believing. It is a more active quality of hope that we carefully contain and nurture. The conviction, not the belief, but the steadfast conviction that you can heal, is a pivotal position to hold for any healing to occur. One must truly wish to heal and be willing to let go of the secondary gains of illness, such as extra attention or a way out of a sticky situation. Healing happens because we are willing to ask for help from God, our personal saints and guides, the soul of our teacher, and the souls of our friends. We ask our own soul to assist. To be willing is an important key. We practice the healing visualizations and chants. We learn what we have to learn.

Twice in my life, doctors give me terrible predictions. The first time they say I will never see again as I sit in the emergency room in New York City with an eye swollen to the size of a golf ball. One side of my face is red and blue. My vision today is perfect. The second time when I ripped muscles in my inner thigh. The doctors say, "You will never dance again." They were wrong. I dance. I am healed. These two episodes help me to relate to my clients as they, too, overcome the words of pessimistic physicians. I know that voice inside that says back, "You are wrong. Just watch!"

When we witness others healing, it gives us more hope for our own healing. We need the support and the encouragement. Because illness or unhappiness is often a result of something going awry in our lives, we need to be willing to change that situation, relationship, or attitude as well.

In short, what we have here is the patient's conviction that they can heal themselves, and secondly, the healer's conviction that you can open to be a conduit of Divine Love and Light.

The essential healing wisdoms that have been shown to me (from the perspective of a healer in training) are these:

- ❖ True healing occurs on the deepest level of the human psyche: our soul.
- ❖ The effectiveness of any healer is based upon his or her spiritual standing, the blessings and transmissions they have received, and the level of consciousness they have cultivated.
- ❖ Ultimately, it is in God's hands.
- ❖ Healing of the physical body may or may not happen. However, the blessings that accompany the healing practice will stay with the Soul as it journeys.
- ❖ For healing to occur, the darkness of negative karma must be cleansed and transformed into light.
- ❖ For healing to occur, the lessons facing the soul must be learned.
- ❖ For healing to occur, the client must actively participate in self-healing.
- ❖ Be not prideful. Be not sad. Clients live and clients die. Be only kind.
- ❖ Divine Love and Light are the highest vibrations available for both healing and blessings.

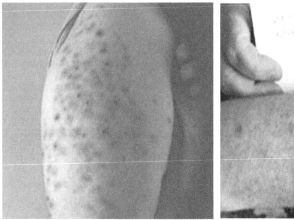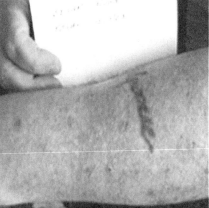

(left) Shows chronic and acute genetic skin condition on both arms when no Power Healing tools are being used by client. (right) Shows effect of 3 months using Power Healing tools with visualization. This is the only modality we use.

Enter Into the Hero Condition

During the first year of my training, I begin to see images of light coming through Master Sha at the focal point of the healing. In time, I see the tips of his fingers extend into the body of the patient rather like laser beam corkscrews into the sickness area. Then, I see darkness pulled out of people and thrown out a window or door to exit the room. A few months later, I see the cellular structure changing from erratic cells to normal cells. I see the transformation to light. Healing can happen in an instant!

These are the images I progressively observe as Master Sha does healing. I am amazed one day, about three years later, when I get feedback that someone is seeing me do the same thing as I have seen him do! This is my first confirmation that his healing abilities are successfully passed on to me.

I am leading a group in a lovely home in Martinez. We are in the "white room" where many spiritual teachers have come before me to offer classes. As is my custom, I ask the recipient, "What did you experience during this healing?" Sharing is important in a group.

On this particular night, I am going around the circle asking each person to share. I am quite startled when a woman reports, "I saw your fingers reaching deep inside her body." I say nothing to them of the meaning of this particular third eye seeing. I just reply, "Good. Anyone else care to speak and share?"

In the next few days, I go to my teacher and tell him what she had seen. He is pleased, because a year prior I had seen him doing the same thing. Part of how Master Sha heals is to reach deep inside

Part of our training is to enter into the hero condition. You ARE the healer. In Western Psychology a counterpart is "act as if." If I am unsure what to do as a healer, then enter into the hero condition and get out of my own way! There are distinct internal steps that allow this to happen:

❖   The willingness to step up to the plate.
❖   The willingness to trust your teacher.
❖   The willingness to forget about yourself. The moment we forget about ourselves, our doubt, uncertainty, insecurity, need to look good, and begin to focus upon the other person in front of us, we instantly make a quantum jump into the role of service.

It is the next few steps that make the distinction between act as if and enter the hero condition. In the latter, you are entering the domain of spiritual healing.

❖ You are now standing in the role of service as a conduit of God's Will. In this space is the foundation of healing. There is a palpable quality of connection with your lineage and your teacher. This is an ancient healing tradition.

❖ You must empty further, breathe slowly, relax, and open yourself to whatever comes.

❖ Enter a state of prayer, invoking whatever God, saint, or Enlightened Master you wish to come and assist.

❖ You become one with the healing saint or deity. You ARE the living presence of that healing saint. There is no separation. Our consciousnesses are merged.

This is a detailed description of how the healer prepares and enters into the space of offering a healing blessing. Many people come to my healing groups because they want the opportunity to go through these steps I have just outlined. They want to practice being the healer. The reason for seeking this opportunity is that, by the time you go through all these steps, you literally are in a state of beautiful golden light. In this state, spontaneous flow comes out of your mouth. You find yourself speaking with the soul of the person you are healing. We all stand in a circle and take turns giving and receiving healing. The presence of intimacy and love within the group is moving. Sometimes, people chant in voices that are deep and free. The soul of the healer experiences a freedom to be expressive, kind, and of service. People want to be these qualities. People want to be of service. It feels wonderful! People cry with joy!

Remote Healing

Healing can be done long distance. It can be focused upon an individual or a group. It can be done over the telephone or by merely holding up one hand and inviting the soul of the person to come in and be present for a healing. Some Chinese Master Healers teach that our intention carries DNA. There is information carried in the DNA, and that is how remote healing works. To Master Sha, remote healing works because everything has a soul. Information is carried through speaking to the soul just as we would normally carry on a conversation.

Each week, I do remote healings for my cancer clients. By the end of these sessions, they tell me they feel peaceful, lighter, and calmer. Their burdens have been lifted and their pain lessens. Some feel their energy increasing and they can re-engage in their lives.

How To Do Remote Healing for Cancer [1]

I speak with my clients for a few minutes, catching up with their progress and whatever issues may be facing them this week. I enter into the hero condition and start the prayer. "Dear God and Heaven's Team, my personal Shi-Fu or saint, dear personal guides of *(client)*, please be with us now. Dear soul, mind, body of *(client)*, please be with us now." Inside and silently, I ask my teacher and his teacher to be with me now. I ask that the soul of the particular healing power I am going to use be with us now. Out loud, I ask my client, "What would you like us to focus upon today?" *(They then add a particular focus for us to address, e.g., I am getting ready to go to my doctor for a CT scan and I am afraid of the results.)*

I begin the healing by first focusing upon the area that is causing the most pain or difficulty. "Dear soul of every cancer cell. You have the power to heal yourself. Do a good job! All cancer cells and all pre-cancer cells, return to normal cells! Symmetrical cells! Healthy cells!" I ask my client to visualize either a golden ball spinning counterclockwise within each cancer cell or I ask them to visualize golden light shooting out in 360 degrees from the area of the cancer. The light shoots out because cancer is a condition of excess energy and blockage. Then, I begin to chant whatever healing tool I am using.

Next, I move to the space between the cells. I ask my client to visualize golden liquid light washing through all the spaces between the cells, opening these spaces so that light and nutrients can be feed to the cells. Here I may chant, "Golden Liquid Light."

After doing this for a minute, I move to the heart chakra. We know this area to be the center of our emotions that need to be balanced and healthy. We also understand that our karma is housed within our heart chakra. I begin to chant or perhaps sing, "Open your heart. Fully open your heart. Feel the golden light healing your heart. Open your heart to the furthest reaches of the universe. Further open and receive God's light." Then I may chant, "God's Light" for a minute or two, adding God's Love in a more quiet and comforting tone. Lastly, I sing without words, the sounds of the blessings that I am guided to do in the moment.

What is happening here is first the healing is done, and then, when there is more space within the person, I move to the blessing. To be effective, it needs to be in that order.

There are many permutations to this basic formula. For example, if the person has received healing programs for themselves, then I will work with what is familiar to them such as a soul software or golden healing ball. I always try to use a modality that my clients use in their own healing practice.

How To Do Self-Healing [2]

It is necessary that the client practice self-healing as a supportive aspect to the work with the healer. I suggest to my clients that they tape a session we do together and replay this at home. This process just described needs to be done as frequently throughout the day as the client can. Three to five minutes each time and a minimum of six times a day is recommended. It is also important to chant as much as you can. Forgiveness of yourself and of others is essential. Lastly, offer prayers of service to all souls in the universe, for their wellbeing, and for light to come to them. In saying prayers, one of the most special times is just before you eat. Ask all souls to come and eat first. By doing this combination of self-healing, you will rapidly regain your strength, clarity, and feel better.

Developing Medical Intuitive Abilities

As your third eye capabilities are developing, the abilities of medical intuitive are a natural progression. One day, I am in a chiropractic office with Master Sha. He is doing a healing. He asks me to watch and then tell the patient what I see. Suddenly, I see the patient's entire spine turn a white golden color. Each disc readjusts, starting at the bottom and quickly moving upward to the base of his skull. I see it is a "spiritual chiropractic adjustment" with rejuvenation of the bones. This is what I tell the patient out loud.

How To Cultivate Medical Intuitive Abilities [3]

You can cultivate your third eye abilities and offer service wherever you can. These Qigong practices include "bone marrow washing."

Body Position
Here you sit with your back straight, feet on the floor about two feet apart. Begin by placing both hands upon your knees, breathe deeply, and relax. Take your right hand, with your palm facing your body, and slowly move it from your pelvis, up your chest, across your left shoulder, and down your left arm. Allow your right hand to lightly brush about 2 inches away from your left arm on the outside and move down to your left hand. When you come to your left hand, turn your left palm upward, slightly lifting it up off your left knee. Then, continuing with your right palm, begin to move, brushing lightly, back up your left arm. You are now on the inside of your left arm. Continue up to your shoulder, to your center of the chest, and now run back down to your pelvis. This completes the right-hand movement.

The second half of the movement is exactly the same, except done with the left hand. The right hand now rests, palm down, on the knee. Your palm will turn upward as your left hand moves towards it, just as you did previously. Your hands will alternate throughout the entire practice.

Breathing
Every upward motion from your pelvis to your chest is an inhalation. From your chest, down your shoulder, to your hand is an exhalation. From your hand to your shoulder is an inhalation and once reaching your chest is an exhalation. In this manner, you are bringing in fresh qi to your body and washing your body. Then, when you exhale, you are removing the dirty or stale qi out of the body, both through the tips of your fingers and the base of your pelvis.

Visualization
The visualization is key to cultivating the ability to see into the body.
1. For perhaps four full cycles of right hand and then left hand, place your eyes in the center of your palm. Use your palm to begin to see the skin of your body and to feel the heat of your body. Sensitize yourself by feeling the different temperatures as

you move your hands. Once you feel you can hold your attention on the skin of your body, you can progress with the second step.

2. Using your palm as your eyes, look deeper into your muscles. Do this for at least four cycles, until you feel you can hold your attention on the large and small muscles.

3. Look even deeper into your body using your palms. Here, you begin to focus upon your organs, intestines, joints, and gradually the bones. You may begin to see the front side of your spine and the bones of your arms and fingers. Stay focused and continue for at least four cycles.

4. Gently begin to return to the layer of the muscles and do this for one to two cycles.

5. Gently continue to return to the skin and surface of your body for one to two cycles.

6. Lastly, just place both palms back upon your knees, breathe, and sit quietly.

The entire practice should take 15-20 minutes.

Who Is the Healer?

The healer is your soul in communion with the Divine.

Inside you, the healer is your soul. You must believe you can heal yourself. You must want to heal yourself. Healers and teachers can have great power and offer special blessings, yet unless you do the work and stand in the place of willingness to heal, the healing will not take place. This may well be the mystery to which Western medicine refers when it cannot account for the body's ability to heal itself, and the state of mind that contributes to some people healing and others not. The golden light and love that comes from the Universe must join with the special light of your soul.

Each person I work with creates their own special program that usually is a mix of traditional medicine and alternative approaches. It is important for people to take control of their healing and to listen to their own sense of what is appropriate for them. My work is to support the internal wisdom in each soul and to encourage it to come forth into action.

Patricia

As a healer always be open for the unknown, the unexpected. I would like to share what happens in a remote healing session with Patricia who had stage IV breast and liver cancer. I worked with her for about a year, sometimes in person. As she became weaker, we spoke every Thursday morning on the phone.

We begin the healing as usual, first chatting about her visit to see family. Then, family comes to be with her. We begin the prayer. She asks me to focus upon an infection that is developing around her port through which she receives chemo. As I speak to the soul of her infected port, I see the presence of Jesus in the woods just outside my window. His beautiful, white, flowing robes glisten with radiant light. There is a golden halo about his head. His arms are outstretched towards us, with light in his palms that is radiating towards Patricia. He picks up the area around her port, the infected tissues, and gently holds them in both hands. His love is so enormous as he holds this infected part of her. The light is all around her tissue. He gently returns this part of her body back into her and smiles at her. It is such a kind, loving, generous, full smile. He then places his hand onto her crown chakra and gives her a direct blessing. There is white light from the heavens coming into him.

Once Jesus is present, and out of respect to Him and the enormity of what is occurring, I tell Patricia exactly what is happening. I leave the usual format of our healing practice. The tears are now streaming down my face as I witness this blessing. I share with her that I have never seen this before. How profound and special is this direct blessing!

Later, I telephone Master Sha to tell him what has happened. I am still in tears as I leave the message on his cell phone. Within the hour, he calls me back to give me more teachings. "Settle down now. You have seen Jesus and felt Jesus run through your hands in Fairfield. Put your logical head aside. You are much better now than three years ago."

Once again, I feel such love for him. It soothes my soul.

I know I am growing, and yet there is so much to learn.

On the Road with Master Sha

In the very early months of my meeting Master Sha, I see with my third eye an image of a large hall in New York City. I am standing on a raised platform made of old wooden planks. There is an oval amphitheater with rows of raised seats. Master Sha is also standing on this stage. We are giving a presentation to a crowd of people. As I am seeing this, Master Sha calls me from the front of the room to share.

This inner vision is a bit of the glue that connects me with Master Sha. He affirms that I am one of his seven Assistant Teachers, and that indeed I will travel with him. And over the next four years, I do travel with him as part of my training.

People come to him for physical healing and spiritual healing. There is such pain and suffering mentally, emotionally, physically… and in people's souls. Hope is what people seek. Master Sha's teachings give many people hope. Hope that they can heal themselves. Hope that he can bless them and relieve their suffering.

A few poignant scenes are hidden from the public. These scenes carry a purity of his intent. I am able to bear witness to these healings.

Corn Belt Healing

On the eve of our departure for this trip to Fairfield, Iowa, March 26, 2002, a small group of Master Sha's students are having dinner on our houseboat. He has just done the dinner prayer when the phone rings. It is the daughter of my dearest friend Liz, telling me she is in the middle of a four-hour operation with a 50/50 chance of survival. As I hang up the phone, Master Sha grabs the moment to immediately deliver a command to her soul. "Let her live!" I have never, in all the time I have been with him doing healings, heard him "command."

I feel torn between driving immediately to Oregon and going with Master Sha to Iowa. At this time, I knew little about the power of remote healing. This is one of those moments in life when you make a big jump and enter into the act as if; you trust that which you do not "yet" know. It is a moment of applying years of training. It is a moment of integrity where the pedal hits the metal. Either you follow the path you have sought throughout your life and are true to yourself, or you bolt out of fear or crisis. This is my life, and these are, and continue to be, my choices. With this mindset, I leap over the obstacle, the spiritual test, and fly with him the next morning to a poor town in the middle of endlessly rolling hills and farmland in Iowa.

Master Sha asks me to record this trip. Here are some of my journal entries.

March 27, 2002

By now, Master Sha's Power Healing book is Number 5 on the Chronicle Book List and Number 12 on Amazon.com. Over 120 people come to Master Sha's introductory event in the public library. They laugh, they cry, their chanting is powerful with a deep resonance. Some who come are devoted students of the Maharishi Center, only a few miles outside town. Spiritually, many of them are advanced. It is quite an experience to be teaching a group at this level.

During the days that come, I am able to watch the minute-by-minute daily life of a Master Healer. It is so very intense. It is hard work. He sees people individually every fifteen minutes, compassionately listening to their stories, their pain, and their hope. "We work hard until midnight, when we rejoin our host and continue talking late into the night."

March 29, 2002

Before dawn, I continue praying for my dear friend Liz. It is Friday night and we do an introduction to our Easter Sunday workshop. About 50 people attend the Soul Series Introduction with demonstrations by both Peter and myself on flow. People ask what is the difference between channeling and flow, and between speaking in tongues and soul language. This leads to a discussion between Peter, Dr. Sha, and myself later on. So much of this is new to me and therefore quite intriguing.

Participants are especially responsive to a long and powerful blessing for the Power Healing book, as Master Sha calls in many spiritual teachers and Enlightened beings to bless his book and then to bless each person in the room. Golden light comes in from hundreds of Enlightened Beings into the book in Master Sha's raised hand, and then the golden beams of light pass into the Message Center of all participants in the room. He says this blessing stores the message of the entire Universe in his book.

March 30, 2002

As his workshop continues, Master Sha gives key teachings:

- ❖ *"The more you give, the more you receive."*
- ❖ *"The message, the soul is IN the mantra; therefore, power healing already knows HOW to heal your knee (or anything). You don't need to tell Power Healing mantra how to heal!" "THE MANTRA KNOWS HOW TO HEAL, BECAUSE THE MANTRA IS A SOUL!!!!!"*
- ❖ *"Pray for the Universe: this is the biggest secret!"*
- ❖ *"To clean karma, give service. Don't complain. It makes more bad karma.*
- ❖ *"Two keys are forgiveness and no complaints! Pray for forgiveness. Give your accumulated virtue to anyone from this life or a past life that you may have a debt to or that you may have hurt."*
- ❖ *"In a spiritual blessing, the Master will give you flowers to nurture your soul for your spiritual journey. Therefore, the smartest student will privately ask the Master to bless his spiritual journey."*

While we are externally engaged in the business of producing a workshop, assisting with individual healings, and intensely talking to one another, my inner life is exploding! Part of the beauty in traveling with such spiritually advanced people is that we can share into the wee hours of the night. Both Peter and Marilyn are also traveling with Master Sha. They have each spent their entire lifetimes on their spiritual paths and are viewed by Master Sha as highly evolved disciples.

March 30, 2002

Working closely with Master Sha, I experience my own mystical moments. I feel a two-foot beautiful stem in deep green rising up out of both my palms. A violet-colored flower appears on each stem with delicate single layered petals. Then small flowers are coming out ALL over my body. My body expands and expands. I am seeing each of the Buddhas as he calls them, coming towards me and parting to each side as they come. When he chants, "Jesus, Jesus," I go back to the time of Jesus and suddenly KNOW that I was one of the women who took care of him during his brief time on earth. A past life regression is occurring.

March 31, 2002

I am unable to reach Liz by phone as she continues to be in ICU. The only way to reach her continues to be in my daily and ongoing prayers for her.

Master Sha continues to give teachings that touch me deeply and I record them:

- ❖ "When you are on a spiritual journey, the purpose of your life is to offer services to the Universe, to offer love, peace, and healing."
- ❖ A key Spiritual Law is, "No complaints. There is a spiritual reason for this. There is a spiritual reason for everything!"
- ❖ "No frustration, no gain. No pain, no gain. No drain, no gain."

Now, one of the most profound experiences I have ever had in my entire life occurs: Master Sha is, once again, asking Peter and me to do flows. He wants us to enter the hero condition of Jesus and become the voice of Jesus. Only moments before, I felt the light and blessing of Jesus upon me. The light penetrated my head and crown. Painful, painful light.

Master Sha must intuitively know what is happening to me, for he asks me to do a flow. Within moments, I completely become Jesus with the Divine and powerfully compassionate light of Christ coursing through my entire being. The Presence of Christ consciousness is fully within me. My body becomes the body of Jesus. My words are His words. His light exudes out from the tips of my fingers and pours out my heart chakra. All of me is now the compassion of Christ consciousness. I shake and cry at the front of the room.

I feel Christ in my body as a light body and suddenly I am hovering over Liz's body in her hospital bed in ICU. Jesus and I hold her in my healing arms. Then, returning to the workshop room, I feel the spikes of the crucifixion in both palms, then the thorns painfully penetrating my head and brow. Then I see Heaven open with golden billowing light. Heaven and the people in this room are in ONE place. The time dimension is seamless and in the NOW. As the light of Jesus enters my crown, it passes down to my heart chakra and radiates out with a single beam of golden light into the heart chakra of each person in the room. This beam of light is the seed of Awakening that touches each person's heart. I am still at the front of the room doing flow.

Midnight Healing

It is approaching midnight following a long day of individual healings and a workshop in the evening. Someone approaches Master Sha asking for help for his daughter. We drive down a darkened street to a house that could have been on the cover of the old Saturday Evening Post—a classic farm belt wooden home. We walk up the old stairs to the second floor where we see a young and somewhat thin blond woman lying on a mattress on the floor. She has been bleeding heavily for three days since giving birth to her young son in this room. The family is poor. There are not many resources to help her recover.

Her father tentatively pauses at the doorway to watch and hope, even pray, for this healing blessing to help her. Master Sha removes his overcoat and kneels down on this bare mattress. He softly speaks encouragement to the young mother. Her story comes forth with her tears. It is a tale of separation, infidelities, pregnancy, and the mixed emotions that come with adolescent motherhood. Her eyes weakly fasten on Master Sha's face and voice. He places his hand upon her head, soothing her, and begins chanting. She relaxes back down upon the mattress and her father gently pulls the blanket over her. Master Sha gently reassures the family that she will recover. They had been so frightened that she would die. The room becomes quiet and peaceful, and the golden light enters.

We walk down the hallway to the next bedroom that is equally bare, except for a bed in which a newborn infant lies quietly sleeping. He is wrapped in several blankets for warmth. The infant is handed to Master Sha, who cradles him gently with such love and gives him a special blessing for strength and a good life. Tears come to Master Sha's eye. I am wondering, what is going on here? We say our goodbyes and go to the van waiting in the darkened street. The teachings begin.

Master Sha and me in Fairfield, Iowa

"What has happened here?" Master Sha poses one of his favorite questions to Peter Hudoba and myself. "Do you know who that baby is?" And, as is often the case, we enter a dimension that I now call The Unknown. I haven't a clue, logically or experientially, as to what he means. The only way to access the information and answer his question is to jump off the cliff, abandon my logical mind, open my mouth, and hear my own answer after it is spoken. This is becoming a familiar way of being taught.

The door to the van closes and Peter and I are speechless. We drive for several blocks. "This is a most special event that has occurred here," Master Sha breaks the silence, "This child was my son in a past life. I needed to give him a blessing. This is really why we came to Fairfield."

So, there is an inner thread for Master Sha as to the purpose of this journey. There is also the outer thread—the stories of people crying, praying, and chanting as we move through the public events. There is a personal thread for myself that is both internal and external. The mystical experience of the spirit of Jesus in me is indescribable. For months, I continue to ask people if they have ever had this happen to them. And there is Liz.

Our time concludes in Fairfield. We did what we came for and now we drive down the road in a snowstorm heading for Chicago. Master Sha chants to the soul of the snowstorm to lessen and allow us a safe journey. Within five minutes, the snowstorm stops, the sun comes out, and the roads dry.

Following an evening presentation at a bookstore, we eat and retire to our rooms. Both Marilyn and I want to talk. We are so touched by his presentation. As we share deep into the night in our Chicago hotel room, Marilyn's knowledge of Christianity and her many years as a nun are deeply helpful.

April 1, 2002

Marilyn and I stay up until 1:30 a.m. as she shares with me her understanding of the women around Jesus. In the car, Peter says all the males in his family have been named after the disciples of Jesus for the past 500 years. Marilyn tells me the stories of Mary Magdalene, The One with No Name, Martha and Mary (the sisters of Lazarus), and the Samaritan Woman. The morning we were scheduled to arrive, Marilyn had had a dream about Master Sha and my third eye experience of last August in seeing Jesus while doing the evening prayer. In Marilyn's dream, she is receiving a message that Master Sha is Jesus.

April 2, 2002

Master Sha's teachings at the breakfast table: OBEY. Obey whom? Obey God. Obey is to have a listening heart. Master Sha says to me, "Aubrey, write a book on your journey to Enlightenment, on your journey at my side, and I will support you by telling people about this book. Do it as flow."

He is intently and emphatically teaching me about obedience! To listen and say yes, no more explanations! I feel inside the subtle holding back I have felt all my life... the basic self-preservation instinct of my ego and its concomitant physical withholding. There is always an explanation to cover up a survival instinct. This must be what has to break open. Master Sha again tells everyone, Marilyn, Peter, how he has knocked me so hard and this is also why I have grown so fast! THE biggest secret to spiritual growth IS TO OBEY!!!!!!

This trip is a spiritual pressure cooker! It is so intense, so remarkable, the openings, the joy of opening to flow in doing service. It is a Yin/Yang experience: the pain of ego reduction and the expansion of consciousness simultaneously!

April 3, 2002

Teachings at lunchtime: How you sign your name affects the success you have or the obstacles you meet. The more clarity, curves, flow, space in your signature, the better. Never end the last stroke with an upward moving line that continues too far… it is an indication that you have trouble ending things.

Midnight eggs and pancakes with Dr. Sha, Marilyn, Peter, and Jack, our host from Fairfield and the Maharishi Center.

April 6, 2002

It is time to part and return home. As I stand in the doorway of the hotel in Chicago, Master Sha says, "Come here, let me bless you. You grow very fast." As we part, I tell Master Sha my way is the path of Divine Love.

Sitting here on this park bench and waiting for the bus, I shall miss my buddies! It has been SO intense and we have been together so closely, 24 hour/day for 11 days!

"Let Her Live!" A Near Death Experience

This story is a Miracle Healing story. This story is about my dear friend, Liz. It contains passages from my diary and from Liz as she begins to be able to write what happened on her side. I feel it is important to document both sides of the story as it unfolds.

She is the one for whom Master Sha gave the command, "Let her live!" She does live. At the time he is giving his command, she later reports feeling the presence of Mother Mary hovering above her, giving her permission to stay or to go. Liz stays.

How can I begin to thank Master Sha? For the saving of my dear friend's life, for the light that shines behind my own eyes, for the opportunity to do such profound service for others, for the unfolding of the spiritual journey.

I know how. Offer Service.

April 5, 2002

I continue to pray for Liz. I tell Master Sha that, for the first time since we have been on this trip, I am able to speak with Liz directly. She sounds awful. She tells me she could go either way and isn't sure what to do. Master Sha immediately does a spiritual herb healing for her. He shoots light across the thousands of miles between us in this van in downtown Chicago and Liz in her hospital bed in Oregon.

April 7, 2002

I am home now in Sausalito. I call Liz. She tells me that two nights ago she had the most remarkable experience: she was cradled all night in Mother Mary's arms. Mother Mary told her she could go or could stay. It really made no difference. Liz decided to stay. She had felt the power of Power Healing enter her and give her the physical strength she so needed to continue to live. She told me the night of her surgery she had been pronounced dead. She hovered above her bed, watching the doctors and nurses move her body. She heard their voices. Before the surgery, she had asked them to pray with her and they did. She heard she was given ten minutes and had to make up her mind. This was the evening Master Sha commanded her soul to live. Today Liz, is home. In five days, I will drive to Oregon to pick her up so she can be with her friends in the Bay Area where her heart is.

Upon our return from the trip to Chicago, I email Liz a copy of the journey, in a sense to complete the loop. She was so present to me, and I prayed for her life. She writes back.

April 8, 2002 (email from Liz)

I am in tears... what other way can I express how deeply your experiences touched me? The insights with Peter and Master Sha are as penetratingly real to me as the experience of our love, sisterhood, and friendship. More continues to unfold for me as I explore the many nuances of this deep spiritual event. Last night, I realized how grateful I am for my disabilities, for only through them have I truly learned to be conscious, present, open to learning. Ah, the learning we both are experiencing... how precious they all are.

Thank you for sharing, dear one. ...I can hardly wait to see you. All is in Divine Order. Tonight, I will chant and pray until sleep takes hold. I love you.

Within five days from our return from Chicago, I take an overnight Greyhound bus up to Oregon, collect Liz in her van, and bring her home to our houseboat, where she lives and recovers for the next three months. She is such a survivor, having survived pancreatic cancer more than nine years earlier.

During these next months, Liz is often out of her body, peacefully exploring the universe. We realize that her ability to determinedly use her will and prayer to survive is important to convey to others. So, Liz and I together try to capture the chronology of Master Sha's healing command, "Let her live!" and Liz's inner experience. This is what we write.

Liz

The surgical team is praying for me... The veil thins and is nonexistent. I'm floating above the room and watching them deal with the monitors and saying, "Oops," "We're losing her," "She's gone." I watch them move my body as though it was a limp dishrag... almost like it was being folded up and put in the garbage can... like there was nothing there.

Me

When your daughter called saying you had only a 50/50 chance of surviving, Master Sha began to pray for you. He actually commanded, "Let her live!" He continued to pray for you for the next five days.

Liz

I'm very conscious of what I'm watching. I'm not quite sure that I'm ready or wanting to be separated from my body completely. The doctor asks me if I'll take the tube as I have a standing DNR. In a very commanding voice, he says, "Here's your choice! You have ten seconds." At that point, I believe they intubate me. I'm conscious of my wrists being tied down as restraints as I slip back into my body. I'm conscious of being completely dysphasic due to the tube. At that point, I leave again.

Me

The next time I speak with your daughter, she wants to let you die. I firmly contradict her position and say NO! Liz is not ready to die. She has work yet to do. I know you are unhappy in Oregon, but that does not mean you want to die now. I can tell your daughter is upset by me so vehemently telling her no.

The next day as I leave for our trip, I am feeling torn. You needed me more than ever before. You needed my love, healing energy, and encouragement to survive. It is a big test to count on the power of remote healing to be as effective as simply being beside her bed. The IC nurses and hospital administrators kept me at a distance, wanting the only contact to be through family. They didn't get that your daughter was letting you go.

Liz

Next thing I recall is waking up two days later with the tube out. The first thing I see are beautiful flowers sent by friends and a small guardian angel that my daughter has placed next to them from my altar at home. My daughter is standing beside my bed, bravely giving me permission to leave this world if I want to. I'm afraid I sharply rebuke her saying, "Don't go there! It's not time!" I'm totally hazed by morphine and have no idea what time of day it is. I have no recollection of the last two days. Morphine has distorted any sense of time and continuum. I know that people have telephoned me and had people in stitches because everything is a non sequitur. I was in the room a day and a half before they discover my lungs were filling up rapidly with pneumonia and once again I left my body. And once again the doctor demanded that I make a rapid decision about the incubation. My daughter said once again she had orders for DNR and I said forget it, I'm not ready.

Liz lives to tell her story for the PBS documentary crew.

Liz had an experience of Jesus hovering over her that happened the same time my soul connected so powerfully with Jesus. She saw him above her. Liz continues to heal and, out of her gratitude to Master Sha, she takes over running his office, answering phones, and producing fliers. She does this for about six months.

Two more years go by, productive and happy ones. Liz lives to see her first grandson born and his arrival seems to complete something most cherished for her. Within a month, her condition turns and she speaks of her readiness to "transition." Because I am her friend, I support her soul's choice, even though I will miss her terribly.

Days later, I am at her side in the hospital. She is agitated, reporting that the peacefulness she had gained has now changed to a new and last-minute effort to live. It is too late. Her body has deteriorated beyond recovery, even for a will as strong as hers. I somehow always knew it would come to this moment, where I am at her side for her passing. I take her hand and leaning close to her frail body begin to chant, "Mary, Mary, Mary, Mary." I remembered from her last near-death experience in the hospital in Oregon that Mother Mary had soothed her. As I chant Mary's name, Liz quiets. She subsides into silence until her full passing the next day. Bless you, Liz, for sharing so deeply with me your love of Mother Mary, for in your last moments, I am allowed to help you connect again. Our friendship has such love and mutual support. I will miss her.

I love you, Lizzie.

Dealing with Death and Dying

As part of my training as a healer, I watch death come to those who are in my healing/blessing groups. I have sought solace from Master Sha to understand more deeply how this comes to pass. Healing may mean the lessening or even disappearing of the physical and emotional pain. Healing may mean that the condition remains and that we are helping the soul to come to terms with this struggle. Healing means learning from the struggle whatever your soul needs to help complete its journey in this lifetime. If these lessons are not learned, we come back around again until the lessons are understood. This is the accumulating of wisdom and compassion.

So, when five cancer clients pass on, how am I to deal with this? Internally, there is grief for I knew each and every one of you. I looked into your eyes and saw your soul seeking guidance and relief. I reached back, giving hope and love. Did I fail you? I have only failed if I set myself up to play God. I did not do that, I merely helped you to deeply reconnect with your own soul and with the Universe. This is the healing of the soul, the very heart of our work.

To The Pioneers of Courage

> *As the green grasses emerge out of the cold earth,*
> *It is winter and yet there is new growth.*
> *In the dark and cold there is new growth.*

I reflect upon sharing these connections with Patricia, a breast cancer survivor. It was her last winter, yet she had the courage to see the new growth.

I reflect upon the woman in the wheelchair, her head bald and hidden under her cap. Once again, looking upward with light in her eyes, unable to clearly speak, yet clearly able to communicate her love.

I reflect upon the devotion of a couple profoundly committed to service during two years of his stage IV cancer, always smiling and so properly dressed, their pain barely showing.

I reflect upon the funny words of a talented gentleman, with his graceful and thin body, sharing his humor only months before passing.

I reflect upon a friend willing herself to health while the onslaught of her body's conditions placed her in a nursing facility. I bring to her a turkey meal with gravy just because she loves it so.

I reflect upon my dearest friend, Liz, a pancreatic cancer survivor for over nine years. I chant to her in her last speaking moments and bring the peace of Mother Mary.

I reflect upon dear Ida, one of Master Sha's Assistant Teachers, a woman of such wisdom, her eyes so deeply shining with a twinkle of inner vision.

Bless all these kind, courageous souls, all victims of cancer, all devoted to healing on the deepest level, the soul. They each knew, in various degrees, that they must make peace within their soul, peace and forgiveness of themselves and others. It was their time to go.

I love each of you. Some of me goes with you.

Please help me to guide, bless, and heal others. Please pass on to me your knowledge from the spiritual realm. May your next lives be easier.

Ida

One of the biggest challenges that faces Master Sha's Assistant Teachers and his close team members is to grapple with this question: How is it that we are "healers" and yet cannot "heal" our closest disciples? I will share only one story and allow a second to remain private.

Ida has been with Master Sha way before many of us came to him. She is a very spiritual woman, highly developed third eye, possessing deep wisdoms, and dearly loves Master Sha. Ida feels she has even been the mother of one of Master Sha's disciples in a past life. As she becomes ill, she keeps her condition hidden from all of us, including her own husband. For reasons we may never know, her cancer is her secret.

Because of her secrecy, our healing team does not do the daily chanting for her that we do for so many other members of the public. She admits only to Peter that she is ill. He immediately flies from Canada to the Bay Area to be at her bedside where he stays for five days, chanting, praying, healing, and giving blessings. Her condition worsens and she goes into the hospital.

I spent eight hours at her bedside that first day following her surgery. Our team has decided to do shifts at her bedside. Her husband does not understand the prognosis of her surgery, because she kept it secret even from him. I find her doctor and ask her to please explain to the family the seriousness of Ida's condition. Even to this moment, Ida kept her family in the dark.

A few weeks go by and Ida joins a teleclass. It is the first time she tentatively approaches this group of healers-in-training. Master Sha asks for someone to read her Akashic Record. I cringe. I recall how devastating my experience is when someone reads my Akashic record in public and tells of events that are awful—that I even to this day question their truth. I know how damaging this experience can be. I also know that Master Sha teaches cancer carries dark karma. So, I see the set-up coming for Ida, weakened by her condition, and so tentatively coming forth for support.

This is very painful. Peter's voice instantly interrupts the phone call before any reading can occur. I then take the moment and make reference to how painful these readings can be—perhaps this is not the moment.

We all recall this moment. Peter is ostracized. I am in trouble. A few of us offer healing prayers and chants each morning for the next weeks, hoping Ida will join us on this one-to-one basis. It is rare that she calls in.

This story is one we might all like to forget because it is so difficult to resolve. However, to the dear soul of Ida, I say I love you, may your soul find the peace, love, and light you so dearly deserve.

**(left to right) Anita Eubank, Shu Chin Su, and Ida Berk
taking a lunch break during the PBS shoot.**

It is not easy to look death in the face.

Master Sha suggests that I bow down in prayer and bring in each person who has passed on, asking God for clarification as to why they have passed.

"Dear God and Heaven's Team, dear Amitabha and Padmasambhava, could you give me guidance now? Dear God of the Almighty Universe and the Unlimited Galaxies of Many Lifetimes, please speak to me now. Help me to understand the passing of this soul."

"My child, you are clinging to form. The Essence of all Life is Light, constantly moving. You misperceive the vessel for the eternal light. Reverse your thinking."

Just as I turn to Master Sha for guidance and teaching, he turns me to the Universal Voice. Clever. I projected there are answers, as if a period at the end of a sentence. Wrong. Master Sha turns me to the Universe Voice so that I can enter into a process: the next step of seeking understanding through accessing and reading the Akashic Record, the book recording all deeds throughout all lifetimes of every soul.

Chapter 15

Up Close and Personal

This is a story for those who aspire to be healers. Sometimes, it gets way too close for comfort.

It all comes so unexpectedly. No matter how many times I hear the teachings on the temporary nature of our existence, I still count on having a life to live, my life— with Tom in our new home and healing center we are building in the country.

It is springtime. Tom is having his routine medical check-up. Everything looks fine. One final check is suggested, a colonoscopy as part of his preventive exam. So, we check into the outpatient clinic where the procedure is done.

While Tom is recovering from the sedation, the doctor enters the clinic room and looks me in the eye. "There is a mass in his colon. It is a tumor. I think it is cancer." I can scarcely believe his words. They enter my ears and then layers of shock won't let his words truly enter my reality. He continues, "I am sorry to give you such shocking news. We will know more when the biopsy results are back."

I feel our lives, our plans, our work, our intention, our hopes and dreams, our future—all pulled out from under us like a rug that is suddenly jerked and we fall down with a thud. My role as healer and loving spouse intertwine in this instant. Tom asks me clearly to make a commitment to keep this private. He poignantly states, "I do not want to be another Ida." He continues, "Do not say a word to Master Sha or anyone else." I feel it is my duty to wholeheartedly follow his bidding—this is his business and his life. However, it also means that I am alone in what now transpires. I am without my teacher and his blessings. I am without my spiritual community. I am on my own and I have to do a good job!

Five days pass quickly. We must be at the hospital by 7 a.m. for surgery. Within the hour, Tom is sedated with various IV's connected to his arm. I lean over him to kiss his forehead as the nurses continue to prep him for surgery. I place my hand on his belly, bringing my prayers for a full lower dan tian (energy center below the navel) to fill with light, giving him the strength to go through this invasive procedure. I tell him I will be with him in spirit the whole time. We part as the impenetrable steel doors separate the surgery unit from the rest of the hospital.

The Healing Begins [1]

It is now 7:45 a.m. I find a spot in a quiet waiting room and ask to close the door for a while. I casually mention the word "chant." That seems to gain me this privacy temporarily. I know I have three hours of pure healing practice in front of me. I know I must be as diligent and focused as possible.

I begin in prayer, asking God and Heaven's Team, countless Enlightened Master Healers, and Master Teachers to come. I feel tears coming up inside, for I am both the healer and the wife. I am the healer and the secondary victim of the illness. How can I be so selfish as to think about how much my own life is being affected? I fight back the tears and continue to focus on the prayer. I carefully call each Enlightened Soul and Healer and Teacher who has ever played any role in our lives to please come now for my dear Tom.

Focus. Focus. Be specific. I ask in detail for each aspect of the surgery to be surrounded by God's Light—the instruments, the scalpel, the clamps, the suture needles, the suctions, the staples. These are only the instruments. I ask the souls of the nurses and doctors to be successful, blessed, and filled with light. I ask the soul of the operation to be successful.

Then there is the procedure itself. First, I ask for each stage to be successful, to be perfectly executed—the initial incision, the moving aside ever so gently all the organs at the front of his abdomen, the cutting of the colon and the rectum, the reconstruction of a new wall that is free from any leakages, the gentle replacing of his organs, and the final suturing of the belly muscles and the skin.

Then, I ask for the results—that all cancer cells and all pre-cancer cells be removed totally, and entirely, from his body, and that these cells transform into their own liberation and into the light. I ask that anywhere within his body that there may be pre-cancer cells or any abnormal cells that they leave his body now. I ask that all his cells be healthy and radiant and cleansed in the light.

Then, I dedicate the merits for his healing. I ask that the merits of my practices, prayers, and service for others be dedicated to his healing. I ask that these merits be dedicated to the healing of all his wounds during this lifetime.

I move in time to a scene in the jungle of Laos where all six members of a special unit assigned to take Tom safely through the jungle are killed. Tom is the only survivor. I move in time to when he had to rescue his own men who were being killed by enemy gunfire from a position high in the karst (mountain hills) surrounding a valley. Tom had to do the job to stop the gunfire. His mission was to kill another human being. I ask God to please, please forgive him for these acts during the time of war when he was barely 26 years old. I ask to take on his karma so that the Akashic Record, the book in the Heavens, may be cleansed. I have learned much from witnessing Ida's soul journey: the inadvisability of taking on someone's karma and yet my love for Tom moves me to seek forgiveness on his behalf.

I feel darkness in my body and rise to go to the bathroom. I start to spit into the toilet and it turns to vomit. I am purging both of us.

I return to my chair in the waiting room and continue. It is now a half hour later. I am tracking the events in surgery. I can see their actions. The initial incision is complete and the job of slowly moving the organs aside has begun.

Suddenly, the presence of Quan Yin comes in. I feel the love, the compassion, the forgiveness literally coming down upon Tom and upon us.

It is so sweet and kind. I return to speaking to all the cancer cells. I see them moving out of his body in a cone shape with the wide end in his abdomen. There is a sucking quality to the golden light.

Yesterday, during our healing group when Sandy, one of my cancer clients was leading a healing for Tom, I saw this golden light in a cone for the first time. Never before have I seen light have a sucking motion. Hours later, when Peter speaks with me, he says he has seen a similar phenomenon. So today, this light is continuing to remove the cancer cells.

Next, I ask Jesus to please come. He places his hands on both sides of Tom's colon and lifts it up and out of his body. I see the intense light coming from his palms. Jesus then asks me to place my hands on the outside of his hands and together we are healing Tom's colon and bathing the entire area in pure light.

(This guidance comes directly from Jesus. At the time, I do not know about the healing procedure called "soul operation." Soul operations are introduced by Master Sha about six months after this event with Tom. The point being guidance can be direct.)

I understand at this time that I am in advance of the actual physical procedure and I am in the realm of prayer and intentionality of outcome. So, I must now slow down. Only an hour has passed and we have two more to go.

I pick up Tom's book on Buddhism to read to his soul. I find pages that are turned down and surmise they must be important to him. They are about the origins of Theravadan Buddhism, which is Tom's way from the early days of the war in Laos. I call in his first teacher, a monk whose monastery was across the Mekong River from the base where Tom's missions were initiated. This is where Tom went to meditate. This teaching brings him each day into the Emptiness.

I then ask the Soul of Emptiness to come and bring teachings to Tom, to fully Enlighten him as a result of this cancer condition and surgery and pain during recovery. I spend time in the Emptiness, and out of this Emptiness comes Sakyamuni Buddha directly to help Tom. I begin to see Tom's other lifetimes and connection with Sakyamuni.

It all makes sense in the spiritual realm. There is a relationship between Tom and Chuang-de Xu, Rinpoche, who is the lineage holder for the original Sakyamuni, the Enlightened Healer and spiritual teacher that I sponsored to come back into this country only four years ago. Rinpoche placed Tom and I together romantically on our first weekend together. Tom and I could feel the magic. Now I see the past soul connections.

Perhaps the reason for this cancer condition is to further strengthen Tom's spiritual journey, to move him to a more full and complete stage of Enlightenment. I pray for this realization to come to pass so that, together, we may offer more service to others. I pray for Tom to take this experience we are going through to bring him to teaching again as he has in the past. I begin to make sense out of all of this.

So, as I open Tom's favorite book on Buddhism, the very book he reads to himself each night before he goes to sleep, I find the Ode to the Lotus Prayer. I read this to his soul. The very last line is dedicated to bring practitioners to the Pure Land of Amitabha. The very same Amitabha that I pray to in all my healing work. The very same Amitabha that Master Sha also emanates. I did not know until this very moment all these connections! I feel so connected with Tom.

I am getting drained and decide to get a cup of coffee. Four hours have passed since we left home without any food. I am feeling dizzy and know I must stay focused.

In the cafeteria, one of the nurses recognizes me from the staff training sequence that I did in the hospital only several months ago. She asks me what I am doing today—is it a training? I tell her I am doing practices for helping my husband who is in surgery. Thumbs up, she gives me back in return.

I return to the waiting room. This is an important moment in the surgical procedure. It is the time of removing the colon section that has the cancer tissue. I am working with golden light surrounding the actual cutting of the tissue as well as golden light surrounding the entire area so that no individual cancer cells have a chance to wander back into Tom's body. I also bring golden light as a washing and cleansing element into Tom through his crown, moving slowly down through the entire body and out his feet.

A nurse gently taps me on my shoulder, saying she was just there in surgery and Tom is doing well. He will be another hour. I must focus for another hour.

I continue in my mind to work with great precision around removing this section of his colon, with the identification of just how far away from the visible tumor to cut, with the golden light encasing and protecting. This is such a crucial part of the surgery. This is the very reason why many cancer clients opt not to have surgery—the possibility that it can spread through the invasive procedure.

Now it is time to begin to suture the colon to the rectum. This is done with staples. I pray that each millimeter of connective tissue be tightly touching and that no leakages can occur. I pray that the scar tissue is thin and that the new wall works perfectly. Then, I see that there is some difficulty reconnecting the front side of the rectum. I work with this to come together more easily. It is giving the doctors some difficulty to make this suture smooth.

It is time to gently and carefully replace Tom's organs into their proper position, to help the excess air leave the abdominal cavity. The inner abdominal muscle and wall must be smoothly sutured, and then the outer skin.

I ask all the Healing Masters to remain with us until the procedure is complete. I continue to thank all the souls who love Tom and have been present. I continue to chant God's Light and God's Love for Tom.

It is now 11:30 a.m., three and a half hours later. I begin to walk in the hallway outside the doors to surgery. The doctor emerges and walks me into the atrium to give his report. "Surgery went well. There were no complications. I will know in two days about the lymph node report. However, I did not see any swelling in the nodes. The cyst I saw on the liver dissolved as I removed it, so I do not think it is cancer. I think it is only a cyst. So, it seems there is no spreading of the cancer. We will know more in two days."

I ask him about the suturing of the anterior near the rectum. "Yes, that was more difficult. It's rather like working under the engine of a car. You have to bend upside down. But it's done and all is well. You can see him in a few hours."

I thank the doctor profusely. I walk out of the hospital and burst into tears of gratitude, relief, understanding, peace, exhaustion, and love. That afternoon, Tom is up beside his bed doing Tai Chi. He tells me, "That wasn't so bad."

Three days pass. Just as we are expecting Tom to be released from the hospital, his pain begins to increase. His fever goes up. I apply cool compresses to his forehead and nape of his neck. At the end of the day, they take him to X-ray to check his abdomen for obstructions. The reports are negative. By the fourth day, Tom is in anguish, even with the continual flow of morphine. Tom goes in for a CT scan. The techs agree to let me accompany him into the room to help with moving his pain-ridden body onto the table. His discomfort level is so painful to witness. I continue, day and night, my healing blessing prayers.

We both are overwhelmed by the intensity and demands of the situation. The CT scan is also negative. Yet his fever increases, nausea sets in, and the pain now is nonstop. There is no respite. The doctor enters the room and tells us we have only hours to agree to an exploratory surgery. Something is very wrong, and the doctor does not know what it is.

The fast-moving conveyor belt of crisis is picking up speed, becoming increasingly precarious. Surgery is set for 9 p.m. I walk in the hall for these hours, doing visualizations of light, calling out to God for help, beseeching Jesus to help heal Tom. I call on all the souls of great saints and Buddhas. I ask my teachers—Master Sha, Master Guo, Rinpoche, Peter, Ida, Tarthang Tulku—please come and help us now.

Midnight comes and goes. The hall is dark and quiet. I am leaning against a corner next to the Recovery and ICU room, waiting, waiting in the still darkness of the night. I force my mind to continually hold the focus of light for Tom. I see him on a gurney, being wheeled into ICU. Tom is so shockingly still. His eyes are closed.

Oh, for so many days, hours, I watch him with his eyes closed and the qi barely moving within his quiet frame of a body. Now, the doctor approaches me and we sit together on a hospital bed in the hallway. "There was a leakage from his colon into his abdominal cavity. We couldn't see it because it occurred shortly after the first surgery and then closed up. The leakage was coming from the lower connection between his colon and rectum."

"Yes," I respond. "Do you recall that I had mentioned, after the first surgery, I was concerned about that spot?"

"Oh, now that you mention it, yes, I do recall. It is rather like climbing under the engine of a car to make a repair," he reiterates.

Inside, I note that my seeing is accurate. Yet there is absolutely no sense of pride about seeing accurately. There is only sadness in seeing Tom's pain.

That night, I am allowed to go into the ICU and assist with Tom's recovery. "Babe, what happened?" These are his first words through the anesthetic fog. I feel our connection. I feel honored that he is giving me his trust, that he is asking me to be his perception and his truth.

"Am I laying on a cabinet?" His back is still hurting from the many days of bumpy hospital mattresses. "Is this a MASH unit?" The room does have an air of disorder and chaos. The nurse is so stressed and uptight that when I call her name, she jumps. I note this classic "startle response" and know I must protect Tom from this kind of jagged care that hovers energetically in the room. It is now 4 a.m. and he is stable in his re-entry into his body.

I drive home looking at the vast night sky, so pristine and simple. I drink in this nourishment. My soul is deeply shocked by these days, and now weeks, of turmoil. I feel we are crossing a deep crevasse on a very narrow footbridge. We cannot afford one more "surprise," as Tom calls them.

Tom remains in ICU for another day. He has more tubes into his body than he did following the first surgery. Again, there is no warning as to what we will find. There is only the sudden reality, just as it has been since the first moment his doctor said he has a tumor and he thinks it is cancer. Now, after the second surgery, an IV line is placed directly into his upper chest. It has three small ports for receiving meds and IV's. His IV pole is filled with four different bags. He has a drainage on one side, making his original incision longer than before. He has a catheter and oxygen. It seems there are tubes in every direction.

The surprise is the colostomy bag that comes directly out of his intestines for elimination. Neither Tom nor I have the ability to ask questions about this bag. Questions such as, "Is it forever?"

Tom's world is now completely focused upon each visit from each nurse or attendant. His world has narrowed. He has no interest, or perhaps even recollection, of the mundane issues in our life. I try to tell him funny stories about the kitties at home. His eyes remain closed and his body still. He does not get up to stand. He just lies in bed. His temperature is elevated. He does not even sip water. Perhaps a single chip of ice will pass his parched lips. The doctor tells me we must go through four days of watchfulness for any abscess.

The narrow and precarious footbridge is ever so delicate and fragile. There are no options or creative solutions. We are on a journey that has picked us up out of our daily lives and catapulted us into this prison of brutality and terror. We both are making efforts to maintain positive energy and positive thinking. This is our agreement with each other. This is part of the reason we have chosen to limit contact with friends; we don't want to counter their shock or negative thinking. We are just too busy fighting our way through this.

Internally, I know I am terrified. I am terrified about losing our lives and our plans. I just want a chance to have a life together. I pray and pray and pray. I pray in the early morning. I cry and talk to God and pray for his healing and recovery. I pray during my sleep. I sit and watch him in his bed and continue to pray and to ask for healing blessings. I give him all the love I can give.

I must get him home! This hospital is no place to recover. I must get him off this morphine! I start cooking chicken soup and bringing it to the hospital. He can't even swallow a teaspoon full. It doesn't taste good. Something inside me rises up. We have got to get him out of here.

By now, I am sleeping nights in the hospital. I bring him sips of any healthy clear liquid I can create at home. One sip at a time. We fight to get the morphine removed. We fight each step of the way, together, for him to survive. Something snaps inside him and he begins to say enough of this. Our goal is to eat just one meal orally, and they will let us go. He does.

It all is a blur now. The recovery at home begins. He is so weak. Yet he is alive. Family come to visit. Friends begin to call. Master Sha calls wondering why he and I have had no contact. "Where have you been?" I tell him about Tom's illness and the surgeries.

He continues obviously upset, "I love you. You are deeply in my heart. I cannot forget you *[Tom]* design system for me. I cannot forget the two of you. When you have a disaster and you do not call me, I feel no good. You should let me know. I can offer a blessing to make things easier.

"I am sending now a soul software to you, a divine golden ball. Aubrey can see. What you need is vitality and energy right now. I send Divine Golden Ball to your abdomen and intestines directly. This is a permanent gift." As he sends this, I see a shaft of golden light go into his tailbone. Tom sees light.

Five months later, there is one more surgery to remove the bag. All goes well. We feel blessed to be regaining our lives. We feel blessed by the help given by so many who sent us prayers and included us in their healing circles. We thank each and every one who was at our side and held us in their hearts. We thank the healing masters who prayed for Tom and even today continue to help him.

Thank you. Thank you. Thank you.

Tom and me, happy and healthy.

Chapter 16

Portals to Enlightenment

This chapter is about the many doorways or portals through which one may realize Enlightenment. Enlightenment is a blessing, a gift from God. Enlightenment is also a gift through our teacher. This gift comes to us and is not within our control. Many offer opinions as to why it does come to us. Perhaps it comes due to our past lives and service. Perhaps it is quite random. I do not know.

However, the effort to cultivate Enlightenment is in our own hands. Here we can take responsibility, action, and do the practices. For the blessing aspect, we can only be profoundly grateful. For the practice aspect, we must be diligent.

We are suffering and seek freedom from this suffering. We also seek wisdom, truth, and understanding of this magnificent and boundless galaxy upon galaxy. Liberation into Enlightenment is available for all sentient beings—worms, humans, plants, and all forms of existence. To be in the human form is considered the best opportunity to focus our minds and hear the teachings that bring us to the portals of Enlightenment, because we are able to listen, cultivate, and realize the truths being presented.

Within this chapter, I will offer a series of ideas, quotes, experiences, and tools intended to be used by the reader as a progressive practice. Each section builds upon the former. Therefore, this chapter is a sequence to be read slowly and applied before moving on to the next practice.

What is Enlightenment?

The actual experience of Enlightenment occurs as our awareness rests in the state of our original nature, reflecting three qualities of our original mind, known as Rigpa—emptiness, pristine luminosity, and powerful undulating movement.

There are many levels of Enlightenment culminating with what is known as a "fully realized being." It is said that with each quantum leap of Enlightenment, the realizations of dimensions expand exponentially. Because I am only at the kindergarten level, I must address my definitions of Enlightenment from my direct experiences to date. Each of my Enlightenment experiences has dramatically changed my perspective, my consciousness, and I return to my daily life as a new me. I must be very clear here. I am suggesting a distinction between my experiences of Enlightenment and categories that are taught by others. For each of us, our experiences may be different from what we are taught or what others describe.

Experientially, I often enter into different qualities of emptiness. These qualities are different depending upon my awareness or how present I am within the sense of "gone far away." If the emptiness is simply one in which I "go to sleep" or have no awareness, this is a lower level of emptiness. If the emptiness is merely quiet, dark, or neutral in tone, and waiting, I call this the Unknown. Conversely, the true Emptiness, Void, or Shunyata experience is startlingly sudden in appearing before me. It is vast, light, infinitely still, and silent. Here, Emptiness is one of the three qualities that reflect an Enlightened Mind.

Years later, I experience the luminosity that is described in Chapter One. The luminosity aspect is the second of the three qualities reflecting an Enlightened Mind. The luminosity is akin to being in the center of the sun—blinding golden and white light from all directions accompanied by a sense of explosion and self is catapulted into every dimension at great speed. The experience of luminosity is all encompassing until there is no distinction between your self and the luminous. As I lose my sense of self that is still feeling explosion, because there is an exploding of a something, I become more and more at one with the luminous bursting light. Then the quality of speed shifts into a more gentle gliding, more smooth, and peaceful into the vastness.

Within the luminosity experience, there is a subsequent state of consciousness where the visual field turns into undulating and powerful movement. This aspect is the third quality that reflects an Enlightened Mind. It is the powerful undulating movement of the light. If you think of the undulating movement that is visible in heat, like the heat waves rising up off a black pavement in the hot sun, you will see the movement or energy that I am describing. Add to the heat wave the power of the center of the sun all in movement. Then multiply these forces of heat, energy, movement into a thousand suns and you will visual this third aspect of your original mind. This is the raw material from which we all originate.

These experiences are profoundly transforming, because they place a different perspective upon all that is usually within our minds. This perspective is vast. This perspective allows me to see more deeply, to have true compassion, and a deep sense of peace.

"It is possible to attain states of Enlightenment that may not be as extensive as Shakyamuni's awakening was, but are nevertheless liberating realizations of one's Buddha potential." (Jack Maguire, *Essential Buddhism, A Complete Guide to Beliefs and Practices,* New York: Pocket Books, 2001.)

In cultures far and wide, historic and current, there are oral traditions holding and preserving the secret teachings as to how one can realize Enlightenment. It is a gift from God. Anyone, at any moment, may receive this gift of spontaneous Enlightenment.

I have thought deeply for many years about the nature of this gift. How can I align myself to have even a chance of receiving Enlightenment, this sweetest gift from God? For some, this gift comes spontaneously. For others, it comes when in relationship with a high-level master.

How will yours come?

Can Anybody Realize Enlightenment?

YES! I say! Anybody can!

We are truly in the midst of a spiritual movement—a movement of spirit, of divine energy from the universe awakening so many people throughout our land. As I talk to people—regular people, not any specific group or religious order or dedicated monks, just "ordinary" people—I find that many of us experience tastes of Enlightenment.

Within traditional lineages, there are those who have dedicated their entire lives to the cultivation of Enlightenment. There are those who realize

Enlightenment while leading a lay life filled with family activities and the pursuit of material goods. Some of the former emphatically state the blessings are to be passed through the lineage only. There are ancient and lengthy discussions about whose way is the right way.

Crucial Considerations

❖ If your realization of Enlightenment arises spontaneously, or arises within a relatively new paradigm as distinct from the well-established spiritual traditions, who will declare your experience to be a genuine Enlightenment? In our modern society, this is quite possible.

❖ Be prepared to know there is spiritual competition and spiritual politics for those who are pioneers in new paradigms from those in more entrenched traditions.

❖ Following the recognition or declaration of your Enlightenment, who will help you cultivate further?

❖ Who will help you understand what stage of Enlightenment you have reached?

❖ How well can you sustain this Enlightened state while leading your daily life?

❖ These considerations are new to our culture as we are no longer living in the age of Buddha or Jesus or the ancient wise ones who lead the way. This is a new time.

The irony is that inherent within every human being is the most pure Buddha nature, Christ nature, God nature, and Divine Light. Once we enter the Oneness, there is no "right way" because there is no "other way." There is no conflict or duality. There is only blessing.

Some say Enlightenment is multi-layered. Some say that with "true Enlightenment" ego is fully transcended, not to return. This implies there is no regression back into states of ego. Yet, I have seen those I consider to be at some level of Enlightenment fall back into ego. This is a debate that reflects the level of Enlightenment rather than a perspective from a particular school of thought. Because there are many levels of Enlightenment, one may use the term "fully realized being" to indicate a very high level of Enlightenment. It goes much like an infant learning to walk—up, down, crash, up, down, crash. Ego, Enlightenment, crash, ego, Enlightenment, crash. Until one day, we master this first step, or kindergarten, layer of Enlightenment. Then life continues and the child now can run, jump, climb, and ultimately dance with grace. This is the same with Enlightenment. We get better at maintaining our balance. We learn to cultivate this consciousness into more advanced stages of realizations.

Portals to Enlightenment: The Possibility

An essential teaching of this state of Enlightenment is in the Heart Sutra, a condensed version of transcendent wisdom taught in Vajrayana Buddhism. For Vajrayana Buddhists, the Heart Sutra epitomizes what I have throughout this book called the journey of the soul to Enlightenment. This sutra, or teaching, gives us the seed idea that there is a lightning path, also known as the path of crazy wisdom, that can bring liberation from countless rebirths in a single lifetime. I offer these ideas as the first portal: the possibility.

Portals to Enlightenment: The Preparation

It is within your personal efforts and commitment that you can prepare for the Enlightenment journey. There is psychological work that will bring clarity and understanding as to your childhood. There is emotional work to come to forgiveness with other people in your life. There is physiological work to strengthen and build your energy centers. There is spiritual work to open spiritual channels and to clear your karma. This is all part of your homework and preparation.

It is also necessary to cultivate proper attitudes, behavior, and thought that lead to purity, compassion, humility, and gratitude. Give service: the more, the better.

Learn to meditate, pray, and chant. These are each ways to connect with the Divine in a soul-to-soul communication.

In the cultivation of these virtues of service, prayer, purity, compassion, humility, gratitude, forgiveness, and love, your soul will accumulate the merits that are needed to bring your soul to the level of Soul Enlightenment.

Soul Enlightenment, as defined by Master Sha, is what I would call a category of Enlightenment rather than an experience. There are many who are identified by Master Sha as having attained this level of soul evolution and standing, who also experience qualities of light and profound blessing. However, it may be interesting to note that research has not yet been conducted to identify what characteristics these students have in common that have been identified as realizing Soul Enlightenment.

Continuing within the paradigm of Master Sha's work, there are nine soul levels prior to Soul Enlightenment. Soul Enlightenment is gained through the accumulation of virtue or service. Soul Enlightenment implies that the soul will not reincarnate and thereby is liberated and will enter into a heaven realm.

Following this stage of Soul Enlightenment are another twelve levels that progressively demonstrate the degree of your purity, service, and transformation. Each of these levels demonstrates greater mastery and spiritual power.

In Master Sha's paradigm, there are three stages of Enlightenment. The second stage is Mind Enlightenment. Mind Enlightenment is our mind resting in a state of its original nature that is emptiness and luminosity. The third stage is Body Enlightenment. Body Enlightenment is when the entire physical body illuminates and rejuvenates each cell until there is a rainbow radiance present at the time of death.

To return to the earlier distinctions between personal experience and categories that I presented at the beginning of this chapter, I want to add these words: without the idea of the possibility of Enlightenment, how could I have moved forward? There is a place for the categories, concepts, the very idea of possibility that points the way. Your teacher brings you to the door. Then, your own personal experience IS what happens as you go through the doorway.

My teacher is the catalyst that brings the next crucial and so highly valued step. Through his blessings, transmissions, karma cleansing, and teachings, I am being prepared to go through the door. I must be willing to listen to his guidance with no prior attachments. Just listen and follow and trust, for he knows more than I know. He brings me the spiritual introductions, to God, to high saints, and to the entire soul world—directly! Then it is God who invites me into the Light.

Portals to Enlightenment: Seed Ideas

Following the introduction of any possibility is defining the goal and a detailed description of how to begin. In the journey of the soul to

Enlightenment, the goal manifests as emotional experiences such as peace, love, and clarity. These are a result of our consciousness gaining an understanding of infinity, of time and space in all directions. While this is beyond our conceptual comprehension, there is something within the very marrow of our bones that understands intuitively. We embrace the paradox: knowing and not yet knowing. This quality of paradox often accompanies higher or more expanded states of consciousness.

When a new experience suddenly overtakes us, even for a nanosecond, we have a taste of the unexplainable, a taste of something new and different. This totally new experience may be without reference in our own minds. By prematurely placing a word or an interpretation upon this new and momentary experience, we lose our pristine closeness to the original nanosecond. If, however, within that nanosecond, we can pause, without returning to our habits of mind, and if we can sustain this pause, we have an invaluable opportunity.

What I am introducing here are the basic building blocks, or the seed ideas, that guide us as we begin.

- ❖ The first seed idea is the possibility.
- ❖ The second seed idea is the paradox.
- ❖ The third seed idea is to suspend any interpretation. To suspend interpretation means to remember to not grasp too quickly, saying to oneself, "Aha, this is what they meant!"
- ❖ A fourth seed idea is to rest in the heart of the experience, one nanosecond and then another nanosecond and then another nanosecond without quickly returning to words and a sense of "I."

These are four examples of seed ideas that will guide you in the more expanded states of consciousness and the new experiences that will come. A seed idea is just like a plant seed. It is embryonic and yet contains the totality. A seed idea is like pollen that inseminates what otherwise would have remained dormant. Having been pollinated with a thought form, a possibility, a concept of potential, this seed idea germinates and comes to life. Initially, this seed idea may be very small, may be words heard in passing. Yet someday, this seed will grow into a tree. The tree matures and bears fruit that feeds the body in the physical universe, and a seed idea matures to bear fruit that feeds our soul. Each piece of fruit also then contains the seed. And so it goes, on and on, in a gigantic recycling.

Inherent within the seed is vast truth. A bare notion can give us great comfort as the actual experiences begin and continue. A seed idea tells us of distinct experiences along the path to Enlightenment.

- ❖ A fifth seed idea is to allow unexpected and spontaneous experiences to mature without grasping ourselves back from them with a thought or any sense of "I."
- ❖ A sixth seed idea is that luminosity (the experience of being totally consumed by infinite light in all directions), is the state of the pure mind. Luminosity offers the opportunity for liberation of the soul to not reenter the recycling of life. For this liberation to occur, the practitioner must be able to recognize and rest in the state.
- ❖ It is key to know that this state may come during your life, and it most definitely will come at the moment of death. This is why we need to recognize it and learn how to remain or rest within it, thereby allowing the liberation of Enlightenment to transpire. While this may be difficult, even knowing these ideas is helpful and gives us a sense of direction.
- ❖ The wisdom contained in seed ideas is invaluable for the journey of your soul.

Portals to Enlightenment: The Here and Now

The presentation of this seed idea requires its own section and will be accompanied by "how to practice" instructions.

Our busy minds, filled with thinking, ruminating, and repetition, leave no space between thoughts to simply be present. Life passes us by because our minds focus upon the past and worry about the future. This absentee condition even causes us to not see, feel, smell, or appreciate what is directly in front of our noses. This busy mind filled with beta thought waves and concepts, accompanied by musical refrains, robs us of our very moment to moment existence.

We need an antidote. We first must learn how to become present to each moment as it unfolds in our daily life.

In retrospect, going back 50 years, several concurrent movements transpired in both the East and the West. The spiritual suppression of Tibet caused His Holiness the Dalai Lama to flee to India for safety, not just for himself but rather for the preservation of thousands of years of meditative studies bringing Enlightenment to the human mind. At the same time in the West, the exploration of inner spaces of the mind was growing into a movement introduced through flower children, psychedelics, meditation, and soon to follow, Humanistic Psychology. The fact that these two movements in the East and the West happened at roughly the same time paved the way for the Eastern traditions to be transplanted in the hungry searching minds in the Western world. In fact, this transplanting was prophesized by the great Buddha Padmasambhava in 700 AD when he said, "When the iron bird flies, the Dharma will come to the land of the red men." The music of the Beatles also paved the way for the Eastern mystics to touch our hearts. Books by well-known American professors who traveled to the East seeking Enlightenment, such as Richard Alpert also, paved the way. He changed his name to Ram Dass, as well as changing his consciousness, and wrote *"Be Here Now."*

The timing was perfect for the concept of the Here and Now to take hold.

The German psychoanalyst Fritz Perls and his wife, Laura, introduced Gestalt therapy in Europe and New York. This approach to psychological healing quickly spread, especially in California when Esalen Institute offered Fritz a permanent home in which to conduct his workshops. The Here and Now captures the two principles upon which Fritz based Gestalt therapy.

Within a decade, a major movement in Humanistic Psychology spread to thousands of students who were granted degrees in Transpersonal Psychology, or the study of transcending the self. At the same time, Indian and Tibetan masters came to the United States and to Europe to establish centers for studying consciousness and the transcendence of the human condition.

From the scientific perspective, a comparable understanding was emerging in the study of quantum field theory. "The conception of physical things and phenomena as transient manifestations of an underlying fundamental entity is not only a basic element of quantum field theory, but also a basic element of the Eastern world view.... Buddhists express the same idea when they call the ultimate reality Shunyata or Emptiness or the Void...like quantum field, it gives birth to an infinite variety of forms which it sustains and, eventually, reabsorbs." (Fritjof Capra, *The Tao of Physics*, p.197-98)

Together, these movements form what is today a significant unfolding of Eastern wisdom as it applies to the Western mind and setting.

- ❖ The absolute foundation of any cultivation of consciousness must first begin by entering into the Here and Now. You must be present.
- ❖ The mind and body must still to then enter the senses. All meditative practices are based upon this foundation.

How To Find the Here and Now [1]

To enter the Here and Now, first breathe deeply, exhaling with a sigh. Now, focus upon feeling your feet upon the floor, then your seat in the chair, and now your hands upon your knees. Repeat this three times saying inside, "Feet, seat, hands. Feet, seat, hands. Feet, seat, hands." Each time, let your full attention go to that area of the body. Be aware of any pulsation in your feet, seat, and hands. Feel the texture of your clothing in these three areas. Feel the thickness of your own body.

This is basic training in focus. It also outsmarts your mind, because we give you something to do. Your thinking will quiet. You have dropped out of your busy head and entered your body. You are now more grounded and centered. Your awareness of sound outside of you will increase. You will feel your own body. Now you are here, and we are ready to begin.

This is a "being" state, rather than a "doing" state.

Portals to Enlightenment: The Boundless Expansion of the Now

What we have just done is an exercise to become present. For many years, people thought by being in the Here and Now was the total picture. It is not. This is a good beginning. It helps us to stop our busy minds, to slow down, to become present, and to cultivate awareness.

- ❖ The Now can itself expand infinitely. It is as if you must first find the microscopic moment in which the Here and Now actually transpires, and then enter into this ever so brief spot that in turn opens.

How to Enter Into the Expanded Now [2]

Where the Here and Now is a point and a place in time and space, the expanded Now melts out into the universe in a multitude of directions. Become fully present through your breathing and your senses. Visualize yourself as butter that is sitting in the warm sun. A gradually melting and softening comes and your form loses its boundaries, becoming larger. With this expanded melting quality, one must now learn how to settle down and rest quietly in this now. "To rest" is to cultivate an intimacy and an openness with the silence. This silence opens like a funnel to the Universe.

"Now" can carry our senses out of our self-orientation and into the Now within every form and sound about us in any given instant. Follow any sound and then see through your hearing. It is as if we begin to ooze out through our senses, beyond our physical body and into a fluid union with other forms.

The quality of awareness of this expanded melting in time and space brings us to a Portal of Enlightenment, a Oneness.

As children, we are more openly connected to the Now. We are joyous in our play simply because we are fully present. All that exists in our play is the warmth of freshly turned summer earth as puffs of dirt pop up between our toes. Time does not exist. There is a flow between our self and the universe. To be able to return to this childlike state with adult appreciation and awareness will enhance our Now. It will become a portal to greater expanded states.

Portals to Enlightenment: Entering the Invisible Energy Bodies

We have several invisible energy body systems. They manifest in our physical body as a network of delicate meridians, larger vessels known as the conception and governing vessels, and chakras containing highly condensed energy centers.

These systems are studied and healing practices applied through a plethora of modalities such as acupuncture, acupressure, medical Qigong movements, yoga, reiki, massage, polarity, Reichian bodywork, and others.

The healing systems found in Traditional Chinese Medicine are recently being researched in Western medical schools, using scientific methodology. Their findings verify the pathways of qi follow our physical circulatory system, culminating in the brain.

Medical intuitives can observe the movement or the blockages of our energy body. Because we live in a society that is so busy, we tend to be out of touch with these energy bodies. A busy mind and a stressful lifestyle become obstacles to discovering and cultivating our energy. Our society values money, outer success, sports, and material consumption. The cultivation of the inner states has been neglected until the spiritual Awakening of the counterculture.

What is lacking is an overall map of how these many approaches not only fit with one another, but also relate to Enlightenment and the Journey of the Soul.

How To Enter the Invisible Energy Body (Part I) [3]

I often introduce any teaching, healing, or blessing session with this Seven Breath Practice.

Now, we will quiet down our body and mind, moving from rapid thinking, or beta activity, into the more relaxed alpha and even theta state. We will take six or seven deep breaths.

Begin now. Inhale slowly. Breathe in the space just in front of you. Now, exhale slowly with your mouth open…down your body, down your legs, and out the base of your feet.

Again, inhale the space in this room, deeply, and exhale, mouth open, down your body, down the insides of your legs and out the base of your feet.

Inhale deeply the space around this building. Exhale, mouth open, down your body like a waterfall washing you clean inside, and out the base of your feet.

Inhale the sky, exhale washing clean like a waterfall in the rainforest, down your body, legs, and out your feet.

Inhale vast peaceful sky. Exhale like a waterfall in the rainforest, washing clean down your body, legs, and out the base of your feet.

Inhale vast peaceful space. Exhale like a waterfall down your body, legs, and out the base of your feet.

Inhale vast peaceful empty space. Exhale down your body, legs, and out your feet.

Sit quietly in this space.

This progressive relaxation and breathing practice opens the musculature, the mind, and the meridians.

First, let me discuss the physiological impact. This breathing flow—from the mouth, down the body, out the toes, into the vast sky, and back to the mouth—is a foundation for purifying the physical system. The entire nervous system switches from sympathetic to parasympathetic within the open mouth exhalation and visualization of space. Within the parasympathetic nervous system, the brainwaves produce alpha, delta, and theta. The parasympathetic nervous system helps us be more relaxed and connected with our senses. These are the brainwaves we produce progressively as stillness comes internally. It is in the stillness that further expansion of consciousness arises. In this manner, a simple breathing practice generates healing, purification, and then expansion. Note that anyone at any time can voluntarily switch from the sympathetic (more related to beta thinking, stress) to the parasympathetic nervous system.

This sets the stage for the energetic impact that produces the further opening of the central channel, the governing channel, and the conception channel.

The central channel (also known as the thrusting channel, chong mai in Chinese, and the Oma Tube to the Tibetans), runs through the center of the body, connecting the perineum with the crown. The open chakras rest like flowers attached to this central channel. The governing channel is the body's superhighway, the yang, du mai, and runs along the spine. The governing channel goes from the tip of the tailbone, up the back, and around the head, ending at the upper palate. It is this governing channel that may open with a Kundalini burst of energy. The conception channel is a yin highway, the ren mai, running from the tip of our tongue down the front of our body to our perineum. There are two important gateways within this teaching: these are small spaces between first, the perineum and the tailbone, and secondly between the upper palate and tip of the tongue. To learn how to conserve energy as distinct from running it out our crown chakra into the universe, you must practice closing both gates. This will enhance your energy and ability to "contain" higher frequencies of electrical charge and light. These practices are often called microcosmic orbit.

How to Enter the Invisible Energy Body (Part II) [4]

As you drop down into your body, you become aware of your belly from the inside. You can feel your abdomen, the thickness or density within your trunk, perhaps even the organs and muscles. You become aware there are sensations such as throbbing, tingling, warmth. Move your awareness into your hands and feet. Feel the tingling like little pinpricks on your skin. The longer your focus rests on these sensations, the more quietness and calmness gradually fill your mind and body. This is a deepening of the stillness.

Become aware of your body pulsating like a sea anemone in a rhythmic undulation. Each pulsation ripples down the tendrils of your arms and fingers, causing gentle multidirectional ebb and flow curving movements. These sensations move throughout your body. Follow these movements. Flow within your own capillaries. Remember, parallel to our capillaries are our meridians. The qi flows through the meridians. By intensifying this flow, we unlock our own energies. NOW you are in your inner energy body.

To clarify this progression: the biggest secret within the foundation of all practices to expand our consciousness is RELAXATION of body and mind. Dropping down into the body and then stilling the mind brings us into our senses. Once our focus is within this subtle level, we can feel our qi in our inner energy body.

Within the Seven Breath Practice detailed above, the mind moves further and further out into vast empty space. Where our mind goes, our qi will follow. Qi follows our intention. Qi carries intelligence. These qualities of qi have been kept secret for a long time. These qualities give an explanation as to how remote healing is done. Therefore, as our mind focuses upon empty space, we begin to move in that direction.

The seventh seed idea is that, first, you focus with intention and concentration to master your practice. Then, you relax your focus and open to receive whatever experience comes.

Portals to Enlightenment: Opening of the Spiritual Channels

Qi is the vital life force that runs through all living matter. Qi runs within the human body, following a pathway similar to the circulatory system as has been previously noted. Qi needs to be intensified and guided through specific channels to assist in the physiological aspect of Spiritual Awakening.

The spiritual counterpart of qi is light. Both qi and light are needed to open our spiritual channels.

Visualize a thick, healthy, green stalk running between your perineum and your crown chakra. Now visualize beautiful bursting ripe flowers hanging off this stalk, each on its own stem. This will give you an image of your chakra system. Qi feeds this system that is a blend of our physical bodies with our spiritual centers. In the Chinese or Indian chakra system, the healthy green stalk is called the Central Channel. The Tibetan system calls this the Oma Tube. The points of condensed energy that are like flowers hanging off this stalk are the chakras.

The activation of each chakra brings many of the physiological sensations described previously within the inner body energy system. As these sensations intensify, they will often be accompanied by pressure, throbbing, pain, and trembling. Usually, the trembling or shaking or even throwing of the body indicates you are still opening and the energy is trying to move through blockages remaining within your chakra system and muscles. It is often a sign that we are still trying to control our experience. As we open and clean out this system, there will be less shaking. As an electrical conduit, you are progressing from 110 volts and upgrading to jolts of 220 volts. It is a process of training, education, practice, and rewiring to feel at home with the intensity of energies that come.

Using a Chinese format for identifying the chakras and their functions, there are five centers, or nadis:

1) Zu Qiao (for creative mind power)
2) Third Eye (for inner eye seeing)
3) Heart (for compassion, soul communication, and direct conversations with God and Buddhas)
4) Lower Dan (for physical powers; also known as the Kath to the Sufis)
5) Snow Mountain (for increasing immune system, strength, and activation of kundalini)

In this format, the body is divided into three primary areas called dans: Upper Dan Tian (from top of head to upper chest), Middle Dan Tian (from heart area to navel), and Lower Dan Tian (from navel to perineum).

To this format, let us add from a Tibetan perspective the crown chakra and perineum (base chakra). The reason to specifically add the crown (top) and perineum (base) is that they are essential gateways. The perineum is a powerful energy center for sexuality, fire and explosives needed to burst open the green stalk or the Oma tube that is directly in front of our spine. The energy that is activated moves up this tube to our crown.

Once at the crown, the energy can burst through and out into the universe. We do not want this kind of exploding, for we wish to guard this precious energy and tame it for our further cultivation. At this point, then we wish to re-circulate the power by using the Chinese Qigong practice microcosmic orbit. Visualize a tube of energy moving from above the crown, down the front of our body, and up the backside in a circulating pattern. The cycle can also be visualized going down the back and up the front. These two directions have different functions and bring different results. Up the back will move the energy and light from the power center at the base of the spine and will feed our third eye abilities. Conversely, moving the energy and light up the front and down the back will aid in the rejuvenation of the physical body and is food for the soul. The latter is a more yin energy, bringing the softness of saints.

We can also visualize this same tube making a slightly larger orbit several inches outside our physical form. Once we graduate this orbit to a much larger size, it is known as the macrocosmic orbit, for it moves in expanding sizes between us, the earth, the sky, and the planets. In a similar manner that energy moves around atoms, the micro and macrocosmic orbits move around us.

In a previous chapter, "Opening Spiritual Channels," I described several experiences of what can occur as a chakra opens and our kundalini awakens. The powers, or siddhis, that accompany these openings are only indications that you are on the right path to Enlightenment. It bears being said again, that if you fall into attachment or pride with any particular ability, this ego grasping can cause you to be sidetracked off the primary goal. Visualize a river that is deep and rapid. As it moves towards its destination, you can be carried along. However, you can also be jettisoned into a back eddy. That which has been given to you as a gift now becomes a prison.

"With the breakthrough of the physical Nadis and Chakras one begins to see the union of space and wisdom: that is, the non-substantial quality of the perceiver." As this sequence of Enlightenment continues *"the sharpness of insight and the notion of 'being wise' are united...the pulsating quality of the energy is diffused...the notion of freedom itself has been freed, so that the true perception of the Dharmakaya* (dimension momentarily experienced at time of death as empty, unconditioned truth) *is seen as extremely realistic... This is the end of the journey, which need never have been made. This is the seamless web of what IS."* (Trungpa, Chogyam, 1972-73) [5]

How To Activate Your Chakra System (5 approaches) [6]

Here are several modalities I have tried. The most powerful and effective will assist you in the opening of our spiritual channels. Here are five approaches:

1. Reichian Breath or Bodywork. This breath work comes the closest to energizing the Eastern chakra locations. There is a systematic removing of body armor (muscular holding) and reliving of past emotional traumas. Then a rush of energy begins to move through that segment of the body. There is a gradual cultivation of ability to sustain higher and more intense energy, as well as greater pleasure and vulnerability. For the physical and energetic aspects of opening ourselves, this approach is highly recommended. For practitioners who are already moving energy, the next stage is the progression of greater electrical charge and then more intense light to flood through the body.

2. The Tibetan practice of d'Tumo breathing builds up pressure in the lower belly that then shoots up the Oma tube to the head. This is done through holding the breath as long as possible while visualizing fire in the belly and ice coming down from the head while doing a sucking motion inside your mouth. The fire and ice meet in the heart. This is a powerful practice that should be done in the presence of someone who can carefully guide you. *[See How To in Chapter 7]*

3. The Qigong practices specifically help to build the sense of qi flow in the body. These practices are most beneficial for containing the energy and moving it in an arc around the body by going up the spine, over the top of the head, down the front, passing the perineum, and then returning to run up the spine again. This direction can be reversed. These are known as the microcosmic orbit.

4. However, the point where the qi flow directly opens the spiritual channels is done in the following manner. Sit cross-legged on the floor. Place your hands on your knees for balance. Begin with your spine straight. Rotate your body slowly in a circle, beginning in a small circle with just your head and shoulders. After you have done this for several turns, include your ribs and waist. Each circle becomes progressively larger. Now, include your hips and let your head come as close to the floor as possible. This last circle is a wide arc. Reverse direction and begin from

your hips going upwards. Again, each circle becomes smaller until you only are moving your head forward, side, back, and side. As you come to a close, sit quietly with your eyes closed, hands on your knees, and spine straight. Go clockwise and then counterclockwise an equal number of times.

5. The Zhi Neng Medicine tradition has many tools for opening our chakras or energy centers. One of the simplest and yet quite powerful is the yin-yang hand position. Place your hands with your left thumb inside right hand touching the palm; right hand closes over top of left hand. This position is to be held at the energy center you are trying to activate (third eye, heart, lower dan tian just below your navel, or snow mountain just at your tailbone). Visualize light coming into this area from 360 degrees. Speak to the soul of that area and ask it to open, fully open. Each center has a helpful sound or chant. For the third eye, chant "EEEEE;" for the heart, chant "ARRRRR;" for both the lower dan tian and snow mountain, chant "JOEJOEJOEJOE."

Portals to Enlightenment: Facets of Space

Thus far, the practices presented have laid the foundation to quiet us, help us drop down into our body and our senses, and to start increasing the energy that is pumping through our body. To open our spiritual channels and our chakras, we need more energy or Qi running through our physiology.

An analogy is we are wired for 110 electrical current and through various practices we increase our tolerance to run 220 through the same system of our physical body. Once we have this increased tolerance, we are ready for more light that comes as part of our consciousness expanding.

Concurrent with the increase of qi and light, we move into different facets of space where there are no thought forms. This is the first practice within this section on space.

I will present here a logical progression of four simple, yet distinct practices that can build one upon another. Cumulatively, they open the mind into its natural state of emptiness, luminosity, and powerful undulating movement of Enlightenment.

To open our minds, we must loosen the grip of control and dissolve the concepts that form is permanent and that "I" am separate and distinct. We need to relax our brainwaves and our nervous system to allow a more fluid relationship with the universe. Within the paradigm of physics, we can easily understand that molecules in gaseous form are more active than in liquid form. And molecules in liquid form are more active than those in solid form. By observing steam, water, and ice, we understand the differences between states of form and the basic nature of transformation. Consider that our physical body, our cells, can subtly transform constantly throughout the day and night in a similar manner.

Consider this contemplation: As you inhale air, at what point does it become you? When you exhale the air in your lungs, at what point does it become part of the universe no longer belonging to you? Once we open to perceiving this constant transformation from form to non-form, we can broaden this formula to see it at play not only within my personal body, but also at play within all aspects of our universe. This will help us to understand that we are part of a process of movement. Within this process, there are particular moments that become doorways to deepen our understanding of the underlying principles of the universe—form and emptiness are interchangeable.

Space Between Thoughts

The contemplation suggested above is a quiet sort of thinking. When you spend time in this more calm and quiet place, you can watch the process of how you think. This is not about what you think or the content of your thinking. Rather, this is like taking a microscope to examine what is going on in your thinking process in this second and now this next second. Therefore, within the Here and Now, within being aware of the present, you focus upon your thinking process.

We are in the habit of having many thoughts, or what is called a busy mind. This busy mind has a grip upon us. It is our rational, cognitive, logical function. There are other functions of the mind that must now come into play for our consciousness to expand. These are the qualities of intuition, discrimination, and awareness. As we find these qualities, we will also find freedom from our own repetitive thinking.

Another way of saying this is that we are now moving from our ego being in control to our soul becoming captain of our ship. Our soul remembers freedom, space, and light. Our soul has, a long time ago, been in limitless emptiness and light. Our soul yearns to return.

This is why we must tame our minds.

How To Find the Space Between Thoughts [7]

First, quiet yourself down, relax, and breathe. Now, turn your focus to your thoughts. In so doing you may see a multi-layered soundtrack. One track has a thought that is concluding. A second track may have a thought that is just starting. A third track may have a thought in the middle. A fourth track may have music. A fifth track may have an image.

We need to observe how these tracks are overlapping. Then, we slow it all down by, once again, relaxing, breathing, and feeling with our senses. Notice your thinking process is a multi-layered soundtrack with several different thoughts all at the same time. Now, add to that there are pictures and possibly music. You may be shocked when you first discover how busy you are inside. A thought will be just beginning as another thought is ending. Gradually, quiet your mind so that there is only one single thought. Watch it rise, grow in full concept, and then begin to recede. This is the moment to catch. Look to the space between your thoughts. This is a moment where nothing has begun to arise as a thought. It is also a moment where the prior thought has completed itself. Between the thoughts is a potential doorway into the Void. Rest in this space without any self-statement or any referent to "I." The longer you can rest here, the greater the possibility that your awareness, not your thinking, can allow you to open further.

> ## *How To Look into the Space Between Forms* [8]
>
> A second focus to cultivate is to look to the space between forms. Let your eyes go loose. Let go of grabbing your focus upon any form. It is a bit like daydreaming, where the eyes also have a loose focus and you are vacantly staring off into space. Now, turn your awareness to the space between all forms. If you are looking out upon trees and grass, look to the space between the trees. Pretend you are a scuba diver and you are swimming in the space between the trees. This will open you to the formless awareness for indeed emptiness is without form.

Space of the Sky into the Emptiness

Space, for our human mind, is about how close many of us can come for a referent to the experience of emptiness. In the following section, I will present three sequential meditations that each build upon the previous one. When practiced in this manner, the results are most powerful.

Once you are resting in stillness or the space between thoughts, you can practice two very high-level teachings: AH Meditation and Sky Meditation (previously introduced). These are from the Vajrayana tradition and were passed on to me through Tarthang Tulku, Rinpoche of the Nygmapa Sect. Usually, these two meditations are carefully protected and given out only to dedicated students. However, Rinpoche chose to do his own experimenting with the Western mind to see if we could realize states of consciousness similar to those of his Tibetan disciples. He provided a two-month intensive course of study in 1972. When used correctly, these two meditations can bring you into the Void, Shunyata, or Emptiness.

AH Meditation

AH is a powerful and profound Tibetan letter. In Sanskrit, the letter AH means the Void, the Emptiness, Shunyata. AH is the sound of the Void.

AH is the shortest version of the Heart Sutra, the essence of Prajnaparamita, the all-encompassing wisdom teachings coming from Shakyamuni Buddha's Enlightenment. It is said that the level of Buddha Enlightenment may be realized only through the teachings of the Heart Sutra. You can see, therefore, that this particular sound has great profundity.

How To Do the AH Meditation (Part 1) [9]

1. This meditation must be done for a minimum of 24 hours to feel its impact. The result will catapult your consciousness further than many other practices. It is well worth this effort. This meditation goes directly into dissolving your self-image.

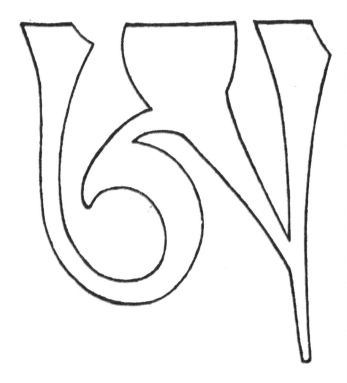

2. Copy this letter on an 8 ½ x 11 piece of plain white paper. Outline the letter AH with a black felt tip pen, making the entire background around the AH black. The AH is to be white against an all-black background. In this way, the AH will stand out visually.
3. Place yourself in a dimly lit room with a candle set to your left side. Place yourself two feet away from a mirror so you can gaze

at your own pupils. On your right side and slightly above your forehead, place the symbol AH on the mirror.

4. Sit quietly and relaxed in front of the mirror. Gaze into your pupils until you are quiet.

5. Now, turn your gaze to the letter AH. Let your eyes follow the outline of the symbol. Trace it in your mind until you feel you have it clearly memorized.

6. Now, let your eyes go loose so that the memory of the complete symbol impacts upon your eyes. This is as if you are looking at the entire image and letting it settle into your memory.

7. Return to the mirror. Look directly into your own pupils. Place your memory of the letter AH upon your pupils. If you feel you are losing the shape, glance again at the sheet of paper. The purpose here is to invoke the Emptiness within your own pupils.

8. Try to see the symbol on the blackness of your own pupils. It is even better when you firmly develop the ability to look at yourself with the AH in the darkness of your pupils. Now you are ready for the second half of this practice.

How To Do the AH Meditation (Part 2) [9]

1. Now, return to the mirror. Put yourself in the mirror looking back at your physical body. You have now entered the mirror image of yourself.

2. Become the pupils in the mirror looking back at yourself where you were originally.

3. Stay in the mirror. There may be visual distortions, images, and blackness. Pay no heed to any of these. Just continue. Try to stay here for the rest of the meditation. You will have a definite shift in your perception of yourself. This, in turn. impacts the mind and shakes us into letting go of the perceptions that limit our mind.

4. Continue for at least one-half hour for a couple of weeks before you move into Part Three: The Sky Meditation. For best results, build the practice to 24 hours.

Sky Meditation

The second, most powerful meditation is the cherished Sky Meditation. I must laugh sometimes, for when I mention this meditation to serious dharma students, they don't want to admit it even exists. It is a secret. However, Rinpoche gave it to us many years ago with full empowerment to teach it to others. It is with deep gratitude to him that I pass this on to you as it happened for me.

How To Do Sky Meditation [10]

1. Go outside or place yourself in front of an unimpeded view of the open sky. Place your body in such a position that you can totally and deeply relax. Close your eyelids halfway. Maintain full awareness at all times. Do not fall asleep.
2. Quiet your mind. When you feel both your body and your mind are quiet and deeply relaxed, focus your eyes on space in the sky. Recall the letter AH from the first part of this practice. Again, this is a quality of invoking the Emptiness or the Void.
3. Let go of the letter AH and focus upon the distant sky and the space. Each moment you feel your eyes grasping or settling upon a particular point in the sky, cut through that point as a knife through butter and go further out into the space. Continue cutting through again and again until there is no grasping. Relax and open.

Do this part of the practice for a minimum of 30 minutes for several months. This is a very high level and secret practice. It is powerful.

[See Chapter 4, "Good Teachers Hurt" under Tarthang Tulku, Rinpoche section to see what happens to me during this practice.] With this practice, I enter the Emptiness that transforms my consciousness for the rest of my life. It is such a distinct experience, different from any other.

Suddenly—oh so suddenly—the vastness comes upon me with an immense power. It comes with a speed from way beyond my awareness of its special dimension. The moment of transition is instantaneous, changing into a smooth, somewhat gliding quality of infinite stillness. A stillness that is notable by the absence of anything at all, a quality of hush as you are invited to listen oh so quietly and attentively. A suspension of all energy, activity, motion, or any quality that previously had characteristics. It is nothing. It is void. It is THE VOID.

I do not know how many minutes, or any time increments, go by. I am in the dimension of neither time nor space. I am completely merged into the nothingness of the Void. There is no me, no thought, no awareness of self. Perhaps some aspect of awareness does yet remain. I ask myself, is there some awareness, because of the next transition during this meditation on the hill.

Portals to Enlightenment: Out from the Emptiness

Thunderously, all emptiness is filled with the image of the Buddha Padmasambhava. I say "thunderously" because of the power of thunder and how it comes from the space of the sky without any warning. Padmasambhava, the great Guru who brings Buddhism from India to Tibet, the great father of the Vajra teachings, appears to me and fills the entire sky. This is a large sky as I am on the hill and there are no obstacles from East to West to South in my view. He is that enormous! He is dressed in fine robes of brilliant color, seated in meditation pose, adorned with sacred crowns and jewels, holding his vajra bell and dorje. These two objects help to identify him. The bell calls us to listen for dharma teachings and the dorje is a symbol for cutting through our ignorance. And he was gone!

I go to my teacher, Tarthang Tulku, Rinpoche to tell him of this experience. He just smiles and says, "I wish I had that good a connection with Guru Padmasambhava!" I know his words are tongue in cheek. It is Tarthang Tulku's connection that brought this powerful experience to me. This is an intuitive knowing. I have no knowledge as to how this phenomenon works.

For my next 30 years, I do daily mantras for Guru Padmasambhava. He has not returned in this manner. Maybe sometime he will. It matters not, for I see his blessing in my daily life on a continual basis. When I seek a parking space, I do his mantra and always find a spot. When I am driving too fast and my intuition tells me there is a police car tracking speeding automobiles, I do his mantra and do not get a ticket. Whenever I drive, I do his mantra. Every morning when I wake up, I do his mantra. When I pray for others, I do his mantra.

When I visit Tibet with my son, the night we arrive is a full moon. We can see from our hotel window the hills and caves that are said to be where Padmasambhava sought retreat and quiet. Our first day in our pilgrimage to this sacred land, we go to the monastery of Padmasambhava and I am able to gaze upon a golden statue over 80 feet high. As I write this passage, there is a hundred-year-old thangka of Padmasambhava above my head.

The experience of Padmasambhava coming to me out of the Emptiness stays with me, daily. This experience is most sacred.

What is the deeper meaning of this experience of entering into The Void and the arising of an Enlightened Master Teacher from out of The Void? This has taken me many years to understand, and I will share this with you now.

The teachings say that when your Shi Fu or Master Teacher comes to you OUT from The Void, this is when you are being taught directly by the Soul World and the Heaven Realm. This connection to the highest saints, buddhas, deities is brought to you THROUGH your physical teacher or Guru. Your teacher is the bridge.

Most of the physical teachers who are lineage holders within their tradition in Buddhism will teach their students about the arising of the Shi Fu. However, they teach that the Shi Fu comes to the guru in retreat or during a special meditation to bring wisdom teachings that, in turn, they will now pass on to the students. They teach their students that this happens primarily to the teacher only. So many of us are led to believe in this hierarchy that is both true and yet misleading.

The teaching from Master Sha regarding Shi Fu (spiritual father) is that while he helps you establish the connection with your own Shi Fu, you have the power at any time to directly hook up and receive wisdom teachings and guidance. His teachings about flow are HOW to communicate with your Shi Fu or any Soul World Enlightened Master Teacher.

This is a most delicate matter. Indeed, it is essential to cultivate a deep respect and gratitude for the bridge, the blessings, and the transmissions that are possible only through a teacher because they are more advanced than we are as students. To cultivate these qualities is a vital part of our opening and aligning with the Oneness of the Universe.

Yet, it is also true that the connection between our own Buddha Nature, and all aspects of the Divine is and always has been in place. We already are connected with the Saints, Buddhas, and highest Enlightened Masters in the Soul World or the Heaven Realm. We need to renew our connection.

We need help to remove the many layers of mud, confusion, conditioning, concepts, and separation that have accumulated within us over countless lifetimes. We need to find those conditions that will remove our obstacles, ignorance, and ego, placing us in auspicious moments that are the Portals to Enlightenment.

There is a delicate balance between needing a teacher to bring us to the door, respecting the blessings and teaching that are given to bring us to that very door, and trusting our own innate connection with the Divine. All mortals have egos. Use your common sense. The ability to hold these ideas that have an energetic push/pull between them is one of the qualities necessary to travel this road. There is no conflict. Open your arms widely and allow different notions to co-exist.

We are connected with the Divine AND we need our teachers AND our teachers are everywhere and everything. Our teachers know more than we do AND the innate wisdom rests within each of us. Paradox is a quality of expanded states of consciousness.

Portals to Enlightenment: Realization of Our Original Nature

What does it mean to (a) have a realization, and (b) to understand our original nature?

A realization means deeply understanding throughout our entire being, a quality of "Aha, I got it!" A realization instantaneously places you on new ground. Beyond internal doubt and self-questioning as to its authenticity, a realization has such a profound clarity that you have no motivation to seek external recognition, approval, or publicity. A realization is unshakable. A realization makes both concepts and belief systems appear as shallow as clothing you put on your body to be stylish. A realization means you are willing to accept your own wisdom and what accompanies it. There is no waffling with personal insecurities or pride.

The actual instant where you accept this realization is a most important step. Here, you enter a new level of consciousness that must be claimed to go further. You acknowledge your nature. You no longer look outward to others to perceive their Buddha nature at the exclusion of your own Buddha nature. It is a mental jump into becoming your own Buddha nature. So, a realization, while it occurs in an instant, must now be integrated to fully become the new ground for further expansion of consciousness.

Original means our place of origin. From whence have we come? This implies a place and a time when you perceive this from the ego conscious state. However, once in a place of "realization of our original nature," part of the wisdom and knowing is that there is no place and there is no time. "No place" undoes all spatial dimensions. "No time" moves us to simultaneity of all occurrences within this nanosecond. This is more enormous than past, present, and future because these three are still linear. Simultaneous time has no time.

From whence have we come? From whence has all that I perceive—the trees, the birds, the earth, the sky—come? An aspect of realization is that trees, birds, earth, sky, and myself are in form that is in the process of decaying and reconstituting, moving between form and formless in differing rates of time. Thus, I may as well be formless wind, for indeed at some point I shall be and have been. Do I not breathe even when in the human form? At what point is my breath me and at what point is my breath merely wind? Form and formless are then facets of a dimension we call time. We now realize time does not exist. Time and form are concepts coming from our limited minds to attempt to understand something from a small and limited consciousness.

According to the scope of our realization, different aspects of this or different levels of consciousness come to us. Hence our realizations come in waves throughout our lives. They can also come in a condensed manner.

We originate from the Source, the purest center of Oneness that creates and subdivides into the entire universe, all galaxies, and beyond. This is our Home. It is beyond any form or dimension and encompasses all form and all dimension.

How To Focus Upon Your Origination [11]

We hunger and long for reconnection with the love, truth, peace, and joy of our original mind. Our origin has no time, no space, no form, no non-form. This does not leave much for a point of origination.

Focus inward and contemplate upon "our origin then has no time, no space, no form, no non-form." You may feel your mind being sucked inward from 360 directions to a tiny point within the center of your brain. Only so much can be pulled inward. Suddenly, there is an explosion of such power and magnitude back outward 360 degrees that you blast open moving up through the top of your head. Blast open! Explode! Fragment into pure light! Melt further. Floating. Quieting.

Enter the Oneness.

Realization of our Original Nature is the understanding of this Oneness in its pristine and undifferentiated Isness. It is with a Pure Mind that our consciousness can open to this high-level wisdom, embracing our innate Buddha nature that arises, is never-ending, luminous, undifferentiated, and empty.

Portals to Enlightenment: The Bardo

What is being discussed in this section pertains to the higher stages of Enlightenment. There are many opportunities to realize various stages of Enlightenment. Because we will all experience death, it is important to include this section of using the stage of our final breath as a practice to liberate our soul.

Liberation is the freedom to no longer be endlessly repeating the cycle of birth and death. To realize the state of Soul Enlightenment is to enter the state of liberation of one's soul, removing you from the cycle of birth and death. This is the purpose of Master Sha's work: to bring all souls into Soul Enlightenment.

The moment of death is an optimal moment of total liberation from the wheel of life, the cycle of death and rebirth. It is optimal because we are freed from our physical body, the heaviness of its pain or constraints. We are freed from our grasping to this life, our goals, families, and material attachments. We have already passed the point of grasping and are moving forward into death.

Having lightened our load, so to speak, gives us greater suppleness as our soul begins to soar. Perhaps you have seen the drawing of Michaelangelo depicting the passage of the soul out of the top of the body. This is where our soul is now poised.

If you have been with a loved one who is at the door of death, you may have witnessed an extraordinary quality of peace. They are already entering the place of their origination. It is beyond seeing the light at the end of the tunnel because there is a recognition of coming Home. The unconditional love, the luminous light, the returning Home moves the soul profoundly. There is bliss and rapture. We see the intrinsic nature of everything, in its *"naked, unconditioned truth, the nature of reality, or the true nature of phenomenal existence."* [12] (Sogyal Rinpoche, 1992)

I quote from this bestselling book because of its simple and essential message that teaches us:

- ❖ HOW to use the experience of death for our liberation.
- ❖ My experience of Luminosity is a taste of the Clear Light state.
- ❖ It is essential to recognize these Enlightenment experiences while we are alive.
- ❖ Fortified by our Enlightenment experiences during our life, we will be better prepared to enter these states upon our death.
- ❖ The key then becomes cultivating awareness EVEN WHEN THERE IS NO EGO, NO SELF, NO PHYSICAL BODY, AND WHEN WE ARE DEAD.
- ❖ We need to practice this while we are alive.
- ❖ To be able to have this experience while still alive brings a familiarity that, if one is able to stay aware and awake as death comes, we will recognize this moment and be able to consciously rest in the luminosity that leads to liberation from countless future lifetimes.
- ❖ How long the soul can rest here is a factor of how diligent has been the preparation of one's practice. This is known as cultivation.
- ❖ *"Liberation arises at that moment in the after-death state when consciousness can realize its experiences to be nothing other than mind itself."* Kalu Rinpoche [13]

Portals to Enlightenment: The Gift

Ultimately, Enlightenment in its many levels is a gift, a culmination of preparation, diligent practices, and blessings from God, the higher spiritual realms, and through your teacher. Yes, I know there is also spontaneous Enlightenment where there is no physical teacher at that particular point in time. May the doorway always be open to this spontaneity!

There are teachings in Christianity—"God helps those who help themselves."—that speak to our role, our hard work, our efforts that invoke the blessing from God. There are also teachings in the Sufi tradition—"Trust in God and tie your camel."—that speak to the simultaneous and often paradoxical relationship between divine trust and using your common sense with fellow human beings. Both of these quotes tell us much about our human predicament while we strive for direct contact with God or the Universe.

It is this very predicament that must be embraced—total love and trust balanced with common sense and effort. The Buddhists might also add the ingredient of non-attachment to the outcome! So, work hard and expect nothing.

When and if the gifts come to you, don't be prideful or identify with them. When you fall into this trap, they stop coming. Instead, be steadfast and compassionate.

The Gift of entry into the Void came to me through the guidance of Tarthang Tulku, Rinpoche. The gift of Luminosity came to me through the guidance of Master Zhi Gang Sha. 30 years were to pass between these events.

Portals to Enlightenment: Universal Service

Unconditional universal service brings the virtue necessary to realize Soul Enlightenment. Virtue is the coin of the realm within the soul world. Virtue counterbalances negative karma.

To offer unconditional universal service means to focus upon others and to forget about your self. Forget the "me, me, me." In so doing, you will discover your heart opens even further and where there was empathy there now is compassion.

In offering universal service to God, to the Divine, to the infinite Source of our creation, we are already in a state of connection and of alignment between our own souls and God. The deepest purpose of our lives is to offer universal service, in this life and in all our lifetimes.

Thus, as a healer of the physical body, be not sad when the person you are helping is passing on into death. At this time, your role is to be a Divine Servant for the transition of that person's soul into the Light. Your role is to help their soul. Be not attached to their body, for that is not your job—that is the job of the Divine. In your alignment to serve God, you are merely the instrument.

Thus, as a healer of the emotions, your job is to help bring clarity of the origins of the person's pain or confusion, and to place that in the greater perspective of the journey of their soul. Help them to understand their lessons, their karma, the karma of their family. Help them to understand that what may be done to them in this lifetime, they may have done to others previously. Help them to understand ALL people come into your lifetime because of karmic connections. These karmic connections need to be seen, cleansed, and forgiven.

Through the act of forgiveness will come the peace and the virtue necessary for Soul Enlightenment. Understand further that Soul Enlightenment is only a baby step. While it brings the possibility to attain liberation and be off the cycle of birth and death and rebirth, you may be called back to service.

Even though you may attain Soul Enlightenment, as a Universal Servant you may return to the earth plane to continue to assist all souls. Be not attached. Be honored to remain until all souls pass before you to enter their boundless Universal Enlightenment. It is a great honor to assist others to go first.

Whatever comes to you, give it away. Whatever blessing comes to you, always thank God and the Divine. Be empty and be of the emptiness. Let go of all that you have gained. Let go of the teachings within this book. Be only of giving thanks.

The revered poet, Santiveda, taught in the 8th century AD that these qualities are to be cultivated for Enlightenment:

- ❖ First grasp the thought of Enlightenment
- ❖ Perfection of Patience

❖   Perfection of Strength
❖   Perfection of Contemplation
❖   Perfection of Wisdom

A Teaching

To perceive another human being as a Buddha or as Christ or as Allah tells us a great deal about the psychological and spiritual state of the beholder.

To perceive a high-level Enlightened being in front of us is a statement about the perceiver as well as the perceived.

To perceive the Buddha nature or the Enlightened nature within every human being is another level of spiritual attainment within the eye of the beholder.

To perceive the Enlightened nature within every sentient being and to hear the teachings coming from all voices is to grant the Oneness its due while we are yet in the human body.

Part IV

A Parable

Chapter 17

The Parable of the Little Soul

The sacred flow comes in the lyrical sweetness of a child's voice. With nary a care in the world, the fullness of the moment is consumed in telling this ancient tale.

Now, consider for a moment that everything you have been taught is placed to one side. Place your beliefs, concepts, thoughts, and opinions on the shelf for a while. Our belief system is the very foundation that guides our life. It is something we chose and yet often is unconscious. Our concepts about our self, our life goals, our relationships, and our expectations are a second tier of our belief system. We are aware of our concepts. For purposes of opening beyond our normal understanding and moving into the space of the unknown, I am requesting that you temporarily place all beliefs, concepts, and prior experiences to one side. With the space that is now created, let us proceed into new terrain.

Let us use the image and analogy of a teacup. I often will work with a cup of tea on my desk. Gaze at this teacup, for it represents our world as we have known it. Realize that most of our lives are spent having *every* conversation inside the teacup. Whenever we wish to solve any issue, we still are within the teacup. The constant inner tapes that run in our mind are inside the teacup. The entire practice of psychology and psychotherapy are inside the teacup. Our religious belief systems are inside the teacup. The physical realities that we create and live by each day and each minute are inside the teacup. This is the world we create.

Now, let it go. Place it on the shelf. Teacup and its contents, place them all on the shelf. Go outside the teacup. The rest of this tale is OUTSIDE the teacup. Outside is a vast space. It is formless. It is fresh. It IS.

Become the innocent child. Let your mind be empty. The world is wondrous once again. Let me tell you a story about your soul.

The Little Soul

One day, the little soul is wandering around wondering, "Which way do I go? Do I take the path to the right? Do I take the path to the left? What path shall I take?" And the soul begins to walk down a path and walk and walk and walk. Then, the little soul sees a sign by the side of the road. The sign says, "50 miles to San Francisco." The little soul has never seen San Francisco and so the soul asks himself, "Could this mean this is San Francisco?" Because the little soul has never seen the actual city, the actual destination, he cannot know the difference between the sign and the city itself.

Well, the little soul decides to keep walking in the off chance that more is to come. Somewhere inside a little voice of wisdom says, "Do not mistake the sign for the path's destination." The sign to San Francisco is the same sign as when the first abilities or powers appear on the journey. These powers are ONLY signs that you are on the path. These signs are very seductive and can cause you to lose your way. The signs are Seductive Siddhis.

So, the little soul keeps walking and walking until he encounters some rocky terrain. Now there are boulders in his path. He turns this way and that way, and there appear many boulders all around him. He is confused and walks in many circles. He backtracks his own footsteps. Deep inside the boulders look like walls around him. The walls are made of steel and reach as high as the sky. "Oh my, what am I to do? I am lost. I am trapped. I cannot get out of these walls. I am constricted so tight. Ow!"

As he cries out in pain, a voice of wisdom again guides him gently, "Walk along the wall. Walk along the side of this wall until you come to the edge of the wall. Peer around the edge. What do you see?"

"Oh," said the soul, "I didn't see the edge of the wall until I walked over there. Now I see the other side of the wall. I can walk farther now!"

And with that, the little soul continues his journey. He walks and he walks until he finds himself in some sand dunes. He walks farther and he is in the desert. Just when he thinks he has found the path again, he instead finds himself way, way in the desert, surrounded on all sides by sand. An image comes to his mind: train tracks are leading into the desert. At the end of the tracks is the little red caboose that was in his childhood book of the Little Train that said, "I think I can. I think I can." But instead of seeing the train on the tracks, he sees only the little red caboose, and the little red caboose has fallen off the tracks and is lying on its side… in the desert.

"Oh dear, this is a terrible state of affairs!" cries out the little soul. He feels so lost and so sad. He even forgets that he is going down a path on a journey. He falls into despair. So many emotions come into him. He doubts himself, that he will ever find his way. He even doubts God. He feels conflict and berates himself for getting lost. He becomes sick in his physical body and feels great pain. He is angry and curses the heavens. He is confused by his own emotions and thoughts. And he feels alone, so terribly alone. He falls into a deep sleep.

From deep inside, that little voice of inner wisdom comes to him as he is sleeping. A little seed of awakening, a memory of something else, a sense of something familiar from a long time ago comes into him in his relaxed state of sleep. These feelings cause him to wake up and stretch. He even stands up, feels his spine flexing, takes a deep breath, and begins to walk again. He continues on his journey.

The little soul begins to contemplate, "What happened to me? Why were all these painful emotions overwhelming me? Why did I get sick?" And so, he begins to ask questions of people he meets. He wants to know if this happens to anyone else. He begins to read books on psychology and the journey of the soul.

One day, he reads a Sufi tale about getting lost in the desert. "Aha!" he exclaims. "That is what happened to me!"

One day, he reads a fascinating book on the Sufi map of personalities known as the Enneagram. "Aha!" he exclaims. "That must have been my ego that was stuck in such pain!" He reads further and almost falls off his chair. "This book is talking about me, about how I see the world. I thought I was different and unique! I was wrong. I am like many other people." And with this insight, he sees himself, like all others, clothed in images created by an ego. This ego is very different from the little voice of wisdom that keeps him going on his path.

And with this new distinction between his own wisdom and his ego, he continues his journey, looking more deeply into the subject.

The little soul, so very thin and tentative in the beginning, is now putting some meat on his bones. It is spiritual meat that makes him stronger and deepens his commitment to seek his own path. The little soul wants to go deeper than his personality and outer layers of facade. So, he takes up various forms of bodywork.

He lies on a couch, naked, breathing chest, belly, and out. All kinds of muscular memories of his early childhood come to the surface as he cries, shrieks, and trembles. Fairly soon, he is quivering all over as his body armor melts and his energy begins to move. His eyes soften and he even feels little openings in his heart. He becomes less afraid to love. He seeks intimacy with friends and lovers. He is beginning to truly open.

As his heart opens, so does his mind. His old way of perceiving his world and even his own family shifts. He can now see reality is not what he thought it was. He has been inside a teacup. Now the world is getting larger and more interesting.

He comes upon the Eastern traditions—the way of the yogis, meditators, samurai, and healers. He finds an invisible energy ball the exact same shape as a basketball so well known to all athletes and sports enthusiasts. Only this ball will never be used in competitive and lucrative worldly arenas. This is the hidden Qi ball, the foundation practice used to heal physical ills.

Now as the little soul plays with his Qi basketball, he discovers he gets very hot. In fact, he starts to quiver and shake. He feels like a red-hot poker is building at the base of his spine. It shoots up to his head and throws him against a wall. "How can this be? I'm a strong man. What is happening to me to be thrown against a wall and land upside down?"

So the little soul decides to pursue martial arts training. He certainly does not want to be caught off guard by some invisible force that throws him like a ragdoll, upside down against a wall. "No way," says the little soul. "I, and only I, am master of my destiny!" This is the way the little soul thinks. He believes he is in control. He wants more strength.

The little soul knows he must learn to tame his mind, to focus and concentrate if he is to have more power and strength. He is in a very Yang mode on this journey. He thinks he has mastered his ego, his physical illness, and his emotional outbursts. He thinks his kundalini energy is awakened as well as his inner energy channels. He thinks he has gained mastery over much of the physical plane. Now he seeks to tame his monkey mind.

His mind will not quiet. His mind wants more mind food, more entertainment, more activity. His mind wants the same Yang energy that is abundant in his body. His ego leads his mind to believe it can be the same food. The teachers of the little soul tell him to relax and quiet down. They tell him to count his breaths and feel his senses. All the little soul can think is, "When will this be over? I want a hamburger!" And the harder the little soul tries to quiet, the more active his ego becomes. The battle lines are drawn.

One day, through an unexpected technique, a skillful teacher outsmarts his ego, and the little soul quite inadvertently has a brief glimpse of the Unknown. The little soul cries at the beauty and the relief. His ego goes into instant analytical mode and attempts to constrain the moment and throw the entire package back into the teacup.

His ego rises up in all its awful glory to retake charge of the little soul. His ego convinces the little soul that he is going to go crazy if he continues down this path. In fact, his ego goes so far as to say that his teacher is crazy. The coup de grace is his ego's insistence that God is dead, or at least has abandoned the little soul.

The little soul falls down into the abyss, a fall only those who have risen from can understand. He tries to grasp at a fleeting root on the way down. His grasping causes the dead root to dissolve. "There is nothing to hang onto!" he yelps in his slide. He does not realize this is precisely the point.

"What is happening to me?" the little soul implores to the heavens, as he lies bruised and cut on his back in the mud. He begins to cry, a lost little soul sobbing under the sky. Gradually, his chest becomes quieter, allowing his lungs to deeply fill with fresh space. He opens his eyes and looks oh so deeply into the sky. His eyes move deeper and deeper into the empty vastness of the night, beyond the stars and planets. He becomes still with a depth of silence and space. He loses track of everything. He becomes part of everything. Silent. Vast.

He lies there for an unknown time. The golden suspension of dawn's early morning light fills the abyss, illuminating the formless and creating forms. The rocks become alive and begin to talk to the little soul. They tell him of an ancient time when he was a fish and they were the rivers and the planet was young.

There appears a river of faces with eyes fleetingly beckoning him, familiar yet strange, for it had been a very long time. "Who are you?" the voice of the little soul hesitantly and humbly queries.

"We are your ancestors," comes the reply. The little soul is so moved, for he recognizes his most dear grandmother who gave him warmth and comfort when he was young. She now wraps him in a golden blanket of gossamer cloth, and he feels such deep peace. She holds him like this for a very long time.

The light climbs higher into the skies and the little soul feels thirst and hunger. He begins to walk down the center of the abyss that transforms into a ravine and then a valley and then opens into meadows.

As he walks along his path, he comes upon women washing clothes by a river. He bends down to wash and sees his face, but it is not his face. It is a new face with eyes luminous and deep. As he sits back to contemplate what is happening to him, the women approach. "Who are you?" they ask.

"Yes, this is a good question. Who am I?" he responds. And with this exchange, the women gather round to hear his story.

The little soul, by now quite transformed, tells his audience of his powers to hear and to see. He sees old souls, his past lives. He can hear the spirits speaking to him. The more he tells his story, the more excited become the women. Surely, this is some magical man or human/god seated in front of them! As the women increasingly attribute special abilities and qualities to him, the little soul comes to believe it himself! "Oh I can see that these women have such a need to believe, such a hope that these gifts are real. I can see into them also," says the little soul to himself. Before long, the little soul is quite proud of himself.

"Do you have a name?" ask the women.

"Yes, I am the Special One with Special Powers." And hearing this title and seeing his siddhis, the women take him to their village where he lives many years. However, one day the little soul realizes many years are going by. He also realizes that he is no longer growing inside… it is all ho-hum—the same old psychic and healing gifts.

Again, a little voice of wisdom, that by now he has learned to identify and listen to, says to him, "My son, you are lost again. You have become prideful about the gifts that I gave you. It is time to return to the main path of your journey." Hearing this message and recognizing the truth, the little soul leaves the village and his following, and continues on his journey.

It took him much contemplation to realize that he was leaving the "Valley of the Seductive Siddhis." Once he realizes this, he is most grateful, for he remembers the teaching that this is a trap. He has been caught in a back eddy and needs to get back on track. It is not much different from when he was lost in the desert, so lost he had forgotten the teachings about being lost in the desert. Then, he sees that both times he was lost. Both times he had forgotten the teachings. Indeed, these are big spiritual tests.

He further realizes that it is contemplation that gives him insight. "This is a Yin energy, most different from my Yang power. Maybe I am more balanced," he hopefully says to himself. "I will keep my abilities, my siddhis more private. I will not be boastful," he vows. With that vow, he suddenly feels a rush of energy through the center of his chest. He feels such a profound sweet quality of love toward all that is around him.

He sits down to allow this precious state to mature in its own way. He is yielding to the unknown, trusting the Divine as it surges into his being. He becomes simultaneously a mother giving birth to the universe and the baby being born between an undulating sky and earth. The unions are in all directions. The intimacy in the touching between earth and sky reveals a delicacy of connectedness. The form and the formless of the wind and the leaves all dance together. The beauty, the peace, the perfection are revealed in front of him and behind him as he is the center and he is the All. He is the silence. He is the vastness. He is the emptiness. He is luminous.

Acknowledgements

I offer my deepest appreciation to the Divine, to being given this human life, to being exposed to the path of Enlightenment, to being born into my family, to birthing my beautiful children and the arrival of my grandchildren, to being loved and supported by friends and dear Tom. I offer my deepest thanks to the Divine for placing me in these settings and giving me these opportunities that are filled with the values of love and service.

I will always thank Master Sha for his continual teachings, blessings, transmissions, challenges, vision, testing, and encouragement, for he is the one who brought me "through the door" to the beginning level of Enlightenment. This realization, albeit it only the kindergarten stage, is the ultimate purpose of this lifetime because from this view I can offer better service. I cannot thank him enough for he is always with me. Tears of gratitude come once again.

I thank, from the bottom of my heart, my two children, Brett and Adam, who in truth raised me. Brett is a serious Buddhist practitioner dedicated to service. Adam is now an attorney, having been identified at age five as a young tulku. They both give my life deep meaning down to the very marrow of my bones. Our moments together are most precious. I thank Eric, my special son-in-law, for his laughter and dedication to family life and his marriage of over 20 years to my daughter. I thank beautiful Dede, my daughter-in-law, for her wise and kind love she gives to all around her.

I thank my dear Tom for his continual emotional support, time, intense graphic assistance, continuous editing, and his presence as one who enters the Emptiness daily. Without the depth and breadth of his knowledge as a doctor of comparative religion, this book could not have been written. His understanding kept me questioning my words, honing its truth.

I thank my parents and grandparents for the many gifts and upbringing they gave me, some of which are described in this book. I thank lovely Andree, my stepmom, for her total understanding and support of this spiritual journey over my entire lifetime. We share many spiritual moments.

I thank my friends and spiritual community, for they are present with me as we all transform, and their stories give credence to the journey we share. In particular, I thank my dear friend, Peter Hudoba. Without his omni-present teachings, piercing questions, and inspiration of Enlightenment, I could not have made the necessary incremental steps, including recognizing my own Buddha nature.

I also thank my teachers, formal and hidden: Lee Sannella, David Deitch, Malcolm "Jerry" Williams, Molly Day, Fritz Perls, Ernie Pecci, Bob Hoffman, Bingkun Hu, Joseph Busey, Claudio Naranjo, Yogi Chen, and Tarthang Tulku,

I thank my editors: Jess Henryes for his initial guidance; Sandy Eastoak for her clarity and breadth; Marcelle Kardush for her gracious assistance especially with "The Psychology of Enlightenment." I thank Melissa Knight for holding the possibility of success in publishing this book, and Diana Gold Holland for her brilliant mind and editorial comments. I thank Sandra Sharpe for her generous encouragement and referrals. I thank Michael McClister and Cheryl Wallace for their efforts in reviewing this material and adding their introductions to key people. I thank Ditta Silbermann for her proofreading. I thank Jean Makanna for her beautiful photographs.

I thank my cats sitting at the computer and my dogs lying at my feet, patiently adding their animal spirit support.

Footnotes

These footnotes give the origin of each teaching tool. Some of these tools come from ancient traditions and are described as carefully as possible and in keeping with how they were taught to me. Other tools reflect my own creativity and the inspiration that I receive. For purposes of acknowledging my teachers and their teachings, I have noted these sources.

Chapter 6, Transforming Darkness into Light

1. *How to Transform Visions of Darkness into Light.* The guiding principles presented here come from Master Sha who always teaches us to say "hello" and be welcoming to any soul. The basic mantra I use, "God's Light" comes from his CD.
2. *How to Do Family Healing.* This is my own creation.

Chapter 7, Opening Spiritual Channels

1. *How to Open Our Spiritual Channels.* This is my own creation (1976).
2. *How to Cultivate the Meditation Practice of "OM AH HUNG."* I have been given the transmissions and the permission to pass these on to others through Tarthang Tulku, Rinpoche. These practices come from Tibetan Vajrayana Buddhism. This is a basic Vajrayana practice in the Nyingma tradition. Received in 1973.
3. *How to Cultivate the Meditation Practice of "WENG AH HUNG."* This is the Chinese version of Weng Ah Hung as taught by Master Sha.
4. *How to Cultivate the Meditation Practice of d'Tumo.* Tarthang Tulku, Rinpoche teaches us d'Tumo breathing. This is the first of a two-part meditation practice.
5. *How to Cultivate the Meditation Practice of "Maha Sukha."* This is the second part of the d"Tumo meditation taught by Tarthang Tulku, Rinpoche.
6. *How to Cultivate Sexual Spiritual Tantra.* This is my own creation.

Chapter 8, Inner Vision

1. *How to Cultivate Inner Vision.* The guidance that follows here comes from my teacher, Master Sha.

2. *How to Cultivate Your Snow Mountain.* The practice for activating your Snow Mountain Area is similar to the formula given above for your third eye and also is guidance from my teacher, Master Sha.

3. *How to Reconnect with Your Abilities as a Child.* This is my own creation.

4. *How to Activate Two Energy Centers as a Unit.* This is my own creation.

Chapter 9, Open Your Heart!

1. *How to Cultivate the Opening of Your Heart.* This is my own creation.

2. *How to Hear with Your Heart.* This is my own creation.

3. *How to Begin Soul Communication.* My early training in the concept of soul-to-soul communication comes from Master Sha. This exercise, however, is a culmination of years as a psychologist and integrates the practice of soul-to-soul communication, moving next into prayer.

4. *How to Do Relationship Healing.* This comes from my own creativity, integrating my training as a psychologist. The sanctuary comes from Fisher Hoffman training. The prayer format is through Master Sha.

5. *How to Open the Heart of a Loved One.* These three in this sequence are based in the teachings of Master Sha to which I add my own inspiration and guidance in the moment. It is a good example of how to work in the state of "flow" as a psychologist.

6. *How to Do Soul Marketing.* This teaching comes directly from Master Sha and shows the many ways to apply soul-to-soul communication in daily life.

7. *How to Enter the Hero Condition.* This is a core teaching of Master Sha's.

Chapter 10, Soul Travel

1. *How to Do Practices for Six States of Consciousness.* These six states come from the Vajrayana Buddhist teachings. I have added points that I believe helpful.

2. *How to Train Your Mind During the Normal Waking State.* This is my own guidance coming to me over time.

3. *How to Connect with Client's Past Lives.* My own teachings that have come as a result of early work with clients more than 20 years ago.

4. _How to Use Sound for Soul Travel._ My own teachings based upon personal experience.

5. _How to Do Sky Meditation to Enter the Void._ Tarthang Tulku, Rinpoche taught me this advanced Sky Meditation and empowered those of us present to pass it on.

6. _How to Heal While in Two Realms._ These are healing sequences that now come to me after learning the basic Power Healing techniques from Master Sha.

7. _How to Teach in the Golden Channel._ Using Master Sha's teachings as a foundation to my further creative work, I offer these presentations. In the teachings of Master Sha this is called sub-divided Soul work.

8. _How to Receive Saints Coming Out from the Emptiness._ These are personal realizations after entering the Emptiness over 30 years ago.

9. _How to Enter Dream Yoga._ This is a teaching coming from Tarthang Tulku, Rinpoche I add my own teaching here as well.

Chapter 11, Blessings and Transmissions

1. _How to Receive Divine Blessing of Nature._ This is based on personal experience and practice.

2. _How to Cultivate Positive Emotions._ This comes from applying Master Sha's chant and tone of "God's Light". After doing this for a couple of years, I then could tell my clients the many, many moments in a day when this chant can be used, and the powerful results it can bring. I add to this foundation practice my own understanding of psychology and the ego. It is a good example of how any healing professional can open the door to spiritual tools in their practice.

3. _How to Cultivate Forgiveness._ _This is b_ased upon a deepening of my understanding of the importance of forgiveness that I learn from Master Sha, I then can create many ways to help my clients. It is rather like taking a wisdom teaching and applying it in my practice in my own unique way.

Chapter 12, Karma: Causality not Punishment

1. _How to Clear Karma Through Offering Yin Service._ This entire section on the many ways to clear karma comes through my training under Master Sha. I have listened to his teachings, his seed ideas, and have directly, or personally experienced each of these, many, many times.

2. _How to Clear Karma Through Offering Yang Service._ This is a second example of teachings from Master Sha.

3. _**How to Clear Karma Through Spiritual Testing.**_ This is a basic teaching from Master Sha that I understand most intimately in my daily life.

4. _**How to Clear Karma Through Prayer.**_ As with the above four examples, this also comes from Master Sha and has touched me deeply.

5. _**How to Clear Karma Through Forgiveness.**_ Same as above.

6. _**How to Clear Karma Through Taking on of Karma by Your Healer.**_ Teaching from Master Sha.

7. _**How to Clear Karma Through Karma the Giving of Virtue.**_ Teaching from Master Sha.

Chapter 13, Expansion Follows Constriction: Spiritual Testing

1. _**How to Move Through Testing of Your Belief System.**_ This understanding is based upon my own experience and guidance over many years.

2. _**How to Address Anger in Spiritual Testing.**_ This is my understanding that comes during my training with Master Sha. In integrating his teachings with the spiritual openings that happen to me as a result, the entire view I have in helping others heal or spiritually awaken is different. Therefore, this tool in a true integration of his teachings with my own unfolding, coupled with years as a psychologist studying the ego. This tool is distinctly different that many training that encourage acting out the anger through yelling, hitting pillows, or writing irate letters as a form of catharsis.

3. _**How to Move Through Family Disagreements in Spiritual Testing.**_ The seed ideas based upon spiritual understanding come through my training with Master Sha. I integrate my clinical and personal experience. The guidance that comes in an actual session with a client is always different and unique to that situation.

4. _**How to Move Through Disagreements with Friends.**_ The same as above.

Chapter 14, Training as a Spiritual Teacher

1. _**How to Do Remote Healing for Cancer.**_ Master Sha teaches us to apply the four powers of Power Healing as well as how to do remote healing using the phone or prayer.

2. _**How to Do Self-Healing.**_ For more precise techniques, please read Master Sha's Power Healing book.

3. _How to Cultivate Medical Intuitive Abilities._ There are specific Qigong practices that will enhance your medical intuitive abilities. I learn this practice through Bingkun Hu, Ph.D., a Qigong Master.

Chapter 15, Up Close and Personal

1. _The Healing Begins._ Everything done in this healing is a combination of everything I have ever been taught, and the guidance that came during these hours directly to help me.

Chapter 16, Portals to Enlightenment

1. _How to Find the Here and Now._ This is my creation that came to me over 20 years ago.

2. _How to Enter into the Expanded Now._ This is my own creation that I have been doing for 20 years with clients and myself.

3. _How to Enter the Invisible Energy Body. (Part 1)_ This is my own creation.

4. _How to Enter the Invisible Energy Body. (Part 2)_ This is my own creation.

5. "The Way of the Buddha: Hinayana, Mahayana, Vajrayana," Ven. Lama Trungpa Tulku, Chakra, A Journal of Tantra and Yoga, Magazine Volume Four, 1972-73, New Delhi, pg. 151 & 152.

6. _How To Activate Your Chakra System (5 approaches)._

    1) Reichian Breath work. I trained under Joseph Busey, Ph.D.on a weekly basis for 5 years. This excellent approach to bodywork was developed by the German psychiatrist, Wilhelm Reich. The division into segments of the body closely corresponds to the chakra system. I found it to be an effective training for opening the chakras.

    2) This practice of d'Tumo comes through Tarthang Tulku, Rinpoche, a high ranking Nyingmapa Tibetan Buddhist master.

    3) This training in Medical Qigong was done under my studies with Bingkun Hu, Ph.D, a Qigong Master and Western Psychologist

    4) This training was also done with Bingkun Hu.

    5) This practice comes through Master Sha in the Zhi Neng Medicine tradition.

7. _How to Find the Space Between Thoughts._ This wisdom teaching comes from Tarthang Tulku, Rinpoche. It is a basic meditation practice.

8. _How to Look into the Space Between Forms._ This teaching, also from Tarthang Tulku, Rinpoche also elaborates upon the former and helps to open the mind to the most basic concept of going beyond form.

9. *How to Do the AH Meditation (Part 1 and 2).* This meditation practice has two parts and is meant to be practiced as a sequence. One to build upon the former after you feel your mind is stable. These are teachings from Tarthang Tulku, Rinpoche that we have been empowered to pass on.

10. *How to Do The Sky Meditation.* This closely held meditation was taught to me by Tarthang Tulku, Rinpoche. It builds upon the above sequence.

11. *How to Focus Upon Your Origination.* In part this sequence comes from Dr. Tom McConnell, spiritual teacher.

12. Sogyal Rinpoche, *The Tibetan Book of Living and Dying,* San Francisco: Harper, 1992, p. 275

13. Kalu Rinpoche, The Tibetan Book of Living and Dying, Sogyal Rinpoche, Harper San Francisco, 1992, pg. 279 & 280.

Credits

Made in the USA
Las Vegas, NV
20 September 2024

95479911R20207